COMMEMORATIVE ISSUE

Limited Edition

No 34.

Author's Signature

Dedicated to the memory of My Father William Leslie Barnes.

Who served in Scorpion Squadron. RAF: 1940 to 1945, and was mentioned in dispatches in Burma.

He died in Hull, July 2001: Deeply missed.

William and Olive Barnes on their Wedding Day; 1940

OTHER BOOKS BY THE AUTHOR

This Righteous War: A History of the Hull 92nd Brigade. 1914 to 1919

The Sign of the Double 'T': The 50th Northumbrian Division in Sicily, 1943 and North West Europe,1944.

ACKNOWLEDGEMENTS

To the following people I owe a debt of gratitude for their help in providing me with information on the fallen.

Malcolm Mann has been collating and cataloguing lists of memorials of war and details of the fallen for many years. Thanks to his hard work and diligence in collecting information from both world wars, much that would have been lost has now been preserved for future generations of Yorkshire men and women. I cannot thank him enough for his unstinting generosity in sharing his work with me and upon his patience when dealing with my many enquiries.

Having visited Reckitts Factory in Hull on various occasions since 1989, Gordon Stephenson and Steve West have been kind and helpful during my periods of work there. Thanks to them I was able to search through the various editions of 'Ours' and other Reckitts publications.

The Commonwealth War Graves Commission web site was a major source of information regarding the final resting places of the fallen.

And lastly to all the people of Hull and farther a field who provided me with material upon their relatives who worked at Reckitts Factory.

Published by Sentinel Press: First Edition
Printed by Hull University Press

FOREWORD

Foreword

In 1914 the Reckitt factory in Hull to which the author refers in this book is represented by manufacturing operations conducted upon three quite separate sites. It will be helpful therefore to remind the reader just what those various sites were and where they were situated.

Firstly, Kingston Works is the name given to the buildings, including the General Office and Works, which grew up around the original starch mill acquired by Isaac Reckitt in 1840 in the area now known as Dansom Lane South. This site remained the Head Office of the business until 1970 when the Head Office was transferred initially to Chiswick in West London and subsequently to Slough in Buckinghamshire. Kingston Works has undergone much alteration in recent times and is now the headquarters and manufacturing site of Reckitt Benckiser Healthcare.

The second Reckitt site to be established in Hull was in Morley Street where a factory was built in 1883 for the production of ultramarine, a major ingredient in laundry blue. That factory became the home of Reckitt's Colours Ltd until that part of the business was sold to Holliday Pigments Ltd in 1994.

The third site, known herein as Canister Works, but often referred to as Stoneferry Works, owed its origins to one John (Tinny) Wilson who established a factory in Stoneferry Road for the manufacture of tin boxes early in the Twentieth Century. With the advent of Brasso in 1905 Reckitt's found itself in regular need of vast supplies of tins for packing this and other products and bought the factory for this purpose in 1907. Much later the factory was converted into a manufacturing site for Reckitt's household products and eventually, following a major reorganisation within the Group, the site was closed down, the land sold and the buildings demolished.

With the 'war to end wars' looming in the summer months of 1914, an outbreak of patriotic fervour swept the nation and it was by no means uncommon for a large proportion of the workforce from establishments such as Reckitt's to answer the call to arms and hasten to serve their King and country. What is perhaps unusual is that, almost a century later, much of what became of so many of those gallant men and women can still be traced in a variety of sources which somehow managed to escape the ravages of another major conflict in the 1940's.

The author began his research for this book in the offices of the firm which employed the subjects of his study. Despite the blitz on the night of 18th July 1941 which knocked out large portions of Kingston Works most of the Company's historic archives survived. I had the pleasant task of making these available to Barrie and was greatly impressed by the enthusiasm with which he went about his task. It came as no surprise to me to learn that he decided to extend his search into other areas where he might track down the part played by each and every one of Reckitt's participants in the Great War. His inquiring mind led him to discover other major collections of war records and, to complete the picture, he set about tracing living descendants of those who took part.

The result of Barrie Barnes' attention to detail is that here we have in a single volume a lasting memorial to those many citizens of Hull who, employed by the city's largest industrial employer at the time, were called upon to face untold tribulations in a conflict the like of which had never been known before and who, in so many instances, paid the ultimate sacrifice. This work will serve posterity well in allowing generations as yet unborn to bear witness to the hardships and sacrifices undertaken on their behalf by their very kith and kin.

Gordon E Stephenson
Archivist, Reckitt's Heritage.

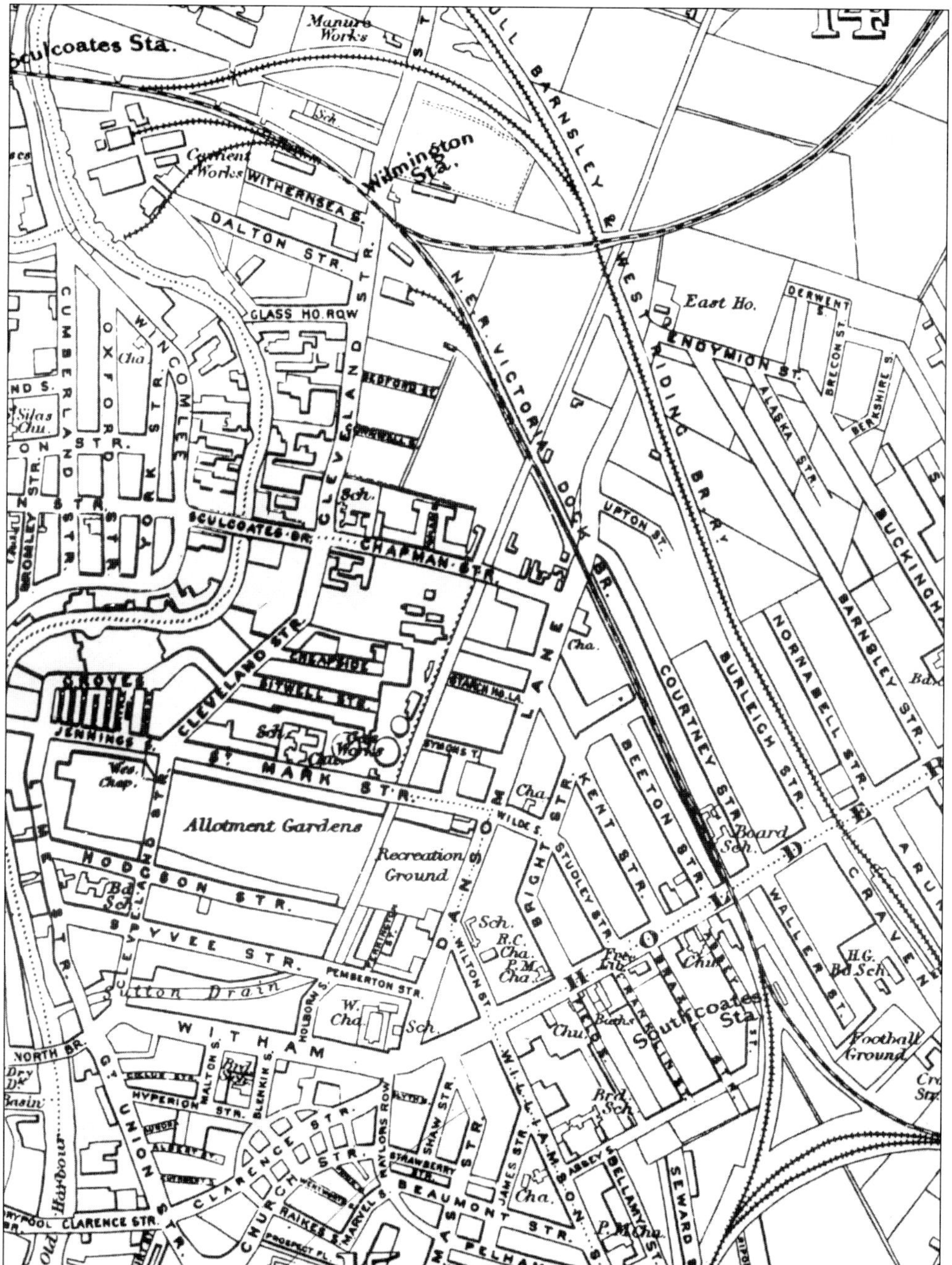

A plan of the Dansom Lane Area of Hull 1840

CONTENTS

Foreword
Authors Introduction
Preface: 1914
Chapter 1: Reckitt's Hospital and its Staff
Chapter 2: 1915 The Fallen and Letters from the Front
Chapter 3: 1916 The Fallen and Letters from the Front
Chapter 4: 1917 The Fallen and Letters from the Front
Chapter 5: 1918 The Fallen and Letters from the Front
Chapter 6: Remembering the Fallen 1920, Memorials
Chapter 7: Reckitt's Employees who served
Chapter 8: The Dansom Lane Shrine
Conclusion: Remembrance 1991

Appendix A: 'Ours' 1920

Appendix B: Men who Succumbed to Ailments in 1920/21

Appendix C: Honours and Awards

Appendix D: Letter from Mr W Aumonier, Memorial Sculptor

Appendix E: Gifts to Returned Service Men

Appendix F: Record of Service by Men of Reckitt's Division of St John's Ambulance Brigade

Appendix G: Employees Contributions

Appendix H: A Complete List of the Fallen

Appendix I: Men Killed during the War but were never featured in 'Ours'

Index

They shall not grow old, as we that are left grow old:
Age shall not weary them, not the years condemn.
At the going down of the sun and in the morning
We will remember them.

They mingle not with their laughing comrades again:
They sit no more at familiar tables at home;
They have no lot in our labour of the daytime;
They sleep beyond England's foam.

But where our desires are and our hopes profound,
Felt as a wellspring that is hidden from sight,
To the innermost heart of their own land they are known
As the stars are known to the Night.

As the stars that shall be bright when we are dust,
Moving in marches upon the heavenly plain,
As the stars that are starry in the time of our darkness,
To the end, to the end, they remain.

Laurence Binyon

A last farewell

Sir James and Lady Reckitt and their Grandchildren at Swanland Manor 1915
Valentine Philip Upton, James Reckitt, Nancie Reckitt, Elizabeth Kathleen Reckitt, Barbara Reckitt, James Bryan Upton

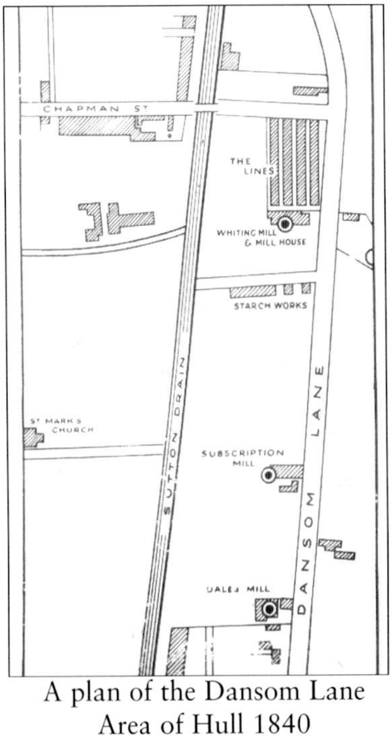

A plan of the Dansom Lane Area of Hull 1840

The General Office and in the background the Kingston Works. 1911. The 'Bird in Hand' Public House, adjacent to the board room at that time, can be seen on the extreme right.

Reckitt's V.A.D. Hospital, Dansom Lane, Hull
(Voluntary Aid Detachment)

The Hospital as it was during 'The Great War'

In 1991 the building was still standing with some additions and was used by the services division. In 1994 it was demolished.

AUTHOR'S INTRODUCTION

On 4th August 1914 Great Britain declared war on Germany, the British Expeditionary Force was sent to France that same month on a wave of euphoria as the population shouted their enthusiasm in an outbreak of patriotic fervour that would not be seen again. The cry was 'it will all be over by Christmas', a sentiment that was to have a hollow ring in the near future. The Germans swept all before them in one great outflanking movement, the B.E.F. advanced to a little town called Mons with still no sign of the enemy and waited.

On a bright and sunny day at the little town of Mons, six German divisions blundered into four divisions of the B.E.F. The Germans were received by a murderous fire from the British and were hurled back again and again with enormous losses. The British retreated to the little town of Le-Cateau and again made a brave stand enabling others to withdraw. They then withdrew to the Marne where the German forces faultered and pulled back, the Allied Forces attacked them in pursuit until the Aisne was reached and the advance slowed. Both sides were exhausted and dug holes in the ground, trench warfare had begun.

On 17th October the First Battle of Ypres opened, this town was the key to the whole Western Front and the ensuing struggle was to be bitter in the extreme. Many of the German troops here were students under the age of twenty and were slaughtered in their hundreds as they assaulted the British line.

The Germans rightly call this struggle 'Der Kindermord'. Or 'Massacre of the Innocents'. The battle was over by 22nd November and the Allied line had held, the old B.E.F. was destroyed at Ypres as fifty thousand men became casualties. The stage was now set for the entrance of the 'New Kitchener Armies' that had been raised during 1914, from the factories, work places, clubs and terraces of England. This study is of the men and women who answered their country's call during that far off time from only one factory, Reckitts. This firm played a major part in the life of the City of Hull for well over a century and when war came its young men were not slow to respond to the call of 'King and Country'. Such sentiments seem out of place today, but we should not judge that generation by our own standards or values, Edwardian man was raised on the principles of duty and sacrifice, England was the center of a great imperial power and the ties of patriotism were strong.

The only men in this study to be killed in 1914 are Charles Edward Myers, George Spires, and Mark Lockwood; all are to be found on the Dansom Lane Shrine, Spires is also to be found in the Reckitt's magazine of 1916, this magazine – 'OURS' – has been a great source of information for this study.

In Hull during September, October and December, 1914, the young men flocked to the colours, Reckitt's factory formed its own company of 100 men, most of them served with 1/4th Battalion East Yorkshire Regiment, (Hull) Territorial Force.

A Recruiting Tram, asking for men for the Hull Pals Battalions, Hull City Centre, 1914.

The 1/4th East Yorks. features prominently in this study because of its local nature, many of its soldiers had been numbered among its ranks long before the war started. It left England for France in April 1915.

The East Yorkshire Regiment had traditionally recruited in this area and many of the men featured in this study will be seen to have been killed serving with one of its numerous battalions. The 10th(Hull Commercials or 1st Hull Pals), 11th (Tradesman's or 2nd Hull Pals), 12th (Sportsmen's and Enthusiasts or 3rd Hull Pals), and 13th (4th Hull Pals) Battalions are of special interest to this study as they were the "Pals Battalions" raised in Hull at the City Hall, 1914. These consisted of local men who enlisted en-mass from Hull's factories, clubs and terraces in answer to Kitchener's call for 100,000 men. A truly popular mass movement that had never been seen before and was not to be seen again.

For Reckitt's factory the immediate effect of the war was the call up of seventy employees, troops were billeted on the Company's premises and the 1907 Social Hall was converted into a military hospital. By 1916 the number of Reckitts men serving was six hundred and forty eight rising to eight hundred and twenty in 1917. Hundreds of Hull's young men still lie in the ground they once fought over, this study is in commemoration of the fallen from only one factory, sons and fathers that answered their country's call and made the ultimate sacrifice.

It was 1990 when first I came across this archive in Reckitt's Library, I browsed through page after page of photographs, mostly of young beardless faces and vowed I would return again to record the sacrifice of these long forgotten warriors. Nearly 2 years later I went back and began to copy letters and photographs from the Reckitts magazines, much of the material here is the result of that work. The Hull Daily Mail published articles on my study and many relatives of the Fallen and men who survived the war allowed me to copy letters and photographs that had been kept in their families since the war.

The Commonwealth War Graves Commission records have been invaluable in my search for information.

Some men I have been able to trace in 'Soldiers Died in the Great War' and the Hull Daily Mail, others through their living relatives. Three men on the Dansom Lane Shrine are to be found in 'OURS' – their photographs are featured here, and some had letters published in 'OURS' and were then killed later in the war. Here they are all presented, with much more information, in one volume. As a historian I find such research exciting as a picture begins to emerge of a part of our social history. Enjoyable it was not, as putting together such a sad little book is a sobering occupation and when I am next on the Western Front the faces of these young men will be with me.

The Hull pals pause at Beverley for a break on their way to Ripon Training Camp: 1915

The 1/4th East Yorkshire Regiment march past the Tivoli Theatre Hull: 1915

Recruits march down Brook Street, Hull, carrying wooden rifles, military belts and dressed in civvies - 1914

Right - Old Soldiers brought back into service to train the new Pals Battalions - Beverley 1915. Two Special Constables stand on the left with a Policeman in the centre

PREFACE

Reckitts' Magazine - September, 1914

The War

Since last we sent our copy to the press for the August number, the Great War has broken out, spreading misery and desolation over almost the whole of Europe.

The efforts of our statesmen and others to preserve an honorable peace have failed, and we are faced with war and all its attendant horrors.

We have not sought it. We are a peace-loving nation and war has been forced upon us. But we believe ours is a righteous cause and we mean to see it through.

Everyone of us can help. The call to arms is urgent and our male employees are responding nobly. Those who have not gone to the front have their part to fulfill. There is money needed for the distress relief fund, a sacrifice of luxuries called for; there is work to be done through the Volunteer Aid Detachment; there are knitting centres where garments are made for soldiers. Each of us must do his or her part, and do it well.

It is hard to see the purpose of war, but if during this period of trial we are drawn closer to our fellow-men and learn to sympathise in others' sorrows; if we are taught the value of self-sacrifice and gain fortitude; above all, if we stop to think whether our fair name as a righteous nation is justified and resolve, each of us, by clean and upright living, to answer in the affirmative and to have the God of righteousness on our side; then this dreadful war will have some compensations.

When war broke out, 113 Army and Navy reserves, Territorials and Ambulance Men attached to the Royal Army Medical Corps, joined the colours.

There has been a ready response to Lord Kitchener's appeal for volunteers, 120 having enlisted to date. A special Works Company has been formed, which will be attached to the 4th Batt. East Yorks. Regiment.

The Directors have decided to supplement the service pay of married men. The difference between the Army pay and wages earned at work has been paid every week since the men went to the front.

Single men with dependents are being treated similarly.

Our Social Hall was offered to the Voluntary Aid Detachment as a hospital, and the firm fitted it up with beds.

Early in August a number of soldiers were quartered in the Boys' Gymnasium.

The Editor - 'OURS'

Chapter 1

Reckitt's Hospitals and its Staff

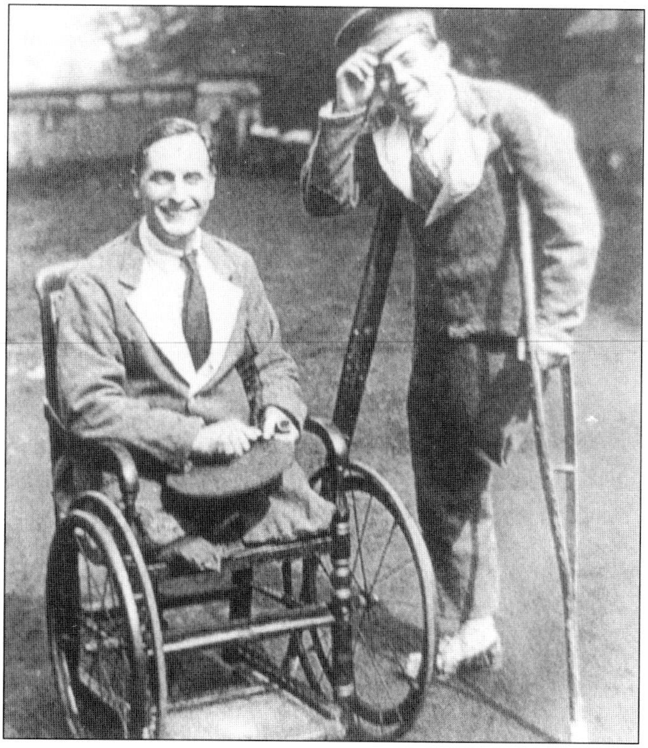

Reckitt's Nursing Division

Reckitt's Nursing Division was formed 12th July, 1912, Miss Hardy being appointed Lady Spt.and Dr. Wales, Hon. Surgeon. Its members were always enthusiastic, practising and studying how to make themselves efficient in First-Aid and Sick Nursing. All were members of the V.A.D. Several of the older members helped at the Rest Station at Paragon Station for some time during the early part of 1915, but as the work at the Hospital grew, and the Air Raid alarms were frequent they were compelled, much to their regret, to give it up.

From the opening of Reckitts Social Hall as a V.A.D. Hospital in 1914 to its closing in January, 1919, much creditable work was done by the members during their leisure time, many doing night duty. Saturday and Sunday always found them busy in wards and kitchen.

The Air Raid work was perhaps the most creditable of all. Thirty-six members were stationed at the various Air Raid Stations in the city. They were unfailing in their duty, always turning out when the alarm sounded. An old member of the Hull Corps remarked to one of the Officers, that he "had never seen such 'stickers', they were always ready with a cheery word and never complained of weariness, no matter how long the watch."

Ten members have been awarded the S.J.A.B. War Badge as follows:- Miss E.M. Hardy, Miss H. R.Thackery, Mrs E. M. Eggleton, Mrs E. Backhurst, Miss H. Marshall, Miss E. Kirby, Miss L. Cullen, Miss E. Farrell, Miss E. Chalmers, Miss M. Westerman.

Four members were accepted for Active Service as follows:- Miss Butler served at the East Leeds War Hospital for a short time, later she went one voyage on the Hospital Ship "Aquatania", finally working at Wandsworth Hospital, London.

Miss Jessie Barcroft was for a long time at Catterick Miliary Hospital, and was later transferred to Rouen, France.

Miss Lily Cullen helped in her spare time at Reckitt's Hospital during the first year, later to be transferred to East Leeds War Hospital.

Miss Ellen Chalmers also helped at Reckitt's Hospital until she was appointed to East Leeds War Hospital.

Names of Members who worked at Reckitt's Hospital and who were on the Air Raid Stations:-

Miss E M Hardy	Miss Frances Frow	Miss Gladys Longhorn
Miss H Ruth Thackery	Miss Emma Farrell	Miss Ivy Teall
Mrs E N Eggleton	Miss Hilda Green	Miss Elsie Thomas
Mrs E Backhurst	Miss Christiana McColl	Miss Daisy Batty
Miss A Yates	Miss Elizabeth Lowe	Miss Ivy Reeder
Miss Elsie Pattison	Miss Eva Selby	Miss Mabel Westerman
Miss Lily Brelsford	Miss Louisa Robertson	Miss Marion Clare
Miss Ethel Kirby	Miss Hilda Tommins	Miss Beatrice Prime
Miss Hilda Marshall	Miss Elsie Barwick	Miss Mary Butters
Miss Edith Sutton	Miss Dora McGavin	Miss Emma McKernan
Miss Lily Thorley	Miss Mabel Charlesworth	

Air Raid Duty Only

Miss Dolly Sorfleet	Miss Ada Smith	Miss Lily Wood
Miss Bertha Payne	Miss Lily McNally	

During the 'Great War' many wounded soldiers and sailors from Hull asked particularly to be sent to Reckitt's V.A.D. hospital, the medical services it provided were first rate and it possessed a pleasing social character. During the whole war period the staff of this hospital worked for the good of the men who had been wounded in the service of their country and quite unobtrusively carried out a noble task.

The hospital was approved by the military authority in November, 1914, and the first patients were received on December 9th the same year. The hospital was open for four years and three months and during that time, 2,910 patients passed through its wards, which were ably staffed by members of the Reckitt's Nursing Division, who in turn were assisted by members of the St. John Ambulance Division.

The hospital catering was carried out by Mr. T. Guest and his staff.

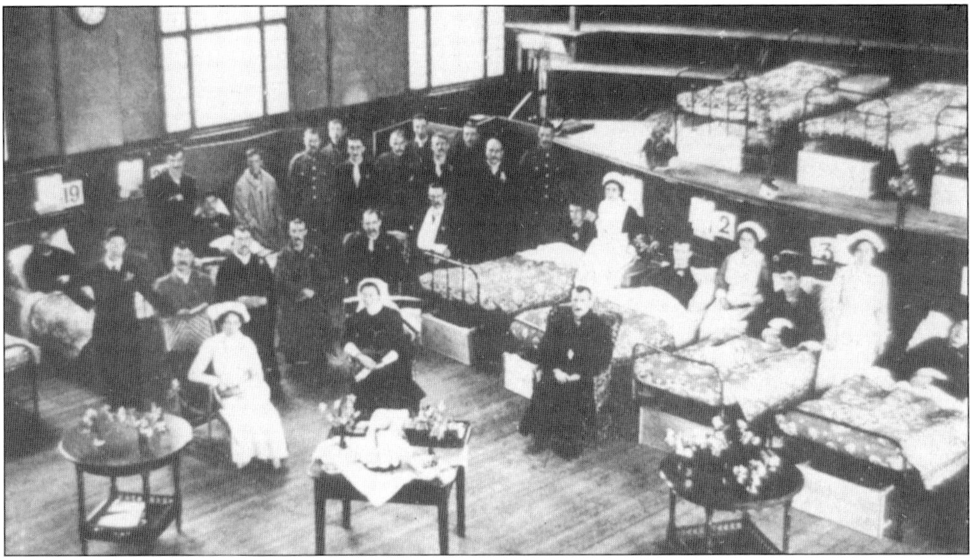

Interior view of the Reckitt's Military Hospital, Dansom Lane, Hull.

Miss Cook and Miss Varey were awarded by the Government the Royal Red Cross for services in hospital work. The medical staff consisted of Dr. J. Divine, J.P., Dr. J. L. Holt, Dr. A. Priest Shaw and Dr. J. H. Kaye (Medical Officer in charge), Corporal A. Layfield acted as quartermaster for the four years. These were assisted by a large staff of voluntary nurses who showed great devotion to duty throughout the war.

Third Row from Top - (Omit two) Miss Hardy, Mr. Findlay, Miss Varey, Dr. Kaye, Miss Cook, Dr. Priest Shaw, Dr. Holt (omit one), Corporal A. Layfield.

Colonel J. W. Tatham, O.B.E., (Humber Garrison Medical Service) wrote the following tribute to the Reckitt's Military Hospital and its staff:

> "The hospital itself and the way it has been managed has been of the greatest assistance, and I do not know how I should have carried on without it. Throughout the time there has been no friction or trouble, and the patients who have been there greatly appreciate the care and kindness bestowed upon them. Many of them have told me they were so well looked after and received so many little extras and kindnesses that Reckitts was the hospital that men wished to get into if they could. It hardly needs my assurance that a great work has been done for the military sick and wounded of the garrison. I have always had pleasant recollections of the hospital and its organisation."

The Hospital Commandant was Mr. P. B. Reckitt, O.B.E., there were 45 beds with a weekly average of 35 patients. The matrons in order were as follows: Miss Tunnard, Miss Cook and finally Miss Evans, all assisted by Miss Varey who was there from start to finish.

A St. John Ambulance Station
Second from right – Nurse Doran McGavin.

Front Row – Miss Cook, Col. Tatham.
Back Row – Dr. Holt, Dr. Divine, Miss Varey, Dr. Kaye, Dr. Priest-Shaw

Nurse Dora McGavin

One of the hard pressed Nurses at Reckitts V.A.D hospital was Dora McGavin, (left)'

She worked at the factory from 1911 to 1955 and was a long serving, and much decorated, member of the Red Cross Society. Dora was born in Glasgow on July 24th, 1895, and her family moved to Hull in 1906, she spent her last years living in Cottingham and died in Hull Royal Infirmary on 31st December, 1981, at the age of 86 years. The following letter was sent to her on 1st January, 1919, by soldiers that had passed through the V.A.D. wards on Dansom Lane, Hull, expressing their gratitude for services rendered and kindness shown:

"To Nurse McGavin,

We, the patients of Reckitt's hospital, feel that we cannot allow this occasion to pass without putting on record our appreciation of all you have done and sacrificed on our behalf.

It is not only for your generous kindness as exemplified by Christmas gifts; nor merely for the leisure you have sacrificed in order to render unstinted and ungrudging service; but for the amiable and gracious spirit in which you have overlooked our roughness and many shortcomings, and for the assiduous attention and charming friendliness you have always manifested in discharge of your duties.

For all of these we feel deeply grateful, and wish to express something of that gratitude although poorly and inadequately, in this way."

The information and photographs regarding Nurse McGavin were given by her niece, Mrs. Brocklebank of Hull.

This photograph was taken at the Morley Street factory, Stoneferry, Hull, and shows nurses and soldiers, Dora McGavin is marked with a cross. The men in light coloured uniforms are in the light blue dress worn by wounded men, the two in khaki have come to say their goodbyes before returning to the western front, knowing full well this may be the last time they will see their friends and colleagues.

When Reckitt's Military Hospital closed down the following letter was sent to Miss Florence Tiplady by Mr. P. B. Reckitt on January 23rd, 1919:

Miss F. Tiplady, the hospital,

As the hospital is closing on or about January 31st, I should like you to take as long a holiday as you think desirable, as during the time you have undertaken duty at the hospital, the work has been very hard, and I thank you for the excellent services you have rendered to all the soldiers who have passed through. I shall therefore be pleased to give you two month's salary, as from the 1st February.

Yours faithfully,

P.B. Reckitt.

Commandant and staff of Reckitt's Military Hospital

Front Row – W. Moon, T. Guest, Miss B. Linney, Miss Walton, Sister Evans, Dr. Holt, Dr. Divine, P. B. Reckitt, Sister Varey, Miss Hardy, Miss Thackray, Miss Kirby.
Standing on the extreme right, second from back (no hat) is Florence Tiplady, who worked on the catering side under Mr T. Guest.
Centre, marked with cross, Nurse Dora McGavin.

Mr T. Guest (Chef) and his staff. Third from left – Miss Florence Tiplady.

The information and photographs regarding Florence Tiplady, later Elvin, were given by her daughter, Miss Cathline Elvin of Hull, who worked at Reckitts from 1940 to 1983,as a Director's secretary.

Mr Harold J. Reckitt, jointly with Lady Helen Johnstone, founded a Hospital at Ris Oranges, Seine-et-Oise. Though the service rendered by this Hospital was for the benefit of French soldiers, efforts were made for a period of four or five months before its establishment to place the Hospital with the British, either at Malta or Alexandria, but these efforts failed. It was eventually made a full French Military Hospital, the first in France to be so honoured.

Its X-Ray Department was one of the best equipped in France, and a number of important discoveries were made. The Hospital was equipped for 207 beds. During the three years it was running 2,400 patients passed through it. It specialised in fractures, more especially fractures of the leg and hip. A large Out-patients' Department for the civil population was run in connection with it.

Mr Harold Reckitt was awarded the French decoration of the Reconnaisance Francaise, 2nd Class.

The hospital building was allocated by the French government in July, 1915. It had been a Jesuit College and unoccupied for ten years.

The first batch of wounded, September 26th 1915. The nursing staff consisted of American volunteers who were glad to assist the allies during the war.

1915

CHAPTER 2

Where are the boys of the old brigade who fought with us side by side.
Shoulder to shoulder, blade to blade fought till they fell and died.
Who so ready and undismayed, who so merry and true.
Where are the boys of the old brigade where are the lads we knew.
Steadily shoulder to shoulder, steadily blade by blade,
Ready and strong marching along the boys of the old brigade.

(Old Marching Song)

The Fallen – Letters from the Front:1915

The inauguration of the Menin Gate Memorial. Ypres.
Inside its great arch 56,000 names are carved onto the walls;
the names of the men who's bodies were never found.

Pte. Walter Stanley Murray, 1/4th East Yorks., Reg. No. 2221, was born in Hull and lived at 93 St. Georges Road. He joined Reckitts on April 4th, 1900, and worked in the Kingston Office. He died on 11th June, 1915, whilst in the line, when His own rifle accidentally discharged. His name appears in the Hull Daily Mail Roll of Honour on 28th June 1915.

Pte. Murray has no known grave and is commemorated on the Menin Gate Memorial, Ypres. Panel 21 and 31.

Pte.Albert Baxter, 1/4th East Yorks., Reg. No. 2450, was born in Hull and entered Reckitts employ on 22nd July, 1909, working in the Kingston Works. He enlisted in Hull early in the war and was killed in action on July 9th, 1915. His name was recorded on the Courtney Street Shrine and appeared in the Hull Daily Mail Roll of Honour on 10th October 1916.

Pte. Baxter was the husband of Mrs L. Baxter of 45 Chestnut Grove, Garden Village, Hull. He is buried in RE Farm Cemetery, Heuvelland, Belgium. 11.D.4.

Pte John Robert Bowden, 1/4th East Yorks., Reg. No. 2535, was born in Hull, joining the firm On May 13th, 1907, and worked in the Saw Mill at the Kingston Works. He enlisted early in the war and was killed in action on April 24th, 1915, Ypres, at the age of 22. His parents were Robert and Betsey Bowden of 3 Berkshire St, Hull. His name appears in the Hull Daily Mail Roll of Honour on May 27th 1915 and April 28th 1916.

Pte. Bowden has no known grave but is commemorated on the Menin Gate Memorial, Ypres, Belgium. Panel 21 and 31.

Pte. Thomas Broadley, 1/4th East Yorks., Reg. No. 3050, was born in Hull, and joined the firm on August 25th 1914, working at the Morley Street Works Hull. He enlisted in Hull and died of wounds on April 26th 1915, at the age of 30 years. He lived at 62 Clarendon St. Hull. His name appears in the Hull Daily Mail Roll of Honour on 14th and 15th May 1915.

Pte. Broadley is buried in Poperinge Old Military Cemetery, Belgium. 11.K.7.

Pte. Arthur Carver, 1/4th East Yorks., Reg. No. 2459, worked on the hoists at the Kingston Works. He was born in Hull and enlisted in Hull. In his 24th year he was killed in action on November 24th 1915. He is recorded in the Hull Daily Mail Roll of Honour of 27th May 1915. His parents were William and Matilda Carver of 78 Thomas Street, Hedon Rd, Hull.

Pte. Carver has no known grave but is commemorated on the Menin Gate Memorial, Ypres. Panel 21 and 31.

Pte. Charles Sydney Elyard, 1/4th East Yorks., Reg. No. 2538, was born in South Newington, Yorkshire, and joined Reckitts on 3rd February 1913, working as a representative. He enlisted in Hull and was killed in action on 6th August 1915, at the age of 24 years. He was the son of Charles and Lydia Elyard of Hull. His name appears in the Hull Daily Mail Roll of Honour on 20th August 1915 and August 7th 1916.

Charles S Elyard is commemorated on the Ploegsteert Memorial. Panel 4. Belgium.

Ely Taylor was reported killed on 20th May 1915 in 'OURS' as serving with the Royal Naval Brigade.This information was to lead me down a blind alley for a long time. After searching for him for years I was browsing through an old Reckitts's Publication when I came across the following: 'Ely Taylor (known as William). It turned out his real name is William not Ely and at last after ten years I found him.

William joined Reckitts employ on October 16th 1908,working as a fitter at the Kingston Works. He served with the Hood Battalion, Royal Navy Division at Gallipoli and lost his life on 7th May 1915, aged 36 years. He left a wife and three children; his home address was 22 Elm Tree Avenue, Garden Village, Hull.

Stoker (1st Class) Taylor is recorded in the Hull Daily Mail Roll of Honour on 21st May 1915: and In memoriam, from his mother, father, sisters and brothers– on 7th May 1917. He is buried in Lancashire Landing Cemetery, Turkey Grave E2

The following letter is from Pte. Frank Lonsdale Miller, 1/4th East Yorks., Reg. No. 1123, and was published in the Reckitts magazine - 'OURS' - in July, 1915:

> "I suppose you will have heard about the gallant deeds performed by the "Mad Mullahs", as the Canadians called us after our attack on the "Huns" position. It was a fine sight to see the "Knuts" advancing. You ought to hear some of the chaps in the trenches offering up a prayer for their safety. I have had some miraculous escapes; my pack was torn completely off my back by a lump of shrapnel; a piece of shrapnel hit me on my hat and broke the wire

rim, and my poor puttees were more "holely than Godly" with the same stuff. The weather here is grand, and I am sleeping in a tent. It reminds me of the Boys' Club camp at Hornsea." Pte. Miller was born in Hull and lived at 28 Laburnum Avenue, Garden Village. He enlisted in Hull early in the war and had worked at Reckitts on the Hoists since May 8th, 1908. His name was added to the growing lists of the 'Fallen' when he was killed on October 13th, 1915. His name appears in the Hull Daily Mail Roll of Honour on 18th October 1915. Pte. Miller is buried in Chapelle – D'Armentieres New Military Cemetery. France. A.3.

Pte. William Wharam, 1/4th East Yorks., Reg. No. 1864, was born in Grimsby, worked in Reckitts Canister Works and enlisted in Hull. He was killed in action on 3rd May, 1915, aged 19.

He was the son of Daniel and Mary Ann Wharam of 40 Providence Row, Beverley Road, Hull.

Pte. Wharam has no known grave but is commemorated on the Menin Gate Memorial, Ypres. Panel 21 and 31.

Trooper J. Hill, Hussars, killed in action, no other details given.

Mr Hill is not named on the Reckitts Rolls of Honour, nor is he to be found in the list of the fallen - 'OURS' - 1919.

Numerous J. Hill's are to be found in the war graves records, however none of them are troopers from the Hussars.

After spending many years looking for Trooper J. Hill I was browsing through an old Reckitts publication and came across a Trooper John Lill, killed in 1915. The factory magazine had spelt his name wrong and at last, nine years later, I found him.

Trooper John (Jack) Lill was killed in action serving with the 20th Hussars on 26th June 1915; age 23 years.

He was the son of John and Rachel Ann Lill of 35 Parrot Street, Hull: his name appears in the Hull Daily Mail Roll of Honour for July 5th 1915 as being killed in the Dardenneles.

On 26th June 1916 he is listed in memoriam as having died of wounds in Alexandria. John Lill is buried in the Alexandria (Chatby) Military and War Memorial Cemetery. Egypt.

201269 Pte. George Lill (brother of John) was killed in action; serving with the 1/4th East Yorkshire Rgt on 16th November 1916. He was posted missing in the Hull Daily Mail on 17th November 1916 and in the lists of the fallen on 29th December the same year. George has no known grave but is commemorated on the Thiepval memorial. Somme. France.

LETTERS FROM THE FRONT

Pte. C Bradley, Labour Corps, joined the firm on October 25th 1909, he wrote home from the front in 1915 and remembered fondly his time at Reckitts Boys Club:

"I am sorry I shall be too old for the club when the war is over, unless the age limit is raised, but I shall always remember the old club and give it a good name. I dare say had it not been for the club I should not have been here today."

Pte. John Henry Collins, East Yorkshire Rgt, joined the firm on 6th October 1910 and worked there until he enlisted early in the war. He started his military career at the front, was later given a cushy job in the mess but preferred to rejoin his pals in the trenches:

> "I have volunteered to go back to the front. They asked me to stay in the mess but I said I was sick of it and wanted to go back."

Pte. John Stone had entered Reckitts employ on October 23rd 1909, and worked there until he enlisted in the East Yorkshire Regiment. He wrote the following letter after being wounded:

> "I arrived at Boulogne on Wednesday morning and got into a nice clean bed. The Sisters there, who are Scotch, are very kind; they brought us all out food and gave us fags into the bargain, sometimes we got fruit and chocolates. I stayed in at the hospital until the Thursday night, when I learnt that I was going to England. I was carried again on the stretcher to the Quay side and put on an Ambulance ship, a fine French boat. I had a splendid trip across the channel to Southampton, and when we landed we were put on an Ambulance train and sent to Manchester, arriving there at 1am on Saturday morning. Sometimes my wound gives me a friendly dig in the side, but I thank God I am still alive."

Pte. James Hopkinson, East Yorkshire Regiment, joined the firm on March 18th 1910. He describes here how his thoughts often turn to home and the old factory:

> "When in the trenches during a lull we sit down and our mind always wanders to home and dear old Hull. Of course we are not always like that, because there is generally a lot of chaffing and fun going on. Sometimes about the time for leaving work at home, somebody will shout 'Bell Oh', and then there's a laugh and we get talking about our mates at work and wonder what they will be doing."

Pte. Ernest Savage, 1/4th East Yorks., had been at Reckitts since 20th June 1910 and had been with the Territorial Force since before the war:

> "I remember the times at Gym., when you used to chaff me about the Terriers, but I never expected we should have the opportunity of being out here, doing our bit for our country."

Pte. Harry Marsden, East Yorks., began working at Reckitts on October 23rd 1911. He joined the army early in the war and describes here his first attack at Ypres, 1915.

> "I shall never forget that first charge we had, when we lost our Colonel and so many officers and men. The lads went splendidly, just as if they were on parade. It was a great charge, or rather attack: for about a mile over open country the gunners had nothing to do but fire at us. As soon as the officer said 'Now, lads!' they were up like one man; bullets and shells coming over and pals dropping by our side. It was a sight to stir any man."

Pte Frederick James Pulsford, 8th East Surreys, joined the staff of the London House on November 4th, 1912; in this letter home he remembers mines being exploded by both sides:

> "I must say we had a fairly good time in billets this time, enjoying a couple of Footer matches and a trip (by ASC motor lorries) to a village a few miles back to a cinema picture house, or rather a barn. It was such a grand change, which we were all thankful for. We again took up our places in the firing-line last Sunday evening, and so far things in general are rather quieter than usual, although last Wednesday morning I thought we were in for another 'lively time.' We were 'standing-to' in case of an attack, when we sent up one of our mines.
>
> Immediately after, the Germans sent up a huge mine, by far the largest I've seen. The trenches fairly rocked like a boat, and a little shelling started but after all nothing of much note ensued. The crater made by this mine was 100 yards x 80 yards."

There is another letter from Pte. Pulsford in the 1916 chapter.

Sapper J. Spruit, Electrician, wrote the following account of a near miss in France. However, he is not recorded in 'OURS' - 1919, on the Roll of Honour of those who served:

"One time I was lying in a ditch on the Fortuin Road, and could see the Germans pouring out of the wood near St. Julien, where the guns were which our fellows re-captured on the next day. It was only about 800 yards away, and didn't I long for a rifle. They saw me climb a pole to reach the end of my wire, which was hanging 8-ft or so up. I had just made the joint when they got a machine gun on me. I came down that pole on the run, I can tell you, with a bullet, which struck the pole first, struck in the thick part of my cap. I have that bullet in my pocket. For nearly an hour I laid beside the pole and daren't move, for every time I showed myself I could hear the pop-pop of the gun and the whine of the bullets; then one of our shells blew the whole thing to pieces, and didn't I run! I did about 400 in record time to the other side of the field, where I could shelter."

Cpl;. J. N. Cowell, Outside Staff, wrote the following letter. However his name is not recorded in 'OURS' - 1919, on the Roll of Honour of those who served:

Night Work.

"In October last the trench warfare commenced in Belgium, and the whole of the 2nd Cavalry Division, of which my squadron formed part, were given bayonets, and we had to do our share in manning the trenches with the Infantry. After leaving our horses a distance of about three or four miles behind the firing line, we would walk up to the trenches carrying all (or nearly all) our worldly possessions. That was really the worst part of the business, for the jolly 'Bosches' would invariably dot the road with a few 'coal boxes' and other interesting things.

One night we were engaged in putting up barbed wire entanglements. We had notified the regiment holding the front line of trenches that we would be out in front of them for some time. We had rather a long job and it was nearly dawn when we started to return. We had only got a few yards towards our own trenches when the bullets started whistling unpleasantly close, the Boshes had spotted us and were trying to make our trip 'some' warm. Eventually it turned out that these few shots were the signal for firing to commence right along the line. Then our people started to respond; we shouted to our troops in the trenches to stop their skylarking and let us come in, but there was nothing doing. We were lying in a field of mangels, and there was nothing to do but worm into these vegetables as far as possible and try to appear like one! When daylight came the firing died down somewhat and by making short rushes, one or two at a time, we eventually reached our trenches, but not without having to convince the Indians (who had relieved the regiment of Cavalry that occupied the trench when we set out) that our intentions were honest and that we were really and truly English. Our dusky friends had been rather dubious of us.

At the present moment I am temporarily HORS-DE-COMBAT through being rather close to a high-explosive shell at the wrong moment."

Sapper John (Jack) Holdsworth, 1/1st E.R.Field Co., Royal Engineers, worked at the Morley Street Works, Hull, and had been with the firm since October 18th 1906. In this letter home he writes of the old times:

"Just a line thanking you for your most welcome letters .... It was quite a pleasure for me to hear from you and dear old Boys' Club, and I am looking forward very much – if I am spared - to the time when we shall all meet again. When I was at home I had all my heart and soul in the Boys' Club. I often think of the time when I used to go to the Gym. and have a real good hours' drill and a good bath on the top of it. We are going into the trenches tonight."

L/Cpl. James Thornton Sanderson, 1/4th East Yorks., joined the Dansom Lane Office Staff on 21st April, 1910, he recounts here how he spent Whit-Monday 1915:

"We spent a rare Whit-Monday; the "Huns" commenced affairs by gassing, which enabled them to get a footing in a certain part of the English trenches. We were called up to reinforce, which is a difficult job in the daytime. We almost reached the line, by crawling, when they trained a maxim gun on us. We read in the papers of the enemy being short of ammunition; it has been a myth. For instance, on the

2nd inst., they bombarded us with huge shells from 3am until the same time in the afternoon, sending them at the rate of two per minute. I am not exaggerating in saying this. The shells shake the whole earth for a long way round, and pieces fly easily 600 yards. I was hit on that date by a piece, but happily it never pierced me. I think the enemy's object was to break up all the communication trenches so that our reinforcements wouldn't reach the line, but we are equal to that sort of business, for many regiments, including ourselves, had been out all the night digging other communication trenches. So, when they bombarded, our men left the first trenches, taking up new positions with maxim guns, and when the enemy came to take possession of things later on, our men opened out with the maxims, and what a mess of them they made."

Pte. Daniel Lang, 1/4th East Yorks., joined the firm and worked on the Hoists at the Kingston Works, he gives a very vivid picture of events as his unit stormed the German positions and earned the nickname 'The Mad Mullahs', given to them by the Canadians and British regulars in recognition of their bravery:

"You would be surprised if you saw the lads laughing and joking while the shells are bursting within a few feet of the trench. I will try to give you a brief account of our doings while I was with the battalion. We left Newcastle on the Saturday, and arrived at Boulogne at about midnight. Here we put up at a rest camp for the night. On the following day we journeyed by train to the place where we were to be billeted for some time. We could hear the continual thunder of the guns, and when darkness came we were all out watching the shells bursting and seeing the starlights go up, illuminating the front for a considerable distance. We got the alarm after we had been there about three days, and it came when we were asleep in the farmer's barn. We fell in as quickly as possible and marched down the main road leading to the front. We were then told we could sleep, as best we could, in a field, while we were waiting for the motor omnibuses. They arrived during the next day, and we were all soon aboard and on our way to the front. We arrived at a rest camp just behind the firing line about 6 o'clock. The Germans were bombarding Ypres when we arrived, and we could hear the shells whistling in the air. The Colonel was standing against our section and he said to us 'they are breaking you in a bit.' We got to bed at last, but we had not been there long when I heard the Sergeant

Major's voice in the doorway 'Fall in.' We fell in and were marched down a road until we came to a hill behind which we stayed for the night. It was there we received our first casualties, by the Germans sending a stray shell or two over. During the next day we got the order to advance in support. We advanced towards the firing line for a bit and then we had to dig ourselves in as the Germans had seen our move and were sending a perfect fusillade of shrapnel. We started to advance again about 4 o'clock in the afternoon, and on our way we passed the Canadians who had been through the mill all the morning and were forced to retire a bit. They were betting we would get wiped out, and I saw tears in the eyes of one or two of them. We kept on advancing, losing one or two men by the shrapnel, but we never wavered. At last we came under rifle fire, and it was after that we lost our men. We had to advance by short rushes, and every time I got up I expected it to be the last. I saw men falling on all sides wounded and killed. The Germans started to run though, and we kept advancing until the regiment we were supporting was back in position. We then lay and waited until it was a bit darker before we left for some trenches. The Germans bombarded these with shrapnel and we had some casualties there. At last we got relived and made our way back to the rest camp. We were congratulated by the General and the C.O.'s of the regular regiments on our splendid feat. The Canadians and the regulars called us the 'Mad Mullahs'. We rested for three days and then we started back for the trenches at dusk. The Germans were again sending shrapnel, and we got orders to dig ourselves further in and deeper. We evacuated these trenches and took up a position in some more which were being heavily bombarded by the Germans. Shells were falling all around the trench and I expected every minute to be blown up. We had been four days in the second trenches when I got wounded. The shell fell in the trench about four feet away from me, blowing one man absolutely to pieces. The next thing I knew was that the trench had fallen in on us, and I had a terrible pain in my left leg. Our comrades soon dug us out and we were shifted to another part of the trench, where one of the lads undid my puttee, and put a field dressing on my leg. I was removed at dusk and at last arrived here where I am being well treated. I think the regiment are going to have a good rest away from the firing line to be reorganised. I forgot to mention my leg is fractured also. Give my best respects to the Club. Wishing them all the best of luck, I remain, your affectionate comrade, Dan."

This anonymous letter is an account of the first action in the war of the 1/4th East Yorks. – Hull Territorials, at Ypres in 1915. Many Reckitts employees had enlisted in this local unit:

British General Headquarters, May 19.
As printed in 'OURS' - 1915

When the story of the battle of Ypres can be written in detail, it will yield one of the finest records of heroism and endurance in the history of the British Army. It is a story of sacrifice and dogged resistance against overwhelming odds, of fragments of battalions refusing to abandon seemingly impossible positions, of individual acts of courage which cannot be surpassed, and the success of a series of "forlorn hopes" which checked an over-confident enemy and saved Ypres. Above all, it is the story of a "soldier's battle" – a battle fought under new conditions which demanded all the initiative and self-reliance of the men who held the salient. The terrors of gas, and the greatest bombardment yet experienced, failed to demoralise them, and they went through the seeming chaos of the new fog of battle coldly determined and undismayed. Captains were leading remnants of battalions, and wounded sergeants commanded ragged companies under a deluge of German shells, while they clung grimly to their battered trenches, yet every man "carried on" without a thought for himself.

THE BRAVERY OF UNTRIED MEN

There were territorial battalions fighting with the deliberation of seasoned regulars, fresh drafts from home that went direct from their newly assigned billets to the firing line, and held their stretch of sand-bagged defences as calmly as though they had been in the field for months, new non-commissioned officers, who never heard the whistle of shrapnel before, directing their men like veterans.

No troops ever behaved more nobly under fire than these men who suddenly found themselves in an inferno of bursting shells. For days and nights they faced an ordeal sufficient to try the stoutest heart – and never did they falter. Some of them came back, but many of them died, and as an officer who commanded some of them told me yesterday: "They died like men." In this way the second battle of Ypres, which began on April 22, and lasted for nearly three weeks, was a British victory, although the shortened salient on the map may make it look like a defeat. It again proved the superiority of the British soldier over his enemy. Whenever the German infantry attempted to storm it was invariably thrown back and only the employment of a vast number of heavy guns, and the expenditure of an almost incredible number of high explosive shells, in addition to the use of gas, gave the enemy the strip of ground which has been added to their line east and north-east of Ypres. At no time did the Germans attempt a great infantry attack. Whenever their infantry came forward in the usual close formation our troops hurled them back again demoralised. They advanced without spirit, depending wholly on their great howitzers, and refusing to press forward when they saw men dropping on every side. Whenever our trenches were occupied it was only after a concentrated shell fire had practically obliterated them from the line.

CAPTAIN EASTON'S HEROISM

I said this was a "soldier's battle." Many individual acts of heroism prove it. Raw Territorial privates and non-commissioned officers, suddenly deprived of officers, fought on their own, and led little parties of desperate men across the shell-swept plain to almost certain death. While the 4th East Yorkshires (Territorial) were being heavily shelled, and it appeared that the entire battalion would be wiped out, Captain Easton, although wounded three times, staggered up and down the trench encouraging the men and refusing to go to a dressing station."

L/Cpl. James Thornton Sanderson, 1/4 East Yorks., worked in Reckitts office, Dansom Lane, joining the firm on 21st April, 1910. Here he writes home about trench life, he was so close to the enemy they could call out to each other:

> "Today (Sunday) is the 4th day in the trenches in a spell we are doing, I am at present on my hour watch. The sun is scorching hot, it is lovely. They are only 250 yards from us. We sit and look through a periscope on the opposite side of the trench, but everything is very quiet, practically no signs of life. At night they work in the front of their trench with impunity, so the other night a couple of sergeants crept out and threw bombs on them, they soon scuttered. They retaliated last night by having a sniper out shooting at our listening patrol, but a few of us on watch at the time let rapid fire go; that cleared him, for no more shots came over. We have only been bombarded once since coming into these trenches. Our trenches are well built, to reach this

firing line we walk down a natural trench known as 'Plank Avenue'. One would walk down here in perfect safety in day-light, it goes back for more than a mile. Sometimes they shout over to us, they know who we are. If we want to annoy them we only have to say 'Has anyone seen a German Band?' They start blazing away when we do."

L/Cpl. George Reginald Atkinson, 13th East Yorks. (4th Hull Pals), joined Reckitts on June 8th, 1905, and was employed in the starch works. Here he encounters a friend from home:

"I saw Happy Hooligan (Hebby) the other day. I asked him if he wouldn't sooner be hay-making at Sutton. He said 'He'd rather be working at Reckitts' for nought.' ... Flan and I are now with the Motor Ambulances, and having the time of our lives."

L/Cpl. Arthur Harrison, Sherwood Foresters, recounts here a close call as his unit took the enemy line and came in for some attention from the German artillery:

" I must tell you all I dare about the big scrap we have been in. Now after going into the trenches we had a lecture, and they told us that we had a very tough job to do, and that General French thought we were his best troops and chose our Division to do it. Well the time arrived, after being put off for a couple of days, and mad with excitement we started off to go to the trenches, which were held by Territorials. Monday morning was selected for the attack. Hours seemed like weeks, and three minutes before the bombardment the Germans opened out just as though they had been told about it. At last the time came for us to start, and just as one gun, our Artillery started. 'Up you go, with the best of luck,' was everybody's cry, and we mounted the parapet. All was over in about 10 minutes, I mean we had completed our work. Now the question was, could we hold the captured trenches? With everyone working as they never worked before, we managed to reverse the parapet and strengthen it. All of a sudden the Germans started to bombard, and, believe me, I never saw anything like it all the eleven months I have been out here. For 16 hours they sent thousands of aerial torpedoes at us, practically flattening the trenches out."

Arthur Harrison entered Reckitts employ in January, 1908.

1916

CHAPTER 3

From Little Towns in a far land we came,
To save our honour and a world aflame.
By little towns in a far land we sleep,
And trust that world we won for you to keep.

THE FALLEN - LETTERS FROM THE FRONT: 1916

The Somme Memorial, Thiepval, France.

On its walls are carved and names of 73,412 men who's bodies were never found.

2nd Lt Percival Bewman Palmer Robinson, King's Own Yorkshire Light Infantry, had been employed at Reckitts on the accounts staff since November 10th, 1910. He was born in Hull at 135 Newland Avenue on 18th June, 1894, attending Newland Avenue School before gaining a five year scholarship to Hymers College, Hull. He entered the college (in Form 3B) in September, 1908, carrying off many scholastic honours, gaining five firsts, including a prize for French given by the Rt. Honourable T.R. Ferens, M.P. Robinson left the college in November, 1910, and entered Reckitts employ.

At the start of the war he was offered a commission in the East Yorkshire Regiment but, preferring cavalry, he joined the 20th Hussars, and towards the end of October was selected for the Dragoon Guards (Queens Bays).

In June, 1915, as cavalry was not then required, there was a call for volunteers to be transferred to the infantry, upon which Mr Robinson journeyed to Hull, and was attached to the 3rd Battalion, King's Own Yorkshire Light Infantry and was made a Lance Corporal. In the August following he was promoted Corporal and then Acting Sergeant. He was gazetted 2nd Lt. in October while in the trenches and returned to England to take up his commission. He joined the 11th Battalion King's Own Yorkshire Light Infantry in November. At this stage in his career he passed various examinations in Military law. He was also successful, after a special course at Otley, in obtaining a certificate which qualified him as a Brigade Signalling instructor. On June 16th, 1916, he went to France, going straight into the line with the 8th Battalion, King's Own Yorkshire Light Infantry. He took part in the start of the Somme Campaign on 1st July, shortly after this he was reported missing. In the Reckitts book of the Fallen – 1919, his date of death is given as 10th July, 1916. In the official records his date of death is 1st July, 1916. He has no known grave but is commemorated on the Thiepval Memorial to the Missing. France.

Pte. George Spires, 1st battalion Coldstream Guards, enlisted at the start of the war at the age of 22 years. He was killed in action at Guinchy on December 22nd, 1914. An officer of the Indian Corps watched the Guards attack on the day and wrote:

"They marched forward without the least hesitation under the most terrific fire as though they were on parade. I watched their progress with the profoundest admiration."

George Spires entered Reckitts employ on April 26th, 1907, his name can still be seen on the Dansom Lane Shrine that is fixed to the factory wall.

Pte Spires has no known grave but is commemorated on the Le Touret Memorial. Pas-De-Calais. France. Panels 2 and 3.

Sapper Charles Darling, Royal Engineers, 1/1st E.R. Field-COY, enlisted at the beginning of the war, he had worked at the firm for five years as a bricklayer under his father, Mr T. Darling, the firm's foreman bricklayer. He was gassed on the night of 30th April, 1916, within only minutes of reaching the trenches and never had time to put on his gas mask. He died on May 9th without recovering consciousness at the age of 23. His younger brother was wounded on the same day. Charles Darling is not recorded on any Reckitts Roll of Honour, nor is he on the list of the Fallen – 'OURS' – 1919. His home address was 67 Craven Street, Holderness Road, Hull and his name appears in the Hull Daily Mail Roll of Honour on 20th May,1916. His last resting place is Bailleul Communal Cemetery extension. France. 11.D.48.

Pte. Frederick J. Chapman, 12th Battalion East Yorkshire Regiment (3rd Hull Pals), Reg. No. 22506, was in the Territorial Force before the war and was born in Hull. He was restrained from enlisting earlier in the war by a sense of duty to a widowed mother. He was originally with the 1/4th East Yorks. but was moved to the 12th later. He enlisted in Hull during the month of February, 1916, under the Derby Scheme and went to France in June. On August 6th of that year he was killed in action at the age of 26. Pte. Chapman entered Reckitts employ on 21st July, 1914.

His home address was 37 Worthing Street, Hull and he appears in the Hull Daily Mail Roll of Honour on 28th August, 1916.

Pte Chapman is buried in the St Vaast Post Military Cemetery. Pas-De-Calais. France.

Pte. Herbert Sellers, 1/4th East Yorks., Reg. No. 4715, joined the firm upon leaving school on 14th February, 1911. He was a member of the works football team, his sister was forewoman in the 'Zebra' machine room and his brother was employed in the packing room but later went to the front. Herbert Sellers was born in Hull, enlisted in Hull in October, 1915, and after only six weeks in France died of wounds in hospital on September 19th, 1916. He was remembered in 'OURS' of that year:

"He was a good lad, manly, gentle and kind, duty's call came to him as to the countless thousands more, and his all too young life was the free response."

Pte. Sellers was 19 years old and is recorded on the Dansom Lane Shrine that still stands. His home address was 23 Pemberton Street, Dansom Lane and he was the son of Charles and Charlotte Sellars of that address.

His name appeared in the Hull Daily Mail Roll of Honour on 25th September, 1916: and he is buried in St Sever Cemetery. France.

Pte. Joseph Ernest Cousins, 7th King's Liverpool Regiment, joined Reckitts on August 21st, 1913, and was employed in the Shinio Branch. This brave young soldier was twice mentioned in despatches and was killed on June 28th, 1916, at the age of 20 years. He was the son of Mrs M Cousins of 54 Sweden Street, Waterloo, Liverpool, and now lies in Wailley Orchard Cemetery, Pas-de-Calais, France.

Cpl. George Edward Hogg, 11th Battalion East Yorkshire Regiment (2nd Hull Pals), Reg. No. 11/63, was born in Hull and joined Reckitts on June 8th, 1911, working in the Lead Mill. He enlisted at the Hull City Hall in September, 1914, trained in England and went to Eygpt in 1915, his unit went to France in March, 1916, to prepare for the Somme offensive. On October 13th,1916, at the age of 23 he was killed in action by shellfire. His Company Commander wrote home the following letter to his parents:

"He was well liked by everyone and all ranks will greatly miss him, a splendid type of fellow, he showed the greatest gallantry in cutting through the wire."

Cpl. Hogg's brother was serving in the trenches at the time of his death, they were both very close, and was so grief-stricken that he had to go to hospital. George Edward was the son of Samuel and Sophia Hogg of 5 Prison Bungalows, Hedon Road, Hull, and now lies in Euston Road Cemetery, Collincamps, Somme. France.

L/Cpl. William A Macpherson, 10th East Yorks. (Hull Commercials – 1st Hull Pals), Reg. No. 10/827, was taken into Reckitts employ on 2nd December, 1903, and worked on the staff of the Insurance Department. He was born in Hull and enlisted at the Hull City Hall in September, 1914. In 1915 he went to Egypt with his unit until all four of Hull's Pals Battalions were moved to France in March, 1916, to prepare for the Somme Offensive. He was wounded on June 4th, 1916, and died the following day in Abbeville Hospital at the age of 26 years. He was buried in Abbeville Cemetery. His colleagues at Reckitts paid him the following tribute in 'OURS' of that year:

"Mac, as he was affectionately termed, held the respect and esteem of all his associates. He was an enthusiastic cricketer and footballer and a member of the works team."

He was the son of James Coppock and Fanny Jane Macpherson of 35 Middleburg Street Hull.

55/113686. Stoker 1st Class Alfred Dean, H.M.S. Invincible was drowned on May 31st, 1916, during the Battle of Jutland at the age of 22 years. The only information on Alfred Dean comes from 'OURS' - 1916.

"Before joining the Navy he was a member of our Boys Club and always spoke appreciatively of his debt to it.

Physically he was a fine fellow and he was to his widowed mother ever a devoted son."

He was the son of Frederick Robert and Sarah Dean of 104 Durham Street, Hull: and is commemorated on the Naval Memorial at Portsmouth.

Alfred Dean is only featured on the Boys Club Roll of Honour, he is not to be found in the lists of the 'Fallen', 'OURS' – 1919, or on the new Rolls of Honour in Reckitts Garden of Remembrance.

Pte. Francis Joseph Scott, 1/4th East Yorks., Reg. No. 3381, was born in Hull and joined the firm on May 24th, 1909, working in the Box Shop. He enlisted in Hull in January, 1915, and went to France the following June. While he was cleaning his rifle a German Sniper killed him on August 4th, 1916, at the age of 21 years. He was the son of Mr & Mrs William Scott of 23 Estcourt Street, Newbridge Road, Hull, and now lies in Bailleul Communal Cemetery Extension. France. 11.F.135. He was remembered in 'OURS' – December, 1916:

"Entering our employ as a boy he attached himself to the Boys Club and showed much ability in manual instruction. He was of an exceptionally gentle, quiet disposition, a temperament – like many another – wholly opposed to the military life. But he proved himself to be, as was said of him, "Cool and calm under fire and every inch a soldier." His brother is a prisoner in Turkey."

Francis Scott was recorded in the Hull Daily Mail Roll of Honour on 9th September 1916.

Pte. Walter Longley joined Reckitts on 18th March 1907, enlisted in January 1915 in the East Yorks. and was sent to France in July 1916 with the 1/5th battalion of the Border Regiment.. He died of wounds on October 1st 1916 at the age of 39 years. In 'OURS' of that year he was reported to be "A man of excellent character and sober habit", he left a widow and four children. Walter was the husband of Edith Longley of 7 The Grove Laburnum Avenue, Garden Village, Hull: and now lies in Dernancourt Communal Cemetery Extension. Somme. France. 111.D.42.

Cpl. Albert Lezanto Andrews, 1/4th East Yorks., Reg. No. 2202, was born in Alnwick, Northumberland and entered the firm's employ on 28th January 1907 working in the Brasso Mill. He enlisted in July 1915 in Hull, was wounded on July, 15th 1916 and died the following day, age 32. He was remembered in 'OURS' – 1916:

> "He felt it was his duty, that simple motive of ten-thousand supreme sacrifices. He was a man of sterling character, of gentle, quiet disposition and studious tastes, and much respected by his fellow workers."

Albert Andrews home address was 191 Dansom Lane, Hull. The son of James and Sabina Andrews of Balfour Street, Hull, he was married to Mrs M A Andrews, and his final resting place is Bailleul Communal Cemetery Extension. France.

Pte. Herbert Emmerson, 1/4th East Yorks., Reg. No. 2216, was born in Hull and entered Reckitts employ on 2nd December 1908, working on the Hoists in the Brasso Department. He was an old member of the Boys Club and played in the works football team. He enlisted in Hull and was killed by shellfire on September 10th 1916, Age 21. the following tribute was paid to him in 'OURS' of that year:

"A manly and modest young fellow, he was an exemplary son, liked and respected by his workmates and in his circle of church associates."

Herbert was the son of Mrs Elizabeth Emmerson of 9 Kingston Place, Witham, Hull. He is buried in Bazentin-Le-Petit Communal Cemetery Extension, Somme. France.

35108. Pte. Edward Sullivan 'C' COY, 16th Battalion Royal Welsh Fusiliers, joined the firm on June 7th 1909 and was a junior member of the London Clerical Staff. He enlisted in December 1915 and was killed on July 11th 1916 during the Somme Battle at the age of 21 years. His sad loss was reported in 'OURS' – 1916."

"His disposition was marked by an unruffled and conciliatory good humour that endeared him to those associated with him, and the news of his death was received with great regret."

Edward Sullivan was the son of Mr and Mrs Sullivan of 56 Marcia Road, Old Kent Road, London: He has no known grave but is commemorated on the Thiepval Memorial to the missing. Somme. France. Pier and-Face 4A.

Pte. John Hinds, 'B' COY, 7th Battalion King's Liverpool Regiment, was employed by the firm on 10th May 1911 and worked in the Shinio Works. He was killed in action on November 26th 1915 at the age of 38 years. He left a widow and three children and was the Husband of Elizabeth C Hinds of 37 Lancaster Street, Walton, Liverpool.

John Hinds is buried in Bethune Town Cemetery. Pas-De- Calais. France. IV.G.8.

S/29105 Pte. George A. Sharman, 1st Battalion Gordon Highlanders, entered Reckitts employ on 21st October 1907 and worked as a fitter in the Canister Works. He was killed on April 1st 1916 at the age of 33. His epitaph in 'OURS' - 1916 read as follows:

"He felt like so many more, that he could not resist his sense of duty, in spite of married responsibilities."

He left a widow and two children, has no known grave and is commemorated on the Menin Gate Memorial to the Missing. Ypres. Panel 38.

Pte. Percival Dalton, 1/4th East Yorks., Reg. No. 2368, was born in Hull and joined the firm on 14th March 1910, working in the printing department of the Canister Works. He was a member of the works football team and also of the troupe of Morris Dancers. The following quote is from the Reckitts Magazine - 'OURS' of 1916:

"He was a good and dutiful lad, his parents have suffered a double loss, for it will be remembered that their elder son, Tom, was killed in May, 1915."

Percival Dalton enlisted in Hull at the start of the war and went to France early in April, 1915, he was reported missing on 24th of that month at the age of 19 years. His body was never found but he is commemorated on the Menin Gate Memorial to the Missing. Ypres. Panel 21 and 31. The Dalton brothers were the sons of Herbert Edward and Mary Ann Dalton of 58 Rendel Street, Grimsby.

Pte. Thomas Edward Dalton, 1/4th East Yorks., Reg. No. 2515, was born in Hull and joined the firm on march 11th 1907 working as a chauffeur. He enlisted in Hull with his brother, Percival, and served with him in the trenches. When he was reported missing Thomas went searching for his brother and was grievously injured in the process. He died of his wounds on 6th May 1915 at the age of 22 years.

Thomas Dalton was listed in the Hull Daily Mail Roll of Honour on 8th May 1916. He is buried in Bailleul Communal Cemetery Extension. France. 11.A.118.

12737. Pte. Reginald B. Gorely, 6th Shropshire Light Infantry, joined the firm on 1st April 1909 and worked on the staff of Introducers. At the beginning of the war he joined the 'Pals Battalion' of the Shropshires and took part in some of the fiercest fighting of the Somme Campaign. He was one of a party of men carrying water to the front line on September 6th 1916 when a shell dropped in the middle of them Killing him instantly. He was 28 years of age. In a letter dated September 13th of that year his Company Commander wrote home to his parents the following moving epitaph:

"Your son was extremely popular with all ranks. As his Company Commander and the only original officer of the Company, may I tell you that I had the highest opinion of him, knowing him as I did for the best part of two years. His death has left us poorer, for men such as he can ill be spared, especially now, when we have need of the best and bravest. Up to the moment of his death he had done some magnificent work. He was fearless in everything. He was amongst those who by their work have made our Regiment and our Battalion one of the most highly spoken of in the field of battle. Beloved by all his comrades, thought extremely highly of by all his officers, his death has been keenly felt and has cast a gloom over all."

Reginald Bertram Gorely has no known grave but is commemorated on the Thiepval Memorial to the Missing. Somme. France.

Pte. Samuel Snow, 1st Battalion East Yorks. Regiment, Reg. No. 16097, had been with the firm for fourteen years, entering their employ on 26th July, 1900. He was born in Hull and enlisted in Hull in December 1914, joining his unit in France in June 1915. He was killed in action on the first day of the Somme Battle, 1st July 1916. The following tribute was paid to him in the Reckitts magazine – 'OURS' – 1916:

"Sam, as he was popularly known, was much liked by his work-mates, and his death came as sad news to them."

Samuel Snow was 34 Years old and left a wife and three children. He was the son of Mr and Mrs Yeaman of 63 Lime Street, Hull. His name was featured on the Spyvee Street Shrine, this no longer exists.

He was listed among the missing in the Hull Daily Mail on 22nd August 1916. On October 3rd, 4th, 14th and 28th 1916 he was in the Hull Daily Mail Roll of Honour as killed. Samuel has no known grave but is commemorated on the Thiepval Memorial to the Missing. Somme. France. Pier and Face 2C.

Pte. Valentine Percival Nasby, 1/4th Battalion East Yorks. Regiment, Reg. No. 1560, worked in the Canister Works and had been with the firm since June 19th 1911. He was born in Hull and before the war was a member of the Territorial Force. He went out to France in April 1915 and died of wounds received on June 17th 1916. The following tribute was paid to him in 'OURS', 1916:

"Of a kind loveable disposition, he was very popular among his fellow workers."

Laurence Nasby, his younger brother, worked at Reckitts but enlisted in 1916 in the 11th Sherwood Foresters, another brother, - Thomas, was with the Hull Commercials (10th East Yorks.). He was killed on 13th November 1916 and has no known grave, but is commemorated on the Thiepval Memorial to the Missing. Pier and Face 2C.

Pte. V. P. Nasby was 21 years old and is buried in the British Cemetery, Bailleul, France. His name appeared in the Hull Daily Mail Roll of Honour on June 26th 1916 and June 18th1917, with fond memories from his Mother, sister Lillie, brothers, Fiancee Elsie and a friend Ida. His name was added to the Lorne Street Shrine and appeared in the Hull Daily Mail in Memoriam, 1st December 1917.

Pte. George Wilson Beckett, 8th Battalion East Yorks. Regiment, Reg. No. 21593, was employed at the Kingston Works on the Hoists and joined the firm on 27th February 1911. He was born in Hull, was a member of the Boys Club and a religious worker. On two occasions he was rejected by the Army but later enlisted under the Derby Scheme and was 20 years old when he was killed on June 13th 1916. A tribute to him appeared in 'OURS', the Reckitts magazine of 1916:

"A highly esteemed young man among those who knew him, his death was much regretted."

Pte. Beckett's home address was 264 Danson Lane, Hull, and his name is recorded on the Dansom Lane Shrine that survives to this day.

His name appears in the Hull Daily Mail Roll of Honour on June 26th 1916 and in the casualty lists for July 3rd 1916. George W. Beckett is buried in Ridge-Wood Military Cemetery. Belgium.

Pte. George Anderson, 12th East Yorks. (3rd Hull Pals), Reg. No. 12/1155, was employed in the Canister Works and had been with the firm since 21st October 1907. He enlisted in December 1914, at the age of 21, went to Egypt in 1915 and France in 1916. On August 28th 1916 he was killed by a sniper and buried just behind the firing line. In 'OURS' of 1916 he was remembered:

"He was an old member of the Boys Club, a good son and of a bright, jolly disposition, he was held in affectionate regard by his fellow workers."

Pte. Anderson was born in Hull. His name appears in memoriam in the Hull Daily Mail August 28th 1917. He is buried in the St Vaast Post Military Cemetery, Pas-de-Calais. France. 111.M.18.

LETTERS FROM THE FRONT

'OURS'

1916

WHEN I COME HOME

When I come home, and leave behind
Dark things I would not call to mind,
I'll taste good ale and home-made bread,
And see white sheets and pillows spread.
And there is one who'll softly creep
To kiss me ere I fall asleep,
And tuck me 'neath the counterpane,
I shall be a boy again –
When I come home!

A poem by Sgt Leslie Coulson, died of wounds : Oct 8th 1916. (published in 'OURS' December 1916). He is buried in Grovetown cemetery. 4½ miles south of Albert.

Acting Company Sergeant Major Clifford Streat, D.C.M., 10th Battalion East Yorks Regiment (Hull Commercials – 1st Hull Pals), joined the firm on October 26th 1908 and worked in the Office. He wrote the following account of the work of the company runner:

> The "runner" is first torn from slumber himself and his duty is probably to spoil the beauty sleep of those of high as well as low estate – even of the Commanding Officer himself – as the alarms and excursions of war demand. The uninitiated "runner" will approach his victim quietly and stand saying "Sir" a dozen times or so in various modulations of voice before touching his man on the shoulder. The experienced "runner", however, failing to extract more than a grunt by a sound shaking, will deftly place his cigarettes under the slumberer's nose – with great effect.

Sgt. John Gates, M.M., 15th Royal Warwicks, entered Reckitts employ on 18th April 1907 and worked on the staff of Introducers. He was wounded in May 1916 and in this letter home describes how he was wounded a second time:

"At one o'clock on Sunday morning our attack commenced. The leading battalion left their trenches promptly in three waves of attackers and we immediately took up their late positions. For a minute the Germans appeared to be taken by surprise, then their machine guns opened fire and the fun started in earnest. Our guns, which had been firing all night, intensified their fire on the Huns' support line. The German big guns opened on us. One shell fell clean on the parapet of the trench. I was wounded in the face and the side."

Cpt. Henry Ellis Hill, M.C., 84th Field Company Royal Engineers and 20th Divisional Headquarters, joined Reckitts on 1st September 1914 and worked on the management of the Kingston works. He tells here of a typical night's work of joining the trenches:

"I set off with two orderlies to set out a trench in "No Man's Land" from one map reference to join up with another division also in "No Man's Land". By night this is not quite so easy as it sounds. Of course a map reference is quite definite on roads and trenches, but if they are obliterated it is quite amusing. About midnight the sappers put them on the job, but the Boche spotted us with his "very" lights, and the men dug in under very heavy rifle fire in what almost amounted to daylight (at about 100 yards range). There were casualties but the men were simply splendid and before we left we had a good trench dug and had done our job."

Pte. Frederick James Pulsford, 8th East Surrey's, joined the London House on November 4th 1912, he was wounded in the Somme Battle, July 1916 and in this letter home describes events:

"Our regiment was the first to go over the top and make the first charge. We got the order at 7.30 a.m. I had my machine gun slung on my shoulder like a rifle. I had no rifle but kept my bayonet. We got a reception from Fritz's machine guns and it was a fairly mad rush. We soon got into the German first line trench and established ourselves there for a breather. It was just as we were leaving the trench to advance on the second line when a piece of shell struck me in the back and at the same time slightly penetrated my chest. I fell back into the German trench and here I lay all day with my wounds bleeding and exposed to the air sometimes I was in my mind, and sometimes I wasn't. A very big German passed me dragging a wounded German with him, but did not interfere with me. About 4 p.m. I was again wounded in the left shoulder by a shrapnel bullet. I have a recollection of a couple of chaps trying to dress my wounds. About 8 p.m. two stretcher-bearers came along and dragged me a little way down the trench and there into a German dug-out."

L/Cpl Albert E. Whitteridge, 146th I.B. Signals, Royal Engineers, worked on the staff of Introducers, joining the firm in February 1912. Private Whitteridge describes here how death would approach from nowhere, even away from the front:

> "I heard the whiz of an approaching shell – it dropped plump into soft ground about twenty yards away and failed to explode. I knew there were more to follow as single shots are rare. By shifting my position I was as likely to move up against one as staying, so without being prompted by any heroic motive I decided to stick it out. It was short and sharp, though at the time it seemed ages – seven more shells came over at intervals of about twenty seconds, sending showers of soft earth flying up which liberally besprinkled the horses and myself. Luckily not a piece of shell touched us. The incident is not much in itself; What made it trying was the impossibility of taking cover and it being in cold blood so to speak. I am writing this in the calm and delightful comfort of the Canadian Hospital at Boulogne where I am mending some broken ribs sustained as the result of a playful tap from my horse's near hind hoof, he having been aroused from his habitual calm by the explosion of a whiz-bang."

Thomas Alfred Bromby, Cpt. – 21st King's Royal Rifle Corps and Adjutant – 2/5th Light Infantry, Indian Army, worked as an Introducer at Reckitts joining the firm on May 4th 1911. In the closing stages of the Somme Battle he was wounded and wrote the following account home in September 1916:

> "About 5 a.m. the Caterpillar "Tanks" moved into position and at 6.20 a.m. we got the order to advance. It was a grand sight to see the men advancing with never a waver, although men were falling all around amidst a perfect tornado of shells and bullets. How anyone could live at all is a marvel. I managed to reach a point about a mile

from our line when I went down with a bullet through the upper muscle of my left arm. I crept into a near shell-hole and waited for six hours before I dare attempt to crawl back to the field dressing station. Every minute I expected to be blown up by the shells which were being put over and which gave the ground an appearance resembling a big ploughed field."

Cpt. Harold Noble, Royal Garrison Artillery, worked at the Morley Street Works, Hull, joining the firm on May 26th 1896. Here he recounts the poor conditions in the trenches and paints a very vivid picture of the sights seen by men at the front during a barrage of enormous proportions. Shortly after writing this letter Cpt. Noble was wounded:

"The great thing in this war is digging – heaps of it – and the shovel G.S. is the chief weapon both offensive and defensive. The barrage immediately preceding the attack of July 14th was the most intense and spectacular of any during the Push. It commenced about 3.20 a.m. The sky was ablaze with flashes, and the din resembled nothing as much as some gigantic foundry or boiler shop in which hundreds of men were working at feverish speed. Occasionally when the guns were altering their range at some prearranged time there would be for perhaps the space of two or three seconds, complete silence, painful in the extreme, more so than the din of the bombardment. As we move forward one sees the effect of our shelling on the appearance of the country. The whole area is a mass of shell-holes, their edges touching. Villages have become heaps of rubbish in which even the direction of the streets cannot be traced. Woods are a mass of broken stumps. One wonders how far this wholesale devastation and ruin will have to proceed before the German line is broken and we can tackle them in the open. Life here is very primitive so far as residence is concerned. A hole is dug, a few pit-props, a sheet or two of corrugated iron, sand bags and a few feet of earth on top of all – and there you are."

Pte. Herbert Farrell, Royal Engineers, and 17th King's Liverpool Regiment, joined the staff of Introducers in May 1910. The following letter was written by him while he was recovering from a wound in Liverpool hospital:

"Even the best of pen-pictures give a poor idea of the "Great

Adventure". Everything is conducted on such matter of fact lines that unless there is a real "strafe" on, it is hard to believe that one is in the thick of it. Our boys are born sportsmen, and nothing will ever beat 'em."

Pte. Edward Wilson Webster, 10th Battalion East Yorkshire Regiment (Hull Commercials – 1st Hull Pals), worked in the Dansom Lane Office, Hull, and had been with the firm since 3rd April 1911. He wrote home a vivid account of a patrol in no-man's land during the Somme Campaign of 1916:

"We took over the front line trenches on August 25th for eight days. My word we HAD a time! Thunderstorms in abundance, trenches like Whirlpools! On the 31st our Officer picked fifteen of us to go with him on a patrol in "No Man's Land" – no equipment, just loaded rifle, gas helmet, and bombs. The Germans at this part of the line were about 150 yards away.

Our duty was to approach the German trench crawling along noiselessly over wretched ground littered with jam tins, old rifles, trip wires, stray arms and legs, numerous decapitated bodies. Over the top we went. Pitch-black night, 11.30 p.m. Shell-holes containing enough water to drown a dozen men. We advanced in line, the leading man heading straight for the German line and the rest of us following behind. I was the ninth man – eight had got through the German wire. I was following and got nearly half-way through the entanglements. We were only ten or fifteen yards away from Fritz when he heard us and we heard him loading his rifle. Guessing that he had discovered us and knowing that to try to fight the host of them that would pour out of the German dug-outs on the alarm being given would be useless, we commenced to make tracks for our own trench – at least the others did. When I turned to go back with them I found to my horror that I was fast to the German wire. I threw off all the well-meaning prayers I could think of, then I gave one big wrench and incidentally succeeded in leaving a piece of German wire in the inside of my left knee. It must have been some "wrench", for it got me clear of the wire and deposited me in one of the nicest shell-holes I have ever seen. Evidently Fritz had heard me, for just as I was falling I got a bullet through my right forearm which knocked my rifle out of my hand. I left them the rifle as a souvenir and cleared off back to our own lines. The bullet also cut the tendon of the last two fingers on my hand."

Later in the war Edward Wilson Webster rose to the rank of Lieutenant.

Pte. George H. Dewick, 10th Battalion EastYorkshire Regiment (Hull Commercials – 1st Hull Pals), worked on the Dansom Lane Office Staff, Hull, and had been with the firm since April 18th 1910. He wrote the following letter while recovering from a wound, or as the troops called it, 'a blighty':

> "We were in the trenches at last, up to our knees in the slimy sludgy mud. We had only been in for a few days, but they were days of incessant rain and no sleep. I was wet through up to my waist. But now I am in beautiful "Blighty" with a wounded foot and I wouldn't have missed what I've seen or been through for worlds."

Lt. Harold Rooms, Royal Garrison Artillery, worked on the Dansom Lane Office Staff, Hull, joining the firm in November 1906. In this letter home he speaks of the war above the trenches:

> "There is no doubt of our superiority in the air and it means everything. You should see our battleplanes travel over the German lines at a terrific speed, then dive down from a great height and rake the trenches with machine-gun fire. It is noticeable how "Fritz" has made a special mark of the churches, but curiously enough the crucifix stands through everything."

Pte. Walter Dresser, R.A.O.G. relates how he "went over the top":

On May 3rd last, the attack was made on the famous 'Infantry Hill', before Monchy le Preux. We were in the support line on the morning of the attack. I was one of the first over in the company. I was detailed for that duty as my section was to join up in connection with the company on the right, which, I am sorry to say, could not be up, as the German artillery fire was terrible.

Somehow I wandered away from my section and went on by myself over our second and then the first line in front of Infantry Hill, where the foremost attack had been stopped by the terrible machine gun fire. I got into a shell hole, where we hid ourselves till six at night. Some did not rejoin our company for two or three days on account of the terrible sniping."Joined Reckitts on 29th February, 1914

1917

CHAPTER 4

If you are able, save for them a place inside of you and save one backward glance when you are leaving for the places they can no longer go.

Be not ashamed to say you loved them, though you may or may not have always.

Take what they have left and what they have taught you with their dying and keep it with your own.

And in that time when men decide and feel safe to call the war insane, take one moment to embrace those gentle heros you left behind.

By Major Michael Davis O'Donnell

The Fallen - Letters from the Front: 1917

Inauguration of the Faubourg D'Amiens Cemetery and Memorial to the Missing – Arras. 31st July 1932.

The cemetery contains 2677 burials.

On the walls of the Memorial are carved the names of 35928 men who's bodies were never found.

Pte. William Rylett, 1/4th east Yorks., Reg. No. 5150, was a metal machinist at the canister works and joined the firm on 19th February 1912. He was killed on July 14th 1916 at the age of 30 and left a widow and two young children. Born in Hull. Enlisted Hull. William Rylett's name appears in the Hull Daily Mail in Memoriam on 8th January 1917 – from his brother George and his sister Girtie. He has no known grave but is commemorated on the Menin Gate Memorial to the Missing, Ypres. Panel 21 and 23.

Pte. Robert Scott, 2238, 1/4th East Yorks, was born in Hull, entering Reckitts Factory on December 11th 1912, working in the canister works. He joined up in Hull early in the war and was wounded in 1915. After recovering from his wounds he was sent back to the front and killed on 25th April 1915 aged 27. Robert left a wife and three children and his name was recorded on the Waller Street Shrine, this no longer exists.

The Hull Daily Mail reported him missing on January 30th 1916. He has no known grave but is commemorated on the Menin Gate Memorial. Ypres. Panel 21 and 31

Sgt. Thomas George Lesar, DCM, 4th Battalion Royal Fusiliers, was on the clerical staff of London House and had been with the firm since March 18th 1912. In this letter home he speaks of his promotion and of the decoration he had just received:

" No doubt you have been wondering what has happened to me. Well, I will now endeavour to explain. First of all I am still keeping fit and well and was promoted Sergeant on June 4th and was straightaway made Platoon Sergeant, and during an attack on June 15th-16th won the D.C.M., which you will no doubt be pleased to hear. One day I hope to be able to let you know how I won it. I hope everyone at Queen Victoria Street is enjoying good health and not having a too hard time; also hope you are receiving good news from the remainder of the boys.

Please excuse scribble, but no doubt you can quite understand why, when one is in a nice small dug-out, with plenty of company and hardly room to sit up, so cheer up!

"Well, I must conclude now, wishing you every success and kind regards to all."

Sgt. Lesar was awarded the D.C.M. for bravery under fire, he carried his wounded officer back to his own lines on the occasion of a trench raid though he also had been wounded in the leg, this occurred on June 15th 1918. He never was able to write home the details as he was killed on 23rd August the same year age 24, serving with the 1st battalion Royal Fusiliers. He was the son of Thomas and Georgina Lesar of 12 Thorpe Road, Stamford Hill, London; and the husband of Rosina Lesar of 39 Belsize Lane, Hampstead, London. His final resting place is Bagneux British Cemetery. Gezaincourt. Somme. France. V1.A.1.

Pte. Henry Pitcairn, Northumberland Fusiliers, was employed at the canister works and had been with the firm since January 12th 1915. He was 34 years old, single and lived at 13 Rensburg Street, Newbridge Road, Hull. He was killed in action on June 16th 1917. His name appears in the Hull Daily Mail casualty lists for 4th and 17th July 1917: and he was the son of the late Henry and Maria Pitcairn. He has no known grave but is commemorated on the Arras Memorial to the missing. Pas-de-Calais. France. Bay 2 and 3.

Pte. Henry Jarrett, in 'OURS' recorded as serving with the 10th East Yorks, but cannot be found in the official records of that regiment. In the Hull Daily Mail casualty lists he is recorded as serving with the 10thbattalion West Yorkshire Regiment (this is correct). Joining the firm on December 6th 1909, he was employed in the stores of the canister works and was an old member of the boys club. He joined up in February 1916, and was 21 years old when he was killed in action on April 23rd 1917. Henry Jarrett lived at 27 Kent Street, Hull. His name appears in the Hull Daily Mail casualty list for 7th June 1917. he was the son of Harry and Ellen Jarrett. His body was never found but he is commemorated on the Arras Memorial to the Missing. France. Bay 4.

In 'OURS' it is recorded that -
Pte. Albert Wells served with the York and Lancs Regiment and was killed on 2nd December 1916 at the age of 32 years. He worked in the paper stores and joined the firm on July 12th 1911. There is no record of this man being killed with the above unit on that date.
There are 113 individuals called Wells with the initial 'A' in the War Graves Records.

Pte. Robert Taylor, 1/4th East Yorks., Reg. No. 2195. He was employed at the canister works and joined the army in August 1914. He joined the firm on May 26th 1913 and was killed in action on September 10th 1916 aged 21 years. Born Dovercourt, Harwich. Enlisted Hull. His name appears in the Hull Daily Mail Roll of Honour on 1st January 1917 and was also featured on the Mersey Street Shrine. Robert is buried in Bazentine-Le-Petit Communal Cemetery Extension. Somme. France.

Stoker William James Stokes was employed at the canister works. His father was Mr W Stokes, late foreman of the lead mill, he joined the firm on February 5th 1908. He met his death when his destroyer, HMS Derwent, struck a mine in the Channel on May 2nd 1917 age 41 years. He was called up as a naval reserve man when war broke out and was the husband of Martha Stokes of 3 Ash Brook, New Buckingham Street, Holderness Road, Hull.

William has no grave but is commemorated on the Chatham Naval Memorial. Kent.

Pte. Herbert Neal was born in Hull and joined the firm of Reckitts on 28th February 1907 working in the lead mill. He joined up at the start of the war at Londesborough Street Barracks, Hull and served in the ranks of the1/4th Battalion East Yorks., Reg. No. 2217. Herbert was a single man and only 24 years old when he was killed on November 8th 1916. His name appears in the Hull Daily Mail Casualty list of 4th January 1917.

Herbert is buried in Bazentin-Le-Petit Communal Cemetery Extension. Somme. France. His older brother John W Neal Reg No 24063 served with the 3rd Battalion Northamptonshire Rgt and died at home of his wounds on 15thAugust 1916, aged 25yrs. John is buried in Hedon Road Cemetery, Hull. Another brother served in the Navy. These boys were the sons of Mrs M Neal of 12 St Paul's Avenue Church Street, Hull

---

Pte . Thomas William Cronk, 1/4th east Yorks., Reg. No. 1633, went out to France under Colonel Shaw, was wounded and afterwards transferred to the 2nd East Yorks. He was killed in the trenches at Givenchy on 10th September, 1916, serving with the 1/4th East Yorks, ATT 2nd Yorkshire Regiment.

He was a member of the boys club and was employed in the canister works. Pte. Cronk was with the Territorial Force before the war and was only 17 when he joined up in the first month of the war. He joined the firm on 2ndJune 1913. The official records state that Pte. Cronk died of wounds. Born Hull. Enlisted Hull. His name is recorded in the Hull Daily Mail Casualty list of 16th November 1916 and was featured on the Barnsley Street Shrine. Thomas William is buried in Gorre British and Indian Cemetery. Pas-De-Calais. France 111.A.8.

Pte William Ernest Cropper, 1st East Yorks., Reg. No. 23978. Died of wounds on May 28th, 1917, and was 30 years of age. He joined the firm on March 24th, 1902, and was employed in the export department, he left a widow and three small children. Born Hull. Enlisted Hull. His name appears in the Hull Daily Mail – 'In Memoriam' – on 28th May 1918: from his widow and children, his father and mother, his brothers Herbert (serving in Italy) and George (serving in France), his sister Alice and brother-in-law Sid. He was the son of Mr and Mrs James Cropper of 61 Rosemead Street Hull and the husband of Elizabeth Cropper of 8 Derwent Avenue, Courtney Street, Hull. William is buried in Bucquoy Road Cemetery, Ficheux, France. 1.J.10.

Pte. Albert Cook, 1st East Yorks., Reg. No. 31044, was accidentally killed in France on February 22nd 1917 Age 28. He joined up in Hull in November 1916 and was a single man. He was employed in the canister works and joined the firm on 8th December 1917. Born Bradford. Albert was the son of Harry and Anne Cooke of 24 Kensington Street, Bradford; he has no known grave but is commemorated on the Loos Memorial. Pas-de-Calias, France. Panel 40 and 41.

35072 Pte. Harold Early enlisted in November 1915 in the 18th Battalion Royal Welsh Fusiliers and was killed in France with the 10th battalion
on 13th November 1916 at the age of 19 years. He joined the London House clerical staff in March 1911 and is buried in Railway Hollow Cemetery, France:

The following letter was published in 1915 in 'OURS' from Pte. Herbert Edward Thackery:

"Our engagement you'll have read about, so it's no use repeating ancient history. Rely on the Reckitts' lads for doing their part. We understand that victory is essential and it's our intention to carry on to the very end".

He was employed before the war on the hoists and joined the firm on December 1st 1910. He was an old member of the boys club and won prizes for swimming and manual work. Pte. Thackery served with the 1/4th East Yorks. in the transport section, Reg. No. 2454 and died of wounds at the age of 20 on November 28th 1916. Born Hull. Enlisted Hull. He is listed in the Hull Daily Mail casualty lists of 5th January 1917. Son of Robert Urwin and Kate Thackery of 58 Bright Street, Holderness Road, Hull. Buried in Becourt Military Cemetery. Somme. France.

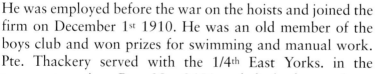

Pte. Albert Turner served with the 12th Battalion Durham Light Infantry, Reg. No. 28558, He was employed on the clerical staff of the canister works and joined the firm in July 1911. He enlisted in May, 1916 and died of wounds at the age of 20 on June 7th 1917. Pte Turners home address was 64 Argyle Street, Hull and he was the son of Mr H S and Mrs M E Turner. He was listed in the Hull Daily Mail Casualty list of 10th July 1917. Albert Turner has no known grave but is commemorated on the Menin Gate Memorial. Ypres. Panel 36 and 38.

Pte. Frederick Goodfellow, 12th Battalion East Yorks Reg.- 3rd Hull Pals – Reg No 12/1341. Enlisted at the Hull City Hall on 1st January 1915 and was killed in action on 13th November 1916. The Commonwealth War Graves Commission gives his unit at the time of death as 1/4th Battalion, I think this is a mistake as the 1/4th were not in action on this date, but the 12th attacked at serre with the Hull 92nd Brigade on 13th November 1916 and his place of burial – Euston Road Cemetery, Collincamps is were many Hull Pals men are buried that were killed on that date.

Frederick left a wife and four children and was mentioned in the Hull Daily Mail casualty list of 4th January 1917: and in memoriam 13th November 1917. Frederick and Theana Goodfellow lived at 3 York Terrace, Bedford St, Hull. After her husbands death Theana moved to 18 Wassand Terrace, Strickland Street, Hessle Road, Hull.

Pte William Henry Bell, 8th East Yorks., Reg. No. 25121, was employed on the cardboard preparation plant and joined the firm on 20th March, 1911. He was killed in action on 3rd May 1917 and left a widow and two young children. Born Hull. Enlisted Hull. William was listed in the Hull Daily Mail Casualty list of 5th June 1917. He has no known grave but is commemorated on the Arras Memorial to the missing. France. Bay 4 and 5.

Sapper George Ely, Royal Engineers, 497th Field COY, joined Reckitts on 5th July 1909 as a motor driver. He enlisted in May 1915 and died of wounds on July 4th 1917. He was 23 years of age and single. Son of George and Agnes Ely, 6 Pemberton Street, Hull. Sisters: Ruth, Alma and Stella. He is listed in the Hull Daily Mail in memoriam on 4th July 1918 and is buried in Canada Farm Cemetery. Ypres. Belgium.

147432 Driver G. Gill, R.F.A. was on the outside staff as a renovator and joined the firm on 23rd June 1913. He enlisted in May 1916 and died of wounds on September 3rd 1917. He left a widow and one child, served with the 37th Division Ammunition Column and is buried in Bailleul Communal Cemetery. France.

Pte. Arthur Farrow, 1st East Yorks., Reg. No. 23089. He was employed at the Stoneferry Works and joined the firm on 17th September 1914. He was 26 years old when he was killed in action on April 9th 1917. He left a widow and a young child. Born Hull. Enlisted Hull. Arthur is featured in the Hull Daily Mail Casualty list of 14th May 1917 and is buried in Cojeul British Cemetery. France.

Pte Leslie C. Foster, 2/8th Sherwood Foresters, 307000 was on the clerical staff of Dansom Lane. He was 18 when he enlisted in May, 1916 under the Derby Scheme. After training at Curragh Camp in Ireland he was sent to France in the following February. He was killed in action on April 7th 1917 age 19. Joined Reckitts on 3rd March 1913. Home Address: 6 Garden Village, Hull. Leslie was featured in the Hull Daily Mail Casualty lists of 21st April and 23rd May 1917 and was the son of Tom Edward and Eliza Ann Foster of 86 Village Road, Hull. He is buried in Vadencourt British Cemetery. Aisne. France.

Letter from Henry Claxton, 1917. Pte. Henry Claxton is taking a course of signalling, which is a pleasant change to the trenches, of which he has had two years' experience:

" I have been sat in the trenches at times when the shells have been whizzing just over my head for at least ten hours at a stretch. But our artillery are splendid. Didn't they show what stuff they were made of in this last push! I shall never forget it. It was great work they did when we went over to take our objective. I lost a good many pals, but I'm still hanging on, and hope to get back to the Old Firm".

Pte. Claxton served with the 16th Battalion Notts and Derby Regiment, before the war he was employed in the packing room and had joined the firm on 20th October, 1891. He died of wounds on November 15th 1917 and was in his 39 year. His home address was 17 Clarendon Street, Hull. Henry is featured in the Hull Daily Mail in Memoriam on 15th November and 17th December 1918; from his sisters Sarah, Ann and Gertrude, nieces and nephews, brother-in-law George and Will in France. Buried in Lijssenthoek Military Cemetery. Belgium.

Pte. John William Watson, Reg. No. 31083, recorded in 'OURS' as serving in 1/4th East Yorks., and having been killed in action. The records show he died of wounds serving with the 1st East Yorks. on July 11th 1917. He worked in the lead mill at Stoneferry, joined the firm on August 12th 1909, was 41 years old and left a widow and four children. Born Hull. Enlisted May 1915 Hull. He is featured in the Hull Daily Mail Casualty list of 5th January, 1918, and is buried in Ervillers Military Cemetery. France.

This letter from Pte. George William Trowell was published in 'OURS', 1917. Pte. Trowell, E.Y.R. son of Mr R Trowell, Packing Room, was wounded in the big advance. He was shot through the shoulder while trying to rescuer some wounded, including a German Officer who had been crying out piteously for 36 hours. "The German snipers were dropping even our stretcher-bearers, and a sergeant-major came to our shell-hole to tell us to come in at dark. They let go at him but missed, the bullet going through the steel helmet of a young fellow with me. It missed his head and, careering down, I got the worst of it." Pte Trowell, 1/4th East Yorks., reg. No. 201821, was wounded in the advance of September, 1916, discharged from hospital and returned to France in January 1917. He was killed in action on April 23rd 1917 age 27. Born Hull. Enlisted Hull. Fiancee: Mabel. He joined the firm on November 6th, 1903, and worked in the saw mill.

His elder brother Pte. John Robert Trowell, 1/4th Battalion Northumberland Fusiliers, at the age of 30 years, was killed in action on September 15th 1916. He took part in the 'great push' of July the same year. John Robert joined the firm on February 4th 1904 and the following tribute was published to him in 'OURS' Christmas, 1916:

"He was of a very quiet, reserved nature. A man of

staunch temperance, principle, of excellent quality of mind and heart, he attained a real degree of self-education. As a member of our Debating Society he proved himself a thoughtful student of modern questions and social movements."

These boys were the sons of Robert and Charlotte Trowell of 81 Laburnum Avenue, Hull. Mr Trowell was the packing room foreman at Reckits and had another son in the forces who was shot through the thigh and a fourth son who served in an anti-aircraft unit.

George William was posted missing in the Hull Daily Mail on 8th June 1917; listed in their Roll of Honour –Missing Believed Killed – on 31st January 1918 and in memoriam, from mother and father, on 23rd April 1918.

Both George William and John Robert feature in the 'In Memoriam' section on 16th September 1918.

George William has no known grave but is commemorated on the Arras Memorial to the Missing. France. Bay 4 and 5.
John Robert is buried in Adanac Cemetery. Miraumont. France.

Pte Leonard Shields, East Yorks. worked in the saw mill, was an old member of the boys club and joined the firm on February 12th 1911. He was 21 years old when he died of wounds in German hands on November 18th 1916. In 'OURS' he is recorded as serving in the 1/4th East Yorks., when he died he was with the 13th East Yorks. (4th Hull Pals) and was taken prisoner when they attacked the village of Serre on the Somme, on November 13th 1916. reg. No. 28085. Born Hull. Enlisted Hull.

Leonard is featured in the Hull Daily Mail Casualty list of 4th January 1917: and in Memoriam 13th November 1917. He is buried in the H.A.C. Cemetery. France.

Pte. Robert Turner, 1/4th East Yorks., Reg. No. 203505, worked in the packing room and had been with the firm since October 14th 1900. He was killed in action on April 23rd 1917 at the age of 32 years. He left a widow and a child (Eric) and lived at 10 Epping Terrace, Rodney Street, Hull. Born Otteringham, Yorkshire. Enlisted Hull.

Robert was posted missing in the Hull Daily Mail Casualty lists on 25th July 1917: and in Memoriam 23rd April 1918. he has no known grave but is commemorated on the Arras Memorial to the Missing. France.

12872. Gunner Herbert Digby Wyatt, New Zealand Field Artillery was on the clerical staff of the New Zealand Office, and joined the firm on June 24th 1912. He died of wounds in France on June 15th 1917 age 21 years. He was the son of Herbert and Ada Wyatt of Marine Parade, Seatoun, Wellington, New Zealand and is buried in Bailleul Communal Cemetery Extension. France.

Pte. Frank Monks, 9th Durham Light Infantry, had been on the staff of the London House for 10 years, first as a boy on the vans and afterwards as a warehouseman, he joined the firm in November 1906. He joined up in July 1916, and was killed in France on March 30th 1917 at the age of 27 years, serving with the 14th Battalion DLI.

He was the husband of Mrs McAniffe (formerly Monks) of 114 Pages Walk. Old Kent Road, London, and is buried in Philosophe British Cemetery. France.

Pte. Edwin Pearson, 11th East Yorks. 2nd Hull Pals, Reg. No. 12/186, was employed in the starch works and had been with the firm since August 28th 1899. He enlisted in September 1914, was wounded on 13th November 1916, and died of wounds on July 15th 1917 in his 38th year, leaving a widow and young family of six. Born Hull. Enlisted Hull.

Edwin's name is featured in the Hull Daily Mail Casualty list of 11th August 1917; and he is buried in Aubigny Communal Cemetery Extension. France.

54/157103. Pte. Raymond Millington was on the Hull staff of introducers, before this he was on the Dansom Lane office staff. In October 1914 he joined the Durham Light Infantry and was later discharged because of a weak ankle. He then joined up again in September, 1915, in the Army Service Corps. On September 1st 1917 he was killed by a bomb dropped from an aeroplane, a fragment of which penetrated his heart while he was asleep. He had been working at Reckitts factory since September 15th 1913.

Raymond served with the Fifth Army Troops Supply Column and was the son of Robert and Alice Millington of 64 Barmston Street, Sculcoates, Hull. He is buried in Mendinghem Millitary Cemetery. Belgium.

Pte. Harold B. Lees, MM, 2nd Battalion Royal Welsh Fusiliers, was employed at the canister works and had been with the firm since May 20th 1914. He was a single man, aged 26 years, and lived at 2 Colonial Street, Hull. As a reservist he joined up on mobilization in August 1914 and was killed by shellfire on July 20th 1916. His death was not officially notified until eight months later and he was awarded the Military Medal posthumously. His name is recorded in the Hull Daily Mail Casualty list of 27th October, 1917. Harold has no known grave but is commemorated on the Thiepval Memorial to the Missing. France.

Pte. Walter Charles Hardy, MM, Reg. No. 28465, recorded in 'OURS' as serving with 1/4th East Yorks and having been killed in action. In the official records he is shown to have been serving with the 6th East Yorks when he died of wounds on July 17th 1917. He enlisted in August 1914 and was wounded in July 1916. When he was killed he was 25 years of age and was awarded the Military Medal posthumously. Employed in the canister works he had been with the firm since September 5th 1913. Born Hull. Enlisted Hull.

He is listed in the Hull Daily Mail Casualty list, with the incorrect Christian name of William, on 11th August, 1917: and again on the 18th August with an incorrect regimental number.

Walter was the son of Walter John and Alice Maud Hardy of 20 Providence Row, Beverley Road, Hull: he is buried in Achiet-Le-Grand Communal Cemetery Extension. France.

1475. Pte. Walter Robinson 2/2nd Field Ambulance, RAMC, was employed on the hoists and had been with the firm since 16th December 1898. He joined up at the start of the war and was killed by shellfire on October 27th 1916, at the age of 31 years. He now lies in Bazentin-Le-Petit Military Cemetery. France. D.II.

Pte. Sydney Woodmansey, 1st Battalion East Yorkshire Regiment, Reg. No. 32926, lewis gun section, was born in Hull, and at the age of 12 years won a scholarship at the Salthouse Lane School and then attended the Grammar School, Leicester Street, for four years. He joined Reckitt's employ on June 2nd 1914, working on the clerical staff at Dansom Lane. Sydney was a regular attender at the Queens Hall, a Sunday School teacher and assistant secretary of the Foreign Missionary Society.

He enlisted on September 3rd 1916, went to France on August 3rd 1917, and was killed in action on October 27th 1917, at the age of 19 years. He was the fourth son of Mr and Mrs J W Woodmansey of 6 Wellington Street, Hull: and the fiancée of Doris Keyworth.

He is listed in the Hull Daily Mail Casualty lists of 13th and 17th November 1917. Sydney has no known grave but is commemorated on the Tyne Cot Memorial. Belgium. Panel 47 to 48 and 163A.

Pte. William A. Piercy, 21st (Tyneside Scottish) Battalion Northumberland Fusiliers, reg. No. 44260, worked at the Stoneferry Works on the Blue Stoves. He joined the firm on September 9th 1897 and was popularly known as 'Dobin'. He died of wounds on April 25th 1917 at the age of 33 years.

He is listed in the Hull Daily Mail Casualty List of 26th May 1917 and was the husband of Mrs F Piercy of 3 Temperance Buildings. Swann Street, Hull.

William is buried in Duisans British Cemetery. Etrun. France.

Pte. Herbert Sedman, 7th East Yorks., Reg. No. 33424, was employed by the firm on December 7th 1898, worked in the starch works and was killed in action on April 13th 1917. He was 36 years of age, married and left two young children. He was born in Hull, enlisted in Hull and lived at No. 5 The Grove, Laburnum Avenue, Hull.

His death is noted in the Hull Daily Mail Casualty lists of 5th and 17th May 1917. He has no known grave but is commemorated on the Arras Memorial to the Missing. France. Bay 4 and 5.

3/9668 Bugler William Cecil Jubb, 9th Battalion West Yorkshire Regiment, was employed in the canister works and had been with the firm since September 19th 1912. He enlisted in August 1914, served in Eygpt, Salonica and latterly France. He was reported killed on September 27th 1916 and was 20 years old. William was the son of Mr and Mrs William Jubb of 6 Arthur's Terrace, Courtney Street, Hull; and now lies in Regina Trench Cemetery. Grandcourt. Somme. France. VI.J.17

Pte. Arthur Cecil Taylor, the Buffs, was employed as a traveller at the London House. He joined the firm on February 16th, 1901, as an introducer and was appointed senior traveller in 1906. He enlisted in March 1916 under the Derby Scheme. His battalion went into action on the Arras front on May 3rd 1917, he was officially reported missing on June 6th at the age of 38. He has no known grave but is commemorated on the Arras Memorial to the Missing. Pas-De-Calais. France. Bay 2.

8133. Pte. Thomas Sanderson, 1/6th Battalion, Northumberland Fusiliers, was employed in the canister works and joined the firm on September 11th 1915. In March 1916 he joined the army and was killed on September 15th 1916. He was a single man, was 35 years old and lived at 66 Laburnum Avenue, Hull.

His name appears in the Hull Daily Mail Casualty Lists of September 17th 1917. He has no known grave but is commemorated on the Thiepval Memorial to the Missing. Somme. France. Peir and Face 10B, 11B, and 12B.

33534 Driver William Rogers, Royal Field Artillery, generally known as 'Peter Miller', was employed in the canister works and had been with the firm since 27th February 1908. He joined the army in September 1914 and was killed by shellfire on July 14th 1916 at the age of 22 years. His death was not reported for several months. He was the adopted son of Mr and Mrs Milnet and appears in the Hull Daily Mail Casualty Lists of July 16th 1917. He is buried in Danzig Alley Cemetery, Mametz. France. Sp. MEM.4.

LETTERS FROM THE FRONT

Quarter Master Sergeant Ernest Oswald Morris, Worcester Yeomanry, joined Reckitts on August 10th 1908 and worked in the office. Here he remembers a close shave:

> "I landed here in March and took part in the second attack on Gaza with my regiment. Since then I have been out on several very interesting reconnaissance's, patrols, etc., one of which was blowing up a railway bridge, when we narrowly escaped being wiped out by Johnny Turk. We had just watered our horses and were moving out of the Wadi River, when down came several bombs. Luckily, they missed us, but caught the next lot, who suffered fairly heavily. In May I was in hospital and the very day I went in the Turks came over and played the very dickens for about an hour. However, I was quite safe in the dug-out.
>
> Please excuse scribble, but no doubt you can quite understand why, when one is in a nice small dug-out, with plenty of company and hardly room to sit up, so cheer up!
>
> Well, I must conclude now, wishing you every success and kind regards to all."

Bombadier Frank Webb Rogers, Royal Garrison Artillery, 194th Siege Battery. He comments on the Reckitts products he sees as he passes through villages:

> "Since being with this battery we have been in action many times, and have moved about considerably. One thing has struck me in the inhabited villages we have passed through, every shop I have been in, that is general store, I have seen Reckitts' Blue, Zebra, etc., stocked and advertised. Just now we are out of range of civilisation, and even if we got paid regularly it is impossible to buy necessities such as soap, smoking material, etc. Still we look forward to the time when we can resume normal conditions, and send in the daily 'Report Sheets' when filled."

He had been with the firm since March 1906.

Cpl. Caborn sends us a vivid account of his experience in "going over the top". The attack was timed for 4am and on taking up their positions he and his companions lay in shell holes for three hours under the enemy's heavy artillery fire.

> "I looked at my watch, it was 3.50. I saw a bright light – it was the signal for our batteries to open fire. There was a flash on the left, then one on the right, and in a few moments the sky for about 12 miles was lit by vivid flashes from our guns. Then shells began to roar over our heads and crash into the German trenches. The German Artillery replied vigorously and so fast did shells pass to and fro over our heads that one would not have been surprised if they had collided in mid-air. In the midst of this terrible inferno our Captain walked calmly in front of his men and said 'Five minutes to go; get ready to advance.' I may forget many things, but I shall never forget the intensity of those words. The gates of Hell seemed open and many a gallant lad offered a silent prayer and gave a fleeting thought of home, and to those who loved them. One young fellow who lay with me in a shell hole with half a 'Woodbine' in his hand said 'Give me a match kid and we will have a smoke before we go.' The next minute we advanced side by side smoking. After the fearful barrage which had been put upon the German first line we felt certain no one could be left alive, but when the barrage lifted Fritz was still there kicking. The whole battlefield was clouded in smoke and fire and it was with great difficulty that we could see the German lines. Bullets were dropping round us like rain and bombs were being hurled in every direction. Finding the opposition was too strong at that point, we worked for another angle and it was while making for the line again I received a bullet in the hand, at the same time splitting my rifle. However, I kept in the fight

for about an hour, when my hand became useless and I retired back to our lines. But my troubles were not yet over, for I had to go through the German barrage to get to the dressing station and when I thought all was safe a shell burst a few yards away and a piece of shrapnel struck me in the back. If it had not been for the contents of my haversack it certainly would have been more serious; but luck was mine. I reached the dressing station and after a few hours waiting I was put on the train for the hospital. Hull, indeed, rose supreme that day, for many of its gallant lads gave their all."

Pte. Caborn served with the 11th Battalion East Yorkshire Regiment, 2nd Hull Pals and is describing his part in the Battle of Oppy Wood, where now stands a large memorial dedicated to the men of Kingston-upon-Hull who died that day – 3rd May, 1917.

Frank Caborn joined Reckitts on January 9th 1911 and worked at the 'Old Mill', Dansom Lane, Hull.

Pte. Arthur Henry Merrifield, 12th Battalion Norfolk Yeomanry, joined the firm as an Introducer in June 1908; he wrote the following letter after convalescing after a bout of illness:

"I am enjoying fourteen days' leave, the first since embarking for active service nineteen months ago. For the first time also I make the acquaintance of my baby girl, now seventeen months old.

Like many of my colleagues and friends, I have had an eventful time and my experiences many and varied. Most of my service has been in Palestine and there I took part in much of the fighting that so successfully broke up the Turkish lines in front of Gaza and Beer Sherba and paved the way for our further successes, such as the capture of Jerusalem. The latter being the most important event of the campaign our regiments took part in and a little extra excitement that I experienced may be interesting.

The day before the attack was one of torrential rains, so that at midnight when the regiment fell in to take up our positions we were soaked through to the skin. With nothing but our haversacks, which contained little else than our iron rations (we having dumped our coats and packs to enable us to more easily climb the hills), we marched to our position, which we reached just before dawn. Our first objective to be taken was the very formidable hill, Neb Samuel, which I believe is the burial place of the prophet Samuel, some 3000 feet high and about four miles to the left of the city of Jerusalem. Just as day began to break we were climbing the slopes of the hill and Johnny Turk was not slow to hear us. Rifles immediately began to spit their bits of lead and shells soon fell thick and fast. One did not realise in that busy hour that the cluster of houses nestling between some other hills on our right was Bethlehem. The day went well for us and by 3 o'clock we were expecting to attack our final objective when we got held up by some Turkish machine gunners on our left flank, bringing our men under enfiladed fire and making our position a precarious one. Here I was detailed off with others to fetch up more rifle ammunition. I had not got far when I was caught sight of by the enemy and bullets from a machine gun fell everywhere around me without actually hitting me. I immediately fell down and crawled a yard or so to a good-sized stone, which very fortunately lay in my path and gave me just sufficient protection by keeping flat on my stomach. Any movement I made brought round me a fresh shower of lead. After about half-an-hour of this I decided to risk it and rolling away from my cover was soon successfully away, although the patient gunner had not forgotten me. Later some fresh reserves on our left cleared this trouble on our flank and the coveted position was ours before the next morning. I may say that this said position had previously been taken and retaken five times."

Sgt. Thomas Clifford Emment, Royal Army Services Corps., joined Reckitts on 1st March 1912 and worked on the outside staff until his enlistment.

"I am now stationed in the wilds of Shropshire. I was transferred here from Woolwich about four months ago and since being here I have been going through a special course of general A.S.C. supply work, which, however, is practically completed now. At the conclusion of this course I expect to be drafted over-seas, probably to France.

In comparison with those who are in the midst of it out yonder, I suppose we are well off. Life is very humdrum here – one day being much like another – but we have no cause to grumble at our lot. In fact, we have some real good times, and in addition to other home-made pleasures we have most enjoyable concerts, in which I have been able to play a male part. This work naturally relieves the monotony of the evenings here.

I would like to take the opportunity of sending my very best greetings to those colleagues with whom I had the pleasure of coming into contact with, accompanying those greetings with a hope that the time is not far off when we shall once again meet round the festive board in our 'civies,' and once again resume our duties for the 'Old Firm'.

I'm sorry I can't relate any exciting experiences, there's an excellent reason for not doing so though – I simple 'ain't 'ad none.'"

Pte. Stanley Wheelhouse, 1st Battalion Royals Berks., had worked on the Reckitts office staff, joining the firm on 9th December 1912. Here he writes from a hospital in Bath.

"On the night of July 22nd – 23rd I was made Officer's orderly and we went 'over the top' the same night. This was my first experience of 'going over' and so you can perhaps guess what I felt like. At 12.30 our artillery put up a very good barrage and we left the trench soon after. About one hundred yards in front of our wire there was only the officer and myself left out of a section of about twenty-five and then we both helped to stop a shell that burst just behind us, but as it was nothing much (or at least we thought it wasn't then) we carried on and finished our job. When things quietened down a bit I found that I had been hit in the left thigh and right hand.

After being taken to about a dozen dressing stations, I arrived at the Casualty Clearing Station about 10am at Trevent, which was then about 36 kilometres behind the line. I was there three days and then went to Rouen, where I had a piece of shrapnel taken out of my left thigh. I spent a week there and heard the 'homely' sound of bombs every night. Left there on August 2nd and came over to England the same night as the 'Warilda' was sunk. We were in the same convoy and I heard all the depth charges dropped and also the explosion of the torpedo. However, on Saturday night, August 3rd, I landed safely in Bath War Hospital. My right hand is quite better now and my thigh is getting on well. It does not affect my walking at all.

Kindly remember me to all at the A.D.V."

Pte. William Booth, Machine Gun Corps – attached to the East Yorks., worked in the canister works and had been at Reckitts since August 10th 1914. He describes a hot corner during an attack:

> "We managed to get our guns placed all right before our attack began. After about a quarter of an hour, suddenly, like a lot of drums beating, our artillery opened a barrage fire and the shells of all sizes screeching through the air mingled with the sounds of violent explosions as they burst. Then the Germans began to send up their flare lights and their gunners soon put up a barrage fire for them. Shells began to burst pretty near us and the smell of high explosives was very marked. Well, our machine guns began their fire, so we were kept busy feeding them, our infantry at the same time attacking the Germans. Fritz put up a terrible barrage fire, which seemed to fall all around us, huge pieces of shell whizzing through the air like the sound of an aeroplane propeller and shrapnel shells bursting overhead."

Pte. George James Chapman, 2/4th King's own Yorkshire Light Infantry, had been employed in the Kingston Works since March 1904:

> "We have a fair amount of amusements, such as pierrot troupes, cinemas and bands of all descriptions, from bugles to orchestral instruments, which make life more bearable when living behind the line for a brief period. We get many exciting episodes at times, as when you are carrying rations up the line and one of your own pals is knocked out by a bursting shell a few yards away from you and you have a narrow shave yourself. It is possible to see the humorous side of things if you can indulge in a good laugh occasionally. I might state that the cigarettes which the workpeople subscribe for are very much appreciated, also the Christmas parcels the firm send out."

Able Seaman Charles Timmons was on the office staff and had been with the firm since September 1914. During the war he served on H.M.S. Colossus and Queen:

> "My quarters in action are down in the 12in. magazine and I am stationed at a searchlight for night action. I was rated A.B. last month and am now going through a course for Acting Seaman Torpedo-man, which I find very interesting."

Rifleman Arthur Banfield Taylor, 20th Battalion King's Royal Rifle Corps, had worked in Reckitts' office since November 18th 1912. He came back from France with a poisoned leg, the result of a blow with an entrenching tool and spent some time in hospital:

> "At present I am at a convalescent camp in the land of Shamrock and have just been marked fit, so that any day I may be sent to England for two or three weeks before again taking my place in the line."

Driver Walter John Lester Elliot, an introducer with Reckitt's since March 27th 1911, he served in the Army Service Corps. In this letter home he reflects on the realities of war:

> "The game of war is a game of chance for all those who are actively concerned in its perpetration. The occasion of this incident happened to be one night when we were delivering ammunition to a battery position. Something had transpired en route necessitating several lorries taking another and unusual route. As we swung round a corner to take the approach to the position, I heard a near explosion and saw a huge column of flame leap into the air. I knew at once that a lorry had received a direct hit. It happened to be a flare shell, which made the lorry an inferno of flame and smoke. By some miraculous dispensation the driver of the lorry was not hurt, but his mate was wounded and badly burnt. The driver, with great courage, succeeded in rescuing the wounded man from what was then a veritable fiery furnace. What happened afterwards would make too long a story and make readers realize too vividly that it did not take place in fairy-land. However, the boys are all fine fellows who carry on with that light-hearted courage and endurance that makes one think sometimes that it is really some sort of picnic or pleasurable adventure, instead of what it is."

Sgt. Tom Nicholson, Royal Field Artillery, 128th Battery, worked at the Hull Office, joining the firm on June 3rd 1905. He was stationed at Muree in India doing clerical work on the staff of the Northern Army:

> "I am once again rattling on the old 'underwood', although in very different surroundings from Chapman Street and Dansom Lane. We have had a very busy time, working in three shifts day and night and seven days a week. We change shifts weekly, so then I have to take my

turn in them all. My being on the staff carries with it the rank of sergeant. Clerical work suits me better than dashing round an 18-pounder at gun drill at Ambala. Incidentally, all the guns in our battery at Ambala were kept in fine polished condition by the use of 'Brasso', which line I also occasionally observe in the native bazaars."

Pte. Arthur Ogden Ainsworth, Northamptonshire Regiment, was employed as an introducer on February 21st 1911. His new experiences he describes very eloquently in this letter home as he looked to the future and the ones he loved:

> "Twenty months ago barracks became my home. It is a desolate and cheerless sort of place, but no doubt the experience has done me good. The variety of men whom I have to live has given me an insight into life of which I was more or less ignorant. I have learnt many lessons, some at no little cost – but, as I have said, gruesome as Army life is, I am not sorry to have experienced it. Above all it has taught me to appreciate the commercial side of life in a degree that only the severance from it could impart, though, like most, I have had more than sufficient of 'khaki-days' and look forward to a renewal of the old times, which I trust will come speedily. The discipline of suffering will find us a world where grumblers will be fewer. The sadness of separation will make re-union sweeter."

L/Cpl. William Alfred Irwin, Army Service Corps – Bridging Transport, was a joiner at Reckitts and joined the firm on March 21st 1911. Here he tells of his work in connection with the lorries proceeding up to the big gun emplacements with iron girders and pit props in preparation for the big push:

> "More often than not under shell fire and in the dark, which is very difficult on shelled roads. As a cyclist I was asked to take the job leading them. The lorries were used in conjunction with the R.E.'s in the Somme advance taking up water pipes. While the R.E.'s laid them – a most unthankful task – the Boches would spot us and send a few over to cheer us up."

Bombardier Laurence Henry Backhouse, Royal Garrison Artillery – 326th Siege Battery – had been employed at Reckitts as an introducer since February 27th 1911. In his letter home he talks of the heavy work involved with the siege battery and of the dangers of being on the receiving end of a barrage:

> "Our worst experience is being 'shelled out' by the German artillery. I don't mind how many shells we send over to Fritz, although on a big howitzer it is very heavy work, but it is when Fritz starts sending them back that one realises the horrors and destruction of war. We can hear the shell coming whistling through the air and can also hear the discharge of the German gun. No one knows exactly where the shell is coming. We make a dive for the dug-out or lay flat on the ground behind anything which offers any cover – and await events. All this happens in a few seconds and our hearts are beating somewhat above normal. Then comes the explosion of the shell and several heads appear immediately afterwards from the dug-out and one question comes from all – 'Where did that one go?' If the shell fails to explode someone is sure to cry out 'Dud', or 'Unobserved' and if there is any immediate danger we 'clear off', with the consent of an officer, to a safer spot until the shelling ceases. Of course, if we are bombarding Fritz at the same time we 'stick it' until ordered off the guns by the O.C. If our position is badly damaged by shell holes and fragments of shell, it means 'pulling out', that is, moving the gun to another position. That is an all-night job. It is all very horrible, this wholesale destruction of life and property, and may it soon end is my everyday wish."

Another letter is featured from Bombardier Backhouse in the 1918 section, after his wounding on service.

Cpl. Frank Harrison, Royal Engineers, joined the firm in October 1904 and was the Secretary of the Boy's club. He served as an electrician in an anti-aircraft unit in France:

> "When I say we have been in action five nights out of seven at some periods, you will know we have been kept busy. We have certainly had some exciting nights and not a few narrow escapes, for apart from the bombs falling quite near, we are often in danger of falling shrapnel from our own guns. On one occasion we were in action four hours, when over 200 bombs were rained in this district and the number of planes taking part in the raid was estimated to be between 30 and 40. I am unable for obvious reasons to tell you of the numerous incidents and achievements, but I assure you 'Archie' is doing good work in France.

We are at present billeted in the loft of a small country house and the 'lady of the house' is what the Cockney calls a 'real lidy'. Many Colonial and British troops have billeted in this neighbourhood and she has picked up a good deal of the English language, or rather 'Tommy' language, for when she desires to express her disapproval of anything we do, her 'flow' would turn a Tyne shipyard plater's helper green with envy. However, the people of France have always treated our section with the utmost hospitality, for we have generally been amongst the country folk.

I have very fortunately been able to keep up a correspondence with many old Boys Club Members and my mail often includes letters from youths in France, Salonica, Mesopotamia, and on the High Seas as well as from many in England. We have lost 22 old members who have fallen for the cause – a glorious record for so humble an institution and whilst we are more than grieved by their loss to us, we are proud to know they have 'played the game'. Their names shall ever be sacred to us, and the knowledge of their deeds shall be an inspiration to us for the higher ideals of our club. May I take this opportunity of expressing my best wishes to all members at home and abroad and trust that by the time these lines are published we may have attained PEACE WITH VICTORY."

Bombardier Henry Woolias, Royal Garrison Artillery, worked in the Brasso works and joined Reckitts on May 25th 1908. He wrote the following letter home:

"A few days ago, when I happened to be engaged on forward observation work, I was a witness of the 'Cannucks' going over the top. First comes the barrage, which reminds me of a firework display on a large scale. Suddenly the noise ceases, and one catches a glimpse of the 'boys' making their way towards the earthly domains of Fritz. Do not imagine for one moment that Tommy Atkins has everything his own way in an affair of this description. But after two years of active service I think I am voicing a general opinion when I say that it is merely a question of time before our enemy finds himself compelled to acknowledge defeat.

Perhaps the people at home imagine the life in France consists of nothing more than danger and excitement. Quite a mistaken idea.

Almost everyone finds some spare moments to devote to the lighter side of life and enjoy the numerous amusements provided by the Y.M.C.A., etc. In the vicinity of my present billet is a large concert hall, erected by the troops, and here on almost every evening one can rest assured of being provided with a few hours' enjoyment. To gaze upon the crowded hall of men, laughing, joking, and joining in the singing with great gusto, would gladden the hearts of their dear folks at home. Just for one brief period operations had to be suspended owing to the activities of the enemy. In his usual inconsiderate manner, he attempted to drown the sound of the piano with the music of his own special brand of 'souvenir.' Only last evening I had the pleasure of witnessing a show which would not have disgraced a 'Blighty' music hall."

1918

Chapter 5

All life, All love's his fee.
Whose perished fire conserves my spark,
Who bought the brightening day for me,
And for himself the dark.

The Fallen – Letters from the Front

A Body Dump - The Somme

20866: Pte. Robert Wright, 18th Battalion Lancashire Fusiliers, had been employed at Reckitts as a bricklayer since 2nd November 1914. He was killed on March 26th 1918 at 35 years of age. He left a widow, Mary, and four young children. Robert is listed in the Hull Daily Mail Roll of Honour of 16th April 1918 and in the Casualty List of 1st May 1918. Home address: 87 Clifton Street, Hull. Robert has no known grave but is commemorated on the Pozieres Memorial. Somme. France.

42618. Pte. Walter Magson, 9th Battalion West Yorkshire Regiment, was employed in the saw mill, joining the firm on 20th September 1912. He was a member of the Boys Club and won honours in physical culture and manual instruction. He enlisted in his 18th year on January 1st 1917 and was killed on 31st July, 1918.

Walter is listed in the Hull Daily Mail Roll of Honour of 24th September 1918 and is buried in Chambrecy British Cemetery. France.

CH/2464. Pte. Sydney Miller, 1st Battalion, R.M.L.I., was on the Reckitts Introducing Staff and entered the service of the firm on 17th May 1909. He was killed at the age of 36 on August 22nd 1918 during the Allied advance, and left a widow and two children.

Sydney has no known grave but is commemorated on the Vis-En-Artios Memorial. France.

Pte. George E. Leak, 1/4th East Yorks. Reg. No. 2452, had been with the firm since 18th December,1911 and worked in the lead pressing department. He was born in Stanley, Yorkshire, enlisted in Hull and was killed in action at the age of 22 on 15th September 1916. He is listed in the Hull Daily Mail Roll of Honour of 16th October 1916 and 'in Memoriam' 17th September 1917.

George has no known grave but is commemorated on the Thiepval Memorial to the Missing. Somme. France.

Gunner John McLoud, 'D' Battery, 330th Bde, Royal Field Artillery, was employed at the lead mill and had been with the firm since 3rd October 1913. He was killed at the age of 32 on October 20th 1917 and was the son of William George and Hannah Sarah McLoud of 91Pelham Street, Hedon Road, Hull.

He was a widower and left a son – John. He is recorded 'in memoriam' in the Hull Daily Mail on 24th October 1918: from his son, mother and father, brothers, Edward and Harold, sisters, Rose Ethel and Violet. John is commemorated on the Tyne Cot Memorial. Belgium.

36868. Pte. Osward Broddle, 13th Battalion, Lincolnshire Regiment, worked in the packing room at Reckitts. He died on April 22nd 1917 at the age of 30 and left a widow and four children. His brother, Sidney Broddle, had been killed on 23rd August 1915. Osward and Sidney were the sons of George and Emma Broddle of Anlaby Common, Hull. Osward was the husband of M Broddle of 10 Roxburgh Street, Hull and is buried in Etaples Military Cemetery. France.

Sidney was killed serving with the 1/5th Battalion King's Own Yorkshire Light Infantry and is buried in Boulogne Eastern Cemetery. France.

Pte. Herbert Mace, 1/4th East Yorks., Reg. No. 201054, was employed at the Stoneferry Works and had been with the firm since October 5th 1914. He was born in Hull, enlisted in Hull and was 20 years of age when he was killed in action on 27th March 1918. His home was at 6 Lendal Terrace, Durham Street, Holderness Road, Hull.

Herbert is listed in the Hull Daily Mail Roll of Honour of 22nd June 1918 and has no known grave, but is Commemorated on the Pozieres Memorial. Somme. France.

4279. Pte. Harry Cobb, 5th Battalion the Border Regiment, was employed in the export department and had joined the firm on February 6th 1911. He enlisted in June 1915 and at the age of 19 years was killed in action on 30th September 1916. He is listed in the Hull Daily Mail Casualty List of 9th September 1916 and was the son of Mrs Annie Cobb of 8 Cambridge Terrace, Cambridge Street, Hull.

Harry has no known grave but is commemorated on the Thiepval Memorial to the Missing. Somme. France.

Gunner James Dobson, Royal Garrison Artillery; 346th Siege Battery wrote the following letter in 1917, he reflects on the strength of the German dug-outs and the state of his own health:

"We are at present in some old German trenches and dug-outs. It is really wonderful the amount of work that has been put into these dug-outs. They are 30 to 40 feet deep, some cemented and others boarded all the way down. It is surprising that they have ever been moved out of them. All the shelling in the world wouldn't get to them when they are in them. I have been troubled with indifferent health, but have been treated exceptionally well by officers and men, and have been given an easy job, that is, spotting the enemy aeroplanes, to give warning to our men to get under cover, so that the Germans should not see anything of what is going on. I am afraid if I had had some of the rough work to do I should have fallen to pieces long before now, so you can tell how I appreciate what the officers and those concerned have done for me."

Before the war James Dobson joined Reckitts on 14th May 1900, he was on the clerical staff of the Kingston Works and was the secretary of the angling club. He died of wounds at a casualty clearing station in France on November 14th 1917 at the age of 38. His home address was 66 Laburnum Avenue, Hull, and he left a wife and two children.

James is buried in Zuydcotte Military Cemetery. France.

806983. L/Cpl. Thomas Edgar Borrill, 2/8th Battalion Sherwood Foresters, had worked in the electricians shop since joining the firm on 21st September 1911 at the age of 14 and was an old member of the boys club, showing great skill for woodwork. He was killed in September 1917 at the age of 20. Thomas is listed in the Hull Daily mail Roll of Honour for 23rd October 1917 as killed in action on 26thSeptember 1917. (This is correct) he was the son of Edwin and Sarah Alice Borrill of 50 Bright Street, Holderness Road, Hull. He has no known grave but is commemorated on the Tyne Cot Memorial. Belgium.

Pte John E Lockham, 7th East Yorks., Reg. No. 33132, was employed at the canister works and had been with the firm since April 1st 1916. He was born in Hull, enlisted in Hull and was killed in action on April 23rd 1917. He is listed in the Hull Daily Mail Casualty List of 23rd May 1917: the war graves registers him as James Lockham who has no known grave, but is commemorated on the Arras Memorial to the Missing. France. As there is only one J E Lockham killed with the East Yorks on that date this must be correct.

931470. Sgt. Albert George Kellett, Royal Field Artillery, 'C' Battery 291st Brigade, worked as an Introducer and had been with the firm since 16th September 1912. He was killed on December 17th 1917 aged 28 years and left a widow and child. He was the son of Mrs Kellett of Leytonstone, London: and was the husband of Eleanor Mary Kellett of 7 Madeira Place, Brighton.

Albert is buried in Cement House Cemetery. Langemark. Belgium.

14786. Pte. Richard Wilson, listed in 'OURS' as serving with 1st East Yorks., however he is not listed in the official records of this regiment. He was employed at the Stoneferry Works and had been with the firm since September 24th, 1914. Enlisting early in the war he went out to France, was twice wounded and transferred to 942nd Area Employment COY – Labour Corps and was with this unit when he was killed on April 27th 1918 at the age of 42. He left a widow, Mary Ann, and two children and his home address was 1 Andrew's Avenue, St Mark's Street, Hull. His parents lived at 73 Arthur Street, Hull. Richard is buried in St Sever Cemetery Extension. Rouen. France.

Pte. Clifford Cooper, 1/4th East Yorks., Reg. No. 200656, wrote home early in 1918 and spoke of the dangers of an enemy barrage:

"You have heard that the Germans are bad shots; well, if you put a knife or anything small above the parapet, I bet you do not have it there a minute before it is splintered to pieces. The worst time I had in the trenches was when we were supports for the Canadians; the shells were practically sweeping the trenches of our men. I am sure they had about 40 guns, because there was one continuous stream of shells from the break of day till dusk. We had three days like that. We were huddled in a hole at

the bottom of the trench for three days without anything to eat, and couldn't get out for fear of being hit with shrapnel. On the 7th day in the trenches we had to retire because we had lost so many men, and the Germans had started using their poisonous gas. How are the boys getting on in the club? I wish I had the chance to spend my time there, I find the good it does now that I cannot get to it, but I expect I shall be too old when this is finished."
Clifford Cooper had been with the firm since October 12th 1909, working on the hoists, at the start of the war he enlisted but was destined never to return home. At the age of 23 he died of pneumonia on August 16th 1918. Born Hull. Enlisted Hull. He is listed in the Hull Daily Mail Roll of Honour for 5th September 1918.
Home address: 74 Bright Street, Hull.
Place of Burial: Etaples Military Cemetery.

A/360245. Pte. Arthur Richard Pullam was on the staff of the Bluebell Polish Company as a representative on the South and East Coasts, and latterly in the City and West End of London. He joined the firm on 1st November 1904. On joining up he went to Egypt in connection with the A.S.C. canteens. On leave in Cairo he was seized with dysentery and died on 15th July 1918 aged 37. He was the son of Charles and Elizabeth Pullum and husband of Mary Alice Pullum of 18 St Kilda's Road, Stoke Newington, London. Arthur is buried in Cairo War Memorial Cemetery. Egypt.

Pte. Edward Sharp is reported in 'OURs' to have served with the 11th East Yorks. (2nd Hull Pals), but is not in the official records of this unit at the time of

his death. He was in fact serving with 31st Battalion, Machine Gun Corps-Infantry when killed in action on June 28th 1918 at the age of 26. Edward Sharp had been with the firm since 20th October 1910 and worked in the Lead Pressing Department. He left a widow – Louie (nee Rickles) and a young son – George, his home address was 155 Buckingham Street, Hull.
Edward is listed in the Hull Daily Mail Roll of Honour of 18th JULY 1918; and is buried in Aval Wood Military Cemetery. France.

290306. Gunner George Henry Saul, Royal Garrison Artillery, 545th Siege Battery, was employed by the firm on 25th January 1912, and worked at the Stoneferry Works. He served through the German East African Campaign and died of wounds in France on October 10th 1918, at the age of 26. He left a widow – Jessie (nee Tether) and two young sons (twins), Bernard and George. His name was listed in the Hull Daily Mail Roll of Honour of 14th October 1918 and his home address was 4 Poplar Grove, Sculcoates Lane, Hull. He is buried in Etaples Military Cemetery, France.Gunner Saul's son George contacted me in early 2001 and gave me the following information regarding his father and family: "My father only came home the once, I remember him bringing home a piece of Ivory – 9" long and 3" wide. My mother used it to prop open the door in summer. He also brought home six ostrich feathers and a pod of what he called 'lucky beans' each was 2" long, black and red at the top. I remember him lying down in front of the fire shivering yet covered with blankets. I asked my Mother what was the matter and she told me he had malaria fever. My uncle, Robert Tether, worked in Reckitt's canister works and came home after the war suffering from the effects of mustard gas poisoning. He was in poor health for years and worked at Reckitts until he died. We lost my other uncle Bernard, he was killed in October 1918 after my father".

Pte. George Charlton, 11thEast Yorks, (2nd Hull Pals), in 'OURS' listed with the 12th but recorded as being with the 11th at the time of his death; Reg. No. 14/60. He was born in Hull, joined Reckitts on September 18th 1914, being employed at the Stoneferry Works, and enlisted in Hull. Pte. Charlton was killed in action on February 20th 1918, at the age of 32. He was a single man and lived at 20 Waterloo Street, Hull. His name is listed in the Hull Daily Mail Roll of Honour of 11th March 1918; and he is buried in Roclincourt Military Cemetery. France.

Pte Harold Lancaster Roberts 2/16th Battalion Queen's Westminster Rifles, had been on the clerical staff of London House since 24th February 1913. He was killed in Palestine on October 31st 1917, at the age of 25. He was the son of John and Jessie Roberts of 28 Fraser Road, Walthamston, London; and is buried in Beersheba War Cemetery. Israel.

390446. Pte. William George Slater, Royal Army Medical Corps; 1/3rd Northumbrian Field Ambulance, was employed by the firm on September 16th 1914. He died from gas poisoning on June 30th 1917 and left a widow Mabel and five children. His home address was 36 Barnsley Street, Hull and he was 33 years of age. His name is recorded in the Hull Daily Mail Roll of Honour of 16th July 1917 and he is buried in Achiet-Le-Grand Communal Cemetery Extension. France.

474360. Driver Gerald Pitts Parker, Royal Engineers, 529 Field COY, had been employed in the Blue Mill since 27th February 1911. He was killed on March 28th 1918 while feeding his horses at the age of 27 years,and left a widow, Miriam, and two children. His family lived at 101 Rosemead Street, Newbridge Road, Hull and he was the son of Robert and Dinah Parker of Ipswich. Gerald is buried in Bellacourt Military Cemetery. Riviere. France.

267842. Rifleman Joseph Markham, 1/7th West Yorks., was employed in the Brasso Mill, joining the firm on August 21st 1895. He was killed in the third battle for Ypres on October 9th 1917, at the age of 34 and left a widow. Joseph has no known grave but is commemorated on the Tyne Cot Memorial. Zonnebeke. Belgium.

81338. Pte. John Simpson, 15th Battalion, Durham Light Infantry, had been employed at Reckitts since July 6th 1914 and worked in the Box Shop.

He died of wounds in hospital on May 29th 1918, aged 18 years and was the son of John Henry Simpson of 1 Spring Cottages, Goodwin Street, Anlaby Road, Hull. John is buried in Terlincthun British Cemetery, Wimille. France.

Lt. George Benjamin Peterson, 1/4th East Yorks; attached to 6th Battalion Dorsetshire Regiment had joined the firm on 16th August 1909 and worked on the clerical staff of Dansom Lane. He was killed by shell-fire on March 31st 1918 while performing his duty as Platoon Officer of the 50th Light Trench Mortar Battery, his age was 22. He was a single man and lived with his parents Elizabeth and Benjamin, at 42 Beech Avenue, Garden Village, Hull, and left a fiancee –Dorothy. His name is recorded 'In Memoriam' in the Hull Daily Mail of 31st March 1919: from his mother, fiancée, sisters and brother Will in France. He is buried in Ribemont Communal Cemetery Extension. Somme. France.

45191. Pte. Thomas Samuel Taylor, 2nd Battalion South Wales Borderers, had been employed at the Stoneferry works since January 26th 1916. He was killed on 16th May 1917 and has no known grave. He is commemorated on the Arras Memorial to the Missing. France.

256212. Gunner Wilfred Dawson, Royal Field Artillery, 'B' Battery 251st Brigade, started his working life on September 1st 1914 and was employed on the hoists. He enlisted at the age of 18 and was killed on 22nd August 1918. He was the son of Annie Dawson of 23 Lee Street, Hull and was 20 years old. Wilfred now lies in Villers-Bretonneux Military Cemetery, Somme. France.

213208. Rifleman Richard Hopper, 9th Battalion Scottish Rifles, had been employed in Reckitts packing room since January 8th 1902. His unit came under artillery fire as they moved up the line, he was hit by shrapnel and killed on 20th September 1917, age 29 years. Richard was the son of James and Elizabeth Hopper of 15 Richard's Terrace, Kent Street, Hull and is buried in Ypres Town Cemetery Extension. Menin Gate. Belgium.

L/Cpl. Edward Chapman, 3rd East Yorks., Reg. No. 28475, worked at Morley Street, Hull, and had been with the firm since 22nd August 1910. He was born in Hull and enlisted in Hull at the start of the war, was wounded four times and died of pneumonia while training as a gymnastic instructor at home on 9th October 1918. He was 24 years old and left a widow Carla and daughter Pansy. Edward is commemorated 'In Memoriam' in the Hull Daily Mail; 9th October 1919 and was the son of Joseph and Annie Chapman of Hull. His home address was 6 Bellamy Street, Holderness Road, Hull and he is buried in Hedon Road Cemetery, Hull.

Pte. Richard A. Hill, in 'OURS' he is stated to have served with 1/4th East Yorks: but there is no trace of him in the official records of that regiment. He was 20 years of age when he was reported wounded and missing on October 1st 1916. No further information was received and it was presumed he was killed on that date. Pte. Hill had been employed at Reckitts since January 4th 1912. He is listed in the Hull Daily mail Casualty Lists of 16th December 1916 as serving with the Border Regiment; this is correct as he was killed on the above date serving with the 5th Battalion. Richard was the son of Richard and Ada Hill of 2 Cicero Terrace, Swann Street, Hull. He has no known grave but is commemorated on the Thiepval Memorial to the Missing. France.

27594. Pte. John James Harvey, Machine Gun Corps, 20th Battalion, attached to the 3rd East Yorks., was employed at the canister works and had been at Reckitts since September 19th 1910. He was killed on April 1st 1918 at the age of 23 years. He lived at 211 James Reckitt Avenue, Hull, and was the son of Mr and Mrs F Harvey of Hull. He is listed in he Hull Daily Mail Roll of Honour for 3rd May 1918 and is buried in Hangard Communal Cemetery Extension. Somme. France.

Pte. Ernest Hotchkin, 12th East Yorks. Reg. No. 12/1225, joined Reckitts on September 18th 1902 and was employed on the hoists. He enlisted in Hull at the City Hall in September, 1914, in the 3rd Hull Pals; in the dying stages of the Somme campaign his battalion attacked opposite Serre on November 13th 1916 and he was killed during the battle. His brother, Frederick, reg. No. 12/1226 was killed on the same day serving with the same battalion. Ernest Hotchkin was born in Hull and was 28 years old. The two brothers are listed in the Hull Daily Mail Casualty Lists of 9th and 13th January 1917. Ernest was the son of Mark and Minnie Hotchkin of Sophia's Terrace, Spyvee Street, Hull and the husband of Evelyn Marsden (nee Hotchkin) of 2 Crofton Avenue, Egton Street, Hull. He has no known grave but is commemorated on the Thiepval Memorial to the Missing. Somme. France. His brother Frederick is commemorated on the same memorial.

Lt. Ivan Hutchinson 5th Battalion East Yorks. Regiment, was on the clerical staff at Dansom Lane and had joined the firm on 1st September 1913. He received his commission in 1914 with the Cyclists Battalion, 5th East Yorks and was promoted to Lieutenant on May 23rd 1918 during the Great German Offensive. In the Allied advance of August 1918 he was shot through the head by a sniper, on the 22nd and killed. He was 21 years old and is listed in the Hull Daily Mail Roll of Honour of 27th August 1918. His home address was 563 Anlaby Road, Hull and his parents were Henry Watson Hutchinson and Gertrude Hutchinson of the same address.

Ivan is buried in Queen's Cemetery. Bucquoy. France.

Pte. William Herbert Woodcraft, Army Service Corps., Reg. No. T4/199519, was employed in the packing room at Reckitts and had been with the firm for twenty six years, beginning his service on 11th January 1890. He was 42 years of age when he died of tuberculosis at Woolwich Hospital on June 2nd 1918. He lived at 26 Thomas Street, Hull, is buried in Hedon Road Cemetery Hull and was the son of the late Zachariah and Elizabeth Woodcraft of 4 The Haven, Garden Village, Hull.

390518. Pte. Frederick Bartholemew Coupland, Royal Army Medical Corps., had been working at Reckitts since September 7th 1914 and was employed at the canister works. He was a single man and at the age of 29 was killed in the act of bandaging a wounded comrade on October 17th 1917. He was the son of Fred and Elizabeth Coupland of 13 Craven Street, Holderness Road, Hull and is buried in St Julien Dressing Station Cemetery, Langemark, Belgium.

T2/13784 Driver George Crockett, Army Service Corps. 6th Reserve Park. Was employed in the Mixing Department of the Shinio Works and had been with the firm since May 22nd 1913. He joined up at the start of the war and was a single man. On the 21st March 1918 he was killed in action, at the age of 25 years. He was the son of Mrs Ellen Crockett of 151 Bedford Bootle. Bootle. Liverpool; and is buried in Nine Elms British Cemetery. Belgium.

L/Cpl. Robert Elsom, enlisted in the 10th Hussars at the age of 15 years on August 7th 1914, later he was transferred to 16th Royal Scots. In the great German offensive of 1918 he was shot in the head and killed on March 22nd of that year. He was 19 years old, worked in the canister works and had been with the firm since July 1st 1914. Home address: 13 Stafford Street, Hull. Robert is listed in the Hull Daily Mail Roll of Honour on 2nd April 1918 and is buried in Bac-Du-Sud British Cemetery. France.

Gunner John Earl, Royal Garrison Artillery, 117th Seige Battery, worked at Reckitts as a joiner and had been in the firm's employ since January 17th 1900. He died of wounds at home on 15th July 1918 age 38, and left a widow Annie and five children. His parents were Thomas W and Francis Earl. His home address was 10 Florence Avenue, Courtney Street, Hull. John is buried in Hedon Road Cemetery. Hull.

722149. Pte. Robert S. Chattey, 2/24th London Regiment, had been a warehouseman at the London House since joining the firm on December 20th 1905. He was 26 years of age when he was killed in Palestine on December 13th 1917, and was a single man. Robert is buried in Jerusalem War Cemetery. Israel.

2nd Lt. Charles Walter Tune, 13th Yorkshire Regiment, was on the office staff of the Kingston Works and had been with the firm since March 29 1910. He was gazetted in September 1917 and was killed on 23 November the same year at the age of 22 years. He was the son of Charles and Annie Everson Tune of Hessle; Hull. His name is recorded in the Hull Daily Mail Roll of Honour for 10th December 1917. Charles Walter has no known grave but is commemorated on the Cambai Memorial. Louveral. France.

Pte. George Thurloe, East Riding Yeomanry, Reg. No. 3075, was employed at the Stoneferry Works, joining the firm on 9th June 1913. During the war he was transferred to the 11th East Yorks. (2nd Hull Pals, his new Reg. No. was 52610) and was killed in action on 28 June 1918. He was born in Liverpool, Lancs., enlisted in Hull and was a single man.

George is buried in Aval Wood Military Cemetery. France.

2nd Lt. Stanley Phillipps Fryer, Worcester Regiment, had been employed as an Introducer since 2nd November 1910. He was 33 years of age when he was killed in France on September 27th 1918. The above information was recorded in 'OURS' some of it is incorrect: Lt Fryer was in fact killed while serving with the 30th Brigade, Royal Field Artillery and had also served with the Honourable Artillery Company in Egypt. He met his death on 27th October 1918; was the son of Herbert and Edith Maud Fryer of Swansea and the husband of Mrs Fryer of 15 George Street, Balsall Heath, Birmingham. Stanley is buried in La Vallee – Mulatre Communal Cemetery Extension, Aisne, France.

238059 Sgt. Charles Hartley, 7th Lincolnshire Regiment was employed at the Stoneferry Works and had been with the firm since he was thirteen, his starting date was 22nd November 1906. He was a single man and was killed in action on July 27th 1918, at the age of 25 years. His home address was 17 Derwent Avenue, Garden Village, Hull. His name appears in the Hull Daily Mail Roll of Honour of 19th August 1918 and he was the son of Henry and Sarah Hartley of Hull.

Charles Hartley is buried in Harponville Communal Cemetery Extension. Somme. France.

44757 L/Cpl. Ernest Downs, 2/7th Manchester Regiment, was employed at the canister works, joining the firm on 1st March 1908. He was killed on March 21st 1918, on the first day of the 'Great German Offensive' at the age of 29 years and left a widow, Elsie, who lived at 8 Florence Grove, Lorraine Street, Stoneferry, Hull.

Ernest is buried in Jeancourt Communal Cemetery Extension, Aisne. France.

Pte. Maurice Walton, 1st East Yorks., Reg. No. 30587, was on the clerical staff of Dansom Lane as an apprentice and had been with the firm since July 27th 1914. He was born in Norton, Yorkshire, and enlisted in Hull in May 1917. On 25th April 1918 he was reported missing and was 19 years old. His parents lived at 5 Albany Street, Hull. Maurice was killed in action on 25th April 1918 and his name appears in the Hull Daily Mail Casualty List of 14th June 1919.

He has no known grave but is commemorated on the Tyne Cot Memorial. Belgium. Panel 47 to 48 and 163A.

Edward Henry Nozedar, 2/1st East Riding Yeomanry, later 12th Battalion Suffolk Regiment. Reg. No. 57463

Edward Henry Nozedar was born on April 3rd, 1899, at 68 Oxford Street, Sculcoates, Hull. He was one of a large family (about 13) belonging to Enoch Nozedar, a general labourer, and his wife Mary Ellen (nee Hill). Edward joined Reckitt's employ on 26th February 1917 and worked in the Canister Works. His sister, Emmie, married Ernest Cockerline who also worked at Reckitt's, joining the firm on April 18th 1916 and was also employed in the Canister Works.

The great nephew of these two men, Mr Stephen Moran of Inverness, provided much information regarding the above, as neither of them appear in the Reckitts Magazine 'OURS', though they are both to be found in the special edition, listing the 'Fallen', of 1919. Mr Moran wrote:

"The photograph I enclose is from a locket which was kept by my great aunt Emmie all her life. The hand on Ted's shoulder is that of his brother Tom. Family memory has it that Ted joined up under age, it is fairly certain he enlisted into the East Yorks. since his medals, which were passed to me by Tom's son, Ronnie, who still lives in Hull, are marked 51172, Pte. E h Nozedar, E. York. R."

Pte. Edward Henry Nozedar was killed by a sniper while serving with the Suffolk Regiment on October 20th 1918 near Espierres near Turcoing, Belgium. He is buried in the churchyard at Espierres (B.441).

Pte. Ernest Cockerline, Reg. No. 57231, served with the 1/5th Battalion West Yorkshire Regiment, was killed on October 11th 1918 and has no known grave. He is commemorated on panel 14, MR 16, (Part 2) of the Vis-en-Artois Memorial, South West of Arras. The two daughters of Emmie and Ernest perished in the influenza epedemic of 1919. Emmie went on to outlive three more husbands but had no more children. Stephen Moran remembers her in her final years:

"I knew great aunt Emmie as a blind old lady with a mind like quicksilver when I was very small, she died in the 60's as did Alice and my Grandfather James Andrew Moran who served with the 12th East Yorks. (3rd Hull Pals) throughout the Somme battles, before being seriously wounded at Serre on 13th November 1916."

'The Hunter Family'

Before the Great War Samuel Hunter was a member of the Territorial Force. He was born in Hull and attended Mersey Street School with all of his brothers and sisters except for Len. His father Mr Leonard Hunter, said he should go to Craven Street School to study for a scholarship. Mr Leonard Hunter worked on the docks as a sworn weigher and died in 1913. Ada and Stanley, being the youngest, were taken into an orphanage at the junction of Spring Bank and Stanley Street, it was demolished only recently. Ada did not come out of it until 1920 and said of her experience there:

"It was 7 years of perfect misery. I was alright at lessons but the boys and girls who weren't very bright got their ears boxed and the stick. There was one boy who stammered, the Headmaster ridiculed him mercilessly and beat him."

The widowed Mrs Susan Hunter lived at 9 Rosedale Avenue, Upton Street, Dansom Lane, Hull, with the rest of her children until they in turn married and left home.

Samuel Hunter married a young woman called Abigail who lived at 9 Malvern Avenue, Ella Street, Newland Avenue, Hull. When they were married they moved to 187 Mersey Street, Holderness Road, Hull. Samuel worked at Reckitts, joining the firm on 2nd September 1914, he was employed in the Canister Works as a stone-polisher. He enlisted in Hull during the war and served as Pte. 33428 with 7th Battalion East Yorkshire Regiment. His brother John also enlisted in the army, his younger brother Len tried to enlist and was told to grow, he returned home for a bowler hat and overcoat and was accepted, serving as Gunner 761280 with the Royal Field Artillery.

Samuel always told Ada that when he returned after the war he would take her out of the orphanage to live with him and his wife. Ada got letters from the boys when they were abroad:

Samuel Hunter before the War

"They used to send us cards from France, but they used to read them before they got to us." Samuel never did return home, he was killed in action on May 12th 1917 at the age of 25 years. His body was never found but his name is featured on the Arras Memorial to the Missing. Len Hunter was killed by shellfire on August 24th 1918 at the age of 20 years and now lies in Cabaret Rouge British Cemetery, Souchez. Plot 8, row N, grave 9.

John Hunter survived the war, seeing active service with the1/4th Battalion East Yorkshire Regiment, he had worked at Reckitts since October 1908 and returned there after the war, working at the Kingston Works on the hoists.

Pte Samuel Hunter

Gunner Len Hunter

Rachel also worked at Reckitts factory and during the war never gave up hope her brothers might still be alive:

Ada and Stanley at the Orphanage

"When prisoners of war began to come home they used to go to the riverside quay and a hooter used to blow. Rachel used to run there to see if Sam or Len were there among them."

Like many other Hull families hope faded for the Hunters. Ada finally left the orphanage in 1920 and the very next day started work at Reckitts. She still lives in Mersey Street (1992).

Ada Prissick.

The Hunter Family before the Great War (The only members missing off the picture are Herbert, who died aged 11 months, and Edith who was not yet born).

1. Rachel
2. John
3. William
4. Samuel
5. Alfred
6. Susan Hunter
7. Leonard Hunter –died 1913. He was the eldest of 10 sons
8. Leonard
9. Stanley
10. Alice
11. Ada

Ernest Wadge worked as the Reckitt's representative in Ontario, Canada. He enlisted in the Canadian Mounted Rifles in early 1916 as a trooper. Quickly he received promotion to Sergeant and then to Lieutenant. He was on outpost duty on the Western Front with a Sergeant and five men when the whole group was killed by a shell which exploded in the middle of their position. Ernest Wadge died on 12th November 1917. Major McEwan, who was in the same squadron stated:

"Lt. Wadge was loved by all, not only for his personal courage, but for his splendid integrity and his fine upstanding manhood."

Ernest is buried in Ypres Reservoir Cemetery. Belgium.

Charles John Nix joined Reckitt's employ on October 21st 1907, and worked in the Canister Works. He was born in Hull and enlisted in Hull at the City Hall during the recruiting campaign of September 1914. He joined Hull's 2nd Service Battalion or 2nd Hull Pals, later to take on the title of 11th Battalion East Yorkshire Regiment, his regimental number was 11/673.

The 11th trained in England during 1915, and was sent to Egypt with the 31st Division in December of that year. No Turkish attack developed here but in Europe events were on the move and the whole Division arrived in France in March 1916, to take part in the Somme offensive.

On the 1st July the 31st Division suffered terribly though the Hull Pals were kept in reserve. In the attacks of 13th November that year the Hull Pals were decimated attacking over the same ground.

In 1917 Nix was promoted to Corporal and took part in the 'Battle for Arras', the Hull Battalions attacked at Oppy Wood, 3rd May 1917 and again their ranks were decimated – yet another black day for Hull. In 1918 the 11th was in the heaviest fighting as the last 'Great German Offensive' was launched and though the allies were pushed back some 40 miles the line held in some of the most desperate actions all along the front. In August of that year the Allies counter-attacked crushing the German front and in countless actions began pushing the Germans back over familiar territory, this was the end for Germany.

Corporal Nix had by this time been awarded the Military Medal and wrote home an account of one incident during his unit's advance. His platoon had spent 24 hours in an advanced post up to their knees in mud and water, the platoon was at last relieved for a well earned rest. The following night, 2 hours before dawn, the command "stand to" rang down this silent trench:

"Coming out of my dug-out I found the trench alive with soldiers. After a hurried preparation water bottles were filled and rations given to every man, we were given four 'pills' (bombs) each and awaited orders. At a given signal we moved forward across 'No Man's Land,' using every precaution against being taken by surprise (for We were to do the surprising). Dawn was just breaking and it was a fine spectacle. We entered the German front line without a hitch and then we 'set our stall out' for any unlikely thing that might happen. We searched high and low for Fritz, in dug-outs and every possible hiding-place and we found no one in the front line. 'Platoon, move forward!' and then we went down the communication trench to the second line. I forgot to mention that the German trenches were like the Old Harbour at Hull –if you did not want to be drowned or up to your neck in mud, you had to walk on top. We reached the second line and then we sighted a few Bosches. Instantly a few of our men sank on one knee and opened rifle fire on them and we saw one roll over and another was wounded. The rest ran for it and got away into the mist. We visited the one who rolled over and found it was an officer, but he was practically dead and we left him. At this point we waited events. We soon heard them. Fritz had just realised he had got visitors and he opened out a barrage of artillery fire on his front line, but thank God, he did not know where we were and we escaped a lot of his fire.

"'Platoon, move forward.' Platoon Commander again yelled, and we moved off under the same conditions as before to the third line and then on to the fourth line. Our Commander ordered us to remain and make ourselves comfortable and we dug ourselves in and made strong points to resist any attack Fritz might make. 'Zip, zip, zip.' the bullets from the German snipers rang around our ears. A shell dropped here and there, but the blood of Yorkshire was up. All was excitement and we took little heed of all. We smoked and smoked and awaited orders. 'Well, boys,' our leader said, 'we have got to retire, our flanks have not been so successful and we're likely to be surrounded.'

Although we had to leave the ground we won, in a few hours' time it was all taken again by our comrades, with a lot more trenches along that front."

Nix was promoted to Sergeant in 1918 and wrote home again later that year revelling in the fact that at last he and his comrades were on the road to victory:

"When I last wrote I really thought we should all be home for this Xmas to tell you all personally our experiences, but it was not to be. We are more up to our eyes in war than ever, but at present we are on the high road to Victory and Peace. I really cannot pick out any real adventure during the past year, for in my mind this year has been one great adventure for all. It seems, as it were, like a clock pendulum swinging backwards and forwards. As I sit here and review the past months over, I feel proud along with the rest of us that we have stood the test and now we are giving Fritz 'big 'uns,' such as he gave us in the early months of the year."

Sergeant Charles John Nix, M.M., had indeed stood the test, he had proved himself a resourceful, committed and brave soldier. He had taken part in many fierce actions during his time in France and was one of the original 'Hull Pals', however he was fated never to return home and was killed in action during the Allied advance on September 29th 1918, less than two months before the Armistice was signed, aged 29. His death was not recorded in 'OURS' magazine but he is featured in the lists of the 'Fallen' – 'OURS' 1919. He was the husband of Mrs Elsie May Nix of 2 Story Street, Hull, and the son of Charles Francis and Annie Mallson Nix of 15 East Street, Church Street, Drypool, Hull.

Sergeant C J Nix. M.M. is buried in Strand Military Cemetery, Comines-Warneton. Hainaut. Belgium VIII. P. 10.

His brother, 200737 Cpl James Nix, worked as a rivet heater in Earle's Shipyard, Hull. He enlisted in Hull in 1914, went to France in August 1915 and was killed in action on 25th May 1918, aged 21, serving with the 1/4th Battalion East Yorkshire Regiment. He has no known grave but is commemorated on the Soissons Memorial to the Missing, Aisne. France.

98927. Driver Henry Binks was the brother-in-law of the Nix brothers, he served 3 years in France with A Battery, 282nd Brigade, Royal Field Artillery. Henry was born in Hull and enlisted in Hull: he died of influenza on Armistace

Day, 11th November 1918 and is buried in Cambrai East Military Cemetery. France. III. A. 8.

Gunner George Hoodless, Royal Field Artillery, 55th Brigade had been at Reckitts since 28th August 1914 before he enlisted. He wrote from Mesopotamia thanking people for sending him gifts and of his wish to return home soon:

"I received the parcel of cigarettes all safe and sound and would express my warmest thanks to the directors and workpeople of Messrs. Reckitt and Sons for their kindness in sending me the parcels since I have been out in this country. I feel that I am not forgotten by the people at home, though such a long way off. Well, I shall be glad when it is all over, as I daresay it will be before much longer now, and then I shall be able to return to work again. I am indeed hoping to be able to do so. I wish to be remembered to all the workmen in the Fitters' Shop. I shall now have to come to a close as the weather is not very comfortable for writing very long, as it is now 120 degrees in the shade."

Sgt. John Gates, M.M., 15th Royal Warwicks, was employed by the firm on 18th April 1907 on the outside staff. In this letter home he gives an account of a trench raid he took part in; he was awarded the Military Medal for his actions:

"The battalion are out for six days' rest when we are informed that the C.O. desires volunteers for special duty. Thirty of us step forward and our names are taken. The day before the battalion takes its place in the line again we are told we have been chosen for a bombing raid on the enemy's lines. A prisoner must be obtained for information. The next four of five days we are busy rehearsing the stunt and out on patrol at night examining the Boche wire and getting proper direction. At last the time arrives when we must essay our task. At 2.15 in the morning we crawl to within 20 yards of the enemy wire and await our barrage which is timed for 2.30 am. Exact to the second our guns open, all calibre of shells whistle over us breaking and destroying the wire entanglements. For one minute our guns play on the object and then lift to his front lines. What a minute! I never dreamt a minute might take so long in passing. Then we are up, dashing madly for the German trench, our guns in the meantime have again lifted and are playing havoc with his support trenches. Into the enemy front line we jump, one party going to the left, the other to the right, another party remaining on top with a machine gun to cover us and take back prisoners. We are very successful, what the guns have left we complete with bomb and bayonet and eventually return to our own lines. We have already sent back the prisoner required. Our casualties have been very slight and we are all very pleased and very tired. For this raid the officer in charge was awarded the M.C., myself and two others received the M.M."

Gunner Laurence Henry Backhouse, Royal Garrison Artillery, 326th Siege Battery, joined Reckitts on 27th February 1911. He wrote the following letter from a hospital in France:

"As you will see from my address I am still in hospital. I was discharged from one hospital and sent to a convalescent camp. After a week there I could hardly walk and was examined by a specialist. The diagnosis was sciatica and I was admitted to this hospital, where I am having electrical and X-ray treatments. I have been here nearly a month and am now progressing slowly but favourably. I am very thin and a mere shadow of my former self, and nothing like the Backhouse who used to perform conjuring tricks in grocers' shops while in quest of orders for Messrs. Reckitts' useful and famous commodities."

Reading Between the Lines: Quoted in 'OURS'

A letter form the Front, written at the time of the "Big Push" 1918, runs as follows:

"Yes, we did move some ... shedding all sorts of things en route. Firing all day, trekking all night; gas for breakfast, H.E. for lunch, and shrapnel as a nightcap.

Shot at everything we could see, and we saw a lot. Fought over places that were all too familiar. We were lucky enough in this phase, but caught it later when we settled for a day; we mustered sixteen all told at the finish.

W... is O.K., but fed up; B... gassed, and in dock, but cheerful; the three new officers are buried somewhere in what is now Germany. Got a fresh lot now, and are still smiling.

We're out at rest at present, eating the asparagus in the garden, and praying that we shan't be sent back before the strawberries are out.

Could tell you a lot, but better not. You would have had the time of your life if you'd been here, and I wish you had."

"The time of your life." We will read between the lines: let us reconstruct the scene.

Imagine a field with a hedge at the back of it. Six big guns are pushed inside the hedge and behind the guns is stacked nearly a barge load of ammunition. Men, naked to their waists, with gas masks over their faces and shrapnel helmets strapped on to their heads, men dazed with the noise and want to sleep, mechanically loading and firing the guns. They are apathetic to danger, but all imbued with the idea of carrying on. No one minds being killed any more than slipping down; it's a nuisance because it stops one working.

Flash! Flash! Bang! Bang! Shriek! Bang! Clouds of dust in the brilliant sunshine. A shell has just landed in No. 2 pit. "Keep on firing!" comes a voice muffled by a gas mask and rendered harsh through a cracked megaphone. Flash! Bang! Answer the other guns. The immediate noise is so great that the guns in the next field might be silent.

The officer left in command knows very little. He has an impression of tiny figures in front running, and he begins to ask himself if they'd better move and if he can get the guns out. Or shall he fight it out? Does it matter much anyway? Over in the ditch six men are building a little bridge in case they must move. They don't seem to be hurrying; perhaps they are too tired.

The wires have all gone. Last orders he got were from the major, "Hang on as long as you can, and get away as late as possible. But get the guns away whatever happens.

Meanwhile Bang! Bang! Bang!

At night the noises increase, the place reeks with gas and the smell of cordite; one stumbles into shell-holes, sometimes over bodies. The maddened horses leap into their harness - it often breaks - another delay. The ponderous guns bump along behind, through ditches and shell-holes, sinking into soft patches here and there; the gunners busy themselves with levers and planks, while the terrified animals sweat and gasp in their excitement and pain. The heavy crash that rocks the ground and blots out everything, the shrieking shrapnel that strikes men and horses down, and the gas,

"How far are the Germans?" A shadowy company of infantry stumbles past in to the cackle of machine guns and bombs.

And the subaltern, caked in mud, not shaved for a week, with one spur only, no belt, his boots torn to pieces, his flesh showing through the tears in his clothing, no sleep or food for days - yes, he's having "the time of his life."

Pte. Roy Vickers, 3rd Battalion East Yorks. Regiment, joined Reckitts on 5th August 1912 and went out to France in March 1918. On the 21st his unit was rushed to the front to meet the onslaught of the 'Great German Offensive', he describes seeing the enemy attacking in massed formation and of how his battalion was pushed back but never broke:

"I was at once rushed up to my battalion, who at that time were in the trenches in front of St. Quenton. You can imagine how cheerful I felt, after being home and enjoying all the home comforts, to be in the trenches again. On the morning of the 21st, about 4 o'clock, the Germans opened a fearful barrage on to our backward areas and our battalion about 6 am received orders to move forward to the front lines with all speed as the Germans were attacking. We hurriedly donned our packs, had ammunition served, and proceeded forward. We lost a lot of men in going forward. At about 11 am we engaged the enemy coming over in massed formation, but could not check him and had to retire to a redoubt. Here we managed to hold him and all the afternoon saw some very fierce fighting. Several times we went over the top to resist his charges and dusk still saw us holding him up. When he found himself unable to proceed any further he started to dig himself in. At the time I was in charge of a Lewis gun and received orders to go out into the front of our redoubt and try if possible to snipe his men. I was just reaching up to get the gun off the parapet when I 'stopped one.' I was hit in the shoulder, chest and neck by pieces of high explosive shell. Of course, that put the tin hat on my little expedition into No Man's Land. I very soon went unconscious and do not remember any more until I woke up in a casualty clearing station. Next day I was evacuated from there on the night and the train was moving out of one end of the village as the Germans were entering the other. It was heavily shelled, but, thanks to Providence, was never hit. From there I went to an American hospital and there found the Yanks very nice fellows indeed. On March 31st I was marked for Blighty and arrived at Shrewsbury on the night of Easter Monday. Here I had a long stop, nearly four months, and had a very fine time. When my wounds were healed I was moved on to my present address for massage, as my left arm is paralysed. They are trying their best to put some life into it, but I am afraid it will always be a very poor arm at the best."

Pte. George H. Adams, Royal Army Medical Corps, worked at the London House before the war as a motor-carman and first joined the firm in October 1906. He found many of the Reckitts goods in evidence in Palestine:

" I am pleased to state I am in the best of health. The heat out here is awful, and one can't do very much in the day-time. I went to Jaffa and the first thing I saw was Reckitts' Bag Blue all round the shops. I smiled to myself, thinking how many I had carried. I also saw Brasso in Jericho and Jerusalem. I may add it is well advertised out here in the towns."

Sgt. Howard Lawson, 4th Battalion Royal West Kents, wrote from Kent:

" I am busy at present on experimental work bearing on the present phase of action overseas. Every energy is bent towards rendering impossible the old stale-mate trench warfare and leads to the art of manoeuvre and speedy decision. More I may not say. As soon as I finish here I shall go back and train N.C.O.'s."

He had been with the firm since 30th August, 1909.

Chapter 6

Upton Street Peace Party: 1919

Remembering the Fallen 1920. Memorials

When the war was over and the Reckitt's community began counting the cost of the conflict it became increasingly important that there be permanent memorials to fallen comrades.

At Reckitt's Factory in 1920 there was a flurry of activity as rolls of the dead were erected throughout the different departments.

A new and very beautiful garden of remembrance was built and at its centre was erected a large white stone memorial fountain featuring the figure of sacrifice and her fallen son.

The following items from 'OURS' 1920 relate to these events and give a picture of a factory in mourning.

'OURS' - 1920

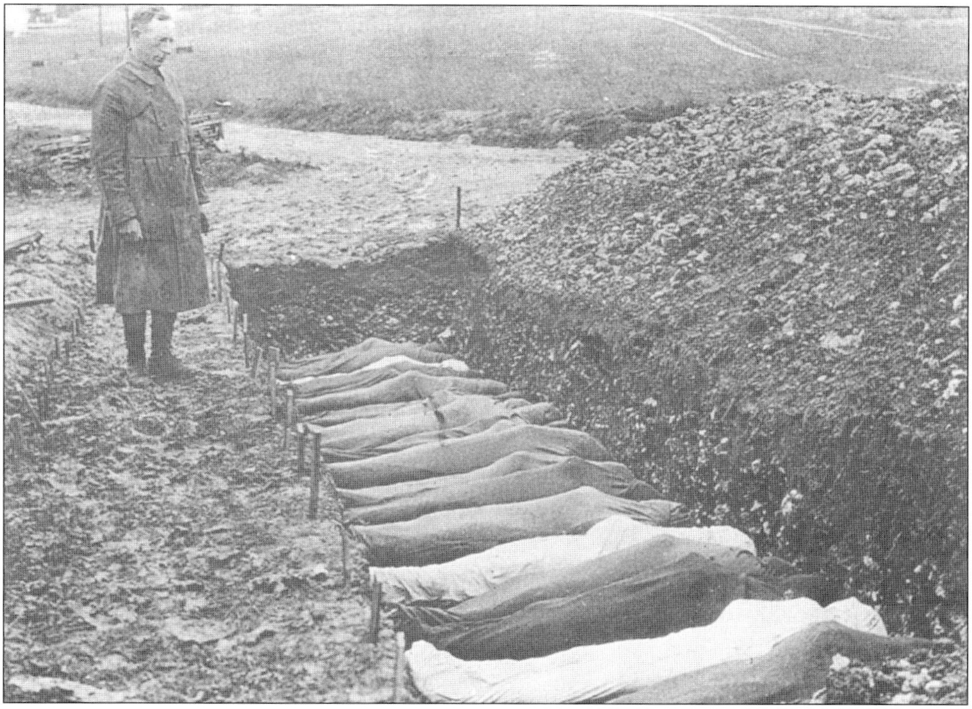

Chaplain T.R. White conducts a burial service over the common grave of 12 men who died in January 1918 at the Red Cross Evacuation Hospital at Fleury-Sur-Aire, France.

The Great War changed people's attitudes to death, what had once been one of the great taboos had become for the population a regular event, men at the front accepted it as a part of their lives, while civilians saw whole sections of their men wiped out in the great offensives. 'OURS' echoed this view as the people of Hull counted the cost of war:

> "Many people thrust aside any though of death, and, unlike Socrates, they shun any discussion of death. Parsons were the only people we allowed to talk to us of mortality; and then we went home to Sunday dinner and dismissed mortality as a remote contingency. We shunned death so much that we invested it with unreal dread, preposterously calling it the 'King of Terrors' and surrounded it with gloomy pomps. We brought up our children to think of death as some unnatural stroke of nature instead of teaching them
> that death is as natural as birth.
>
> The Great War has altered us. We who have seen a million of our strong men in the morning dew of their springtide pass gaily out of life cannot decently or with any sense of perspective beat our breasts on the comfortable, love-attended, gently nursed deaths of our middle-aged friends or our middle-aged selves. We have seen death overwhelm the young, joyous and hale; we cannot grieve so much when death comes as a kindly release of the pains and weakness of the middle-aged and elderly."

The Unveiling of Employees Memorial Tablets 1920

The works council, elected in 1920, wished to provide an employees memorial consisting of a roll of honour, upon which the names of the 'Fallen' would be inscribed. It was decided that £250 should be expended for that purpose. A competition was thrown open to employees for the best design, seven designs were submitted and two of them were judged to be of outstanding merit, one by Ernest G Atkinson of the Canister Works and the other by Mr H T Peak of the Kingston Works. These two designs were placed in the hands of Mr Aumonier, master mason, who embodied the best points of both into one feature. It was found that two tablets, of the same design, would be needed to contain the 153 names of the 'Fallen'.

The unveiling ceremony took place in the Reckitt's Institute, Dansom Lane, Mr A B Reckitt led the ceremony and the following groups were in attendance: All Directors and Management, members of the works council, the Foremen's and Forewomen's standing committee, the departmental committees of the council and all ex-servicemen.

The Gathering in the Reckitt's Institute

Mr Rimmington and Mr Arthur B Reckitt addressed the gathering in the Institute building with Mr Reckitt unveiling the tablets, after which he spoke of the sacrifices made by the employees and the debt owed to the men who returned home:

"They had travelled a long way in the valley of the shadow of death, had experienced many horrors and much mental anguish, and though they had not laid down their lives, had yet borne the great brunt of the war."

After a short silence the ceremony was concluded by the singing of the National Anthem.

These finely executed memorials have long since disappeared.

Mr Rimmington and Mr Arthur B Reckitt address the gathering. The tablets can be seen clearly behind them.

The Memorial Tablets

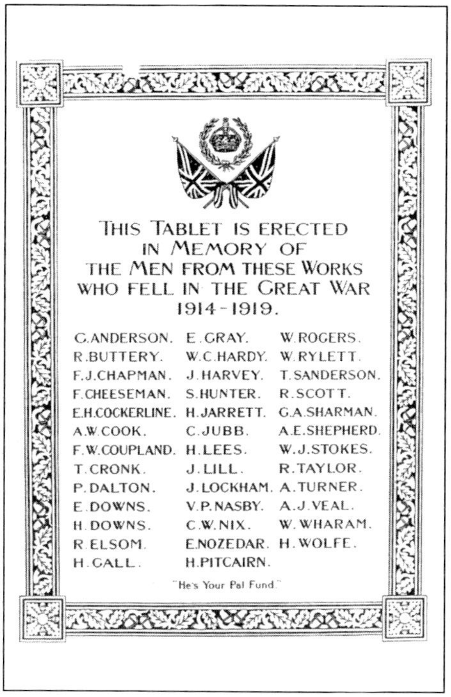
THIS TABLET IS ERECTED
IN MEMORY OF
THE MEN FROM THESE WORKS
WHO FELL IN THE GREAT WAR
1914 - 1919.
G.ANDERSON. E.GRAY. W.ROGERS.
R.BUTTERY. W.C.HARDY. W.RYLETT.
F.J.CHAPMAN. J.HARVEY. T.SANDERSON.
F.CHEESEMAN. S.HUNTER. R.SCOTT.
E.H.COCKERLINE. H.JARRETT. G.A.SHARMAN.
A.W.COOK. C.JUBB. A.E.SHEPHERD.
F.W.COUPLAND. H.LEES. W.J.STOKES.
T.CRONK. J.LILL. R.TAYLOR.
P.DALTON. J.LOCKHAM. A.TURNER.
E.DOWNS. V.P.NASBY. A.J.VEAL.
H.DOWNS. C.W.NIX. W.WHARAM.
R.ELSOM. E.NOZEDAR. H.WOLFE.
H.GALL. H.PITCAIRN.
"He's Your Pal Fund."

Roll of Honour Tablet of the Canister Works

Immediately after the two minutes' silence on November 11th there was a very simple, but none the less impressive ceremony at The Canister Works. This was the unveiling of a beautifully executed Memorial Tablet, bearing the names of the thirty-eight men from these works who fell in the War. All the ex-service men were asked to be present, and they lined up silently while Miss Dunn unveiled the Memorial; then the Last Post was sounded.

"The Brass was fixed to the wall near the entrance where everyone in the works must pass each day; here it will perpetually remind us of the gratitude and admiration we owe to those who made the supreme sacrifice that we might remain free. These men have, of their own free will, and for the sake of others, foregone the happiness of life and faced the last enemy of mortal man; and therein they have the advantage over us, who, whether we will or not, have some day the same enemy, we hope in less terrifying form, to face."

The Brass was purchased out of the balance of the Canister Works "He's your Pal Fund."

‘OURS’ 1920

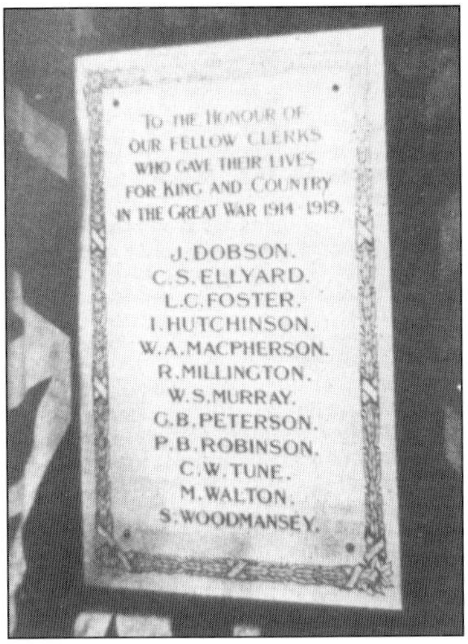

The Glorious Dead

On the page is a photograph of the Brass Memorial Tablet placed on the wall of the General Office by the Staff in memory of their colleagues who have given their lives in the war.

“On November 11th, the first anniversary of Armistice day, the tablet was decorated by a laurel wreath, and around it at 11o’clock, took place the impressive ceremony in accordance with the King’s request – a beautiful idea – that for two minutes “the thoughts of every one may be concentrated on reverent remembrance of the dead.”

No one who gathered round that shrine that morning is likely to forget those tense two minutes, charged as they were with deep emotion, with sharpened realization of the tragedy of young lives cut off in their bright morning and with thought of our debt to them. Moments too, that were filled with the remembered grief of those who had known the bitterness of loss within their own family circle. In the bowed, silent assembly, stood a visitor and stranger, much moved, who had himself suffered the death of one son, and had two others seriously injured, and who expressed afterwards his thanks for the privilege of participating in the commemoration.

The hush of profound silence was broken by the bugle call of “The Last Post” sounded by Mr A V Coates, and the staff returned to the duties of the day after the most moving ceremony that has ever been witnessed amongst them. Throughout the Works all machinery was stopped, and for the “two minutes” a reverential silence reigned.”

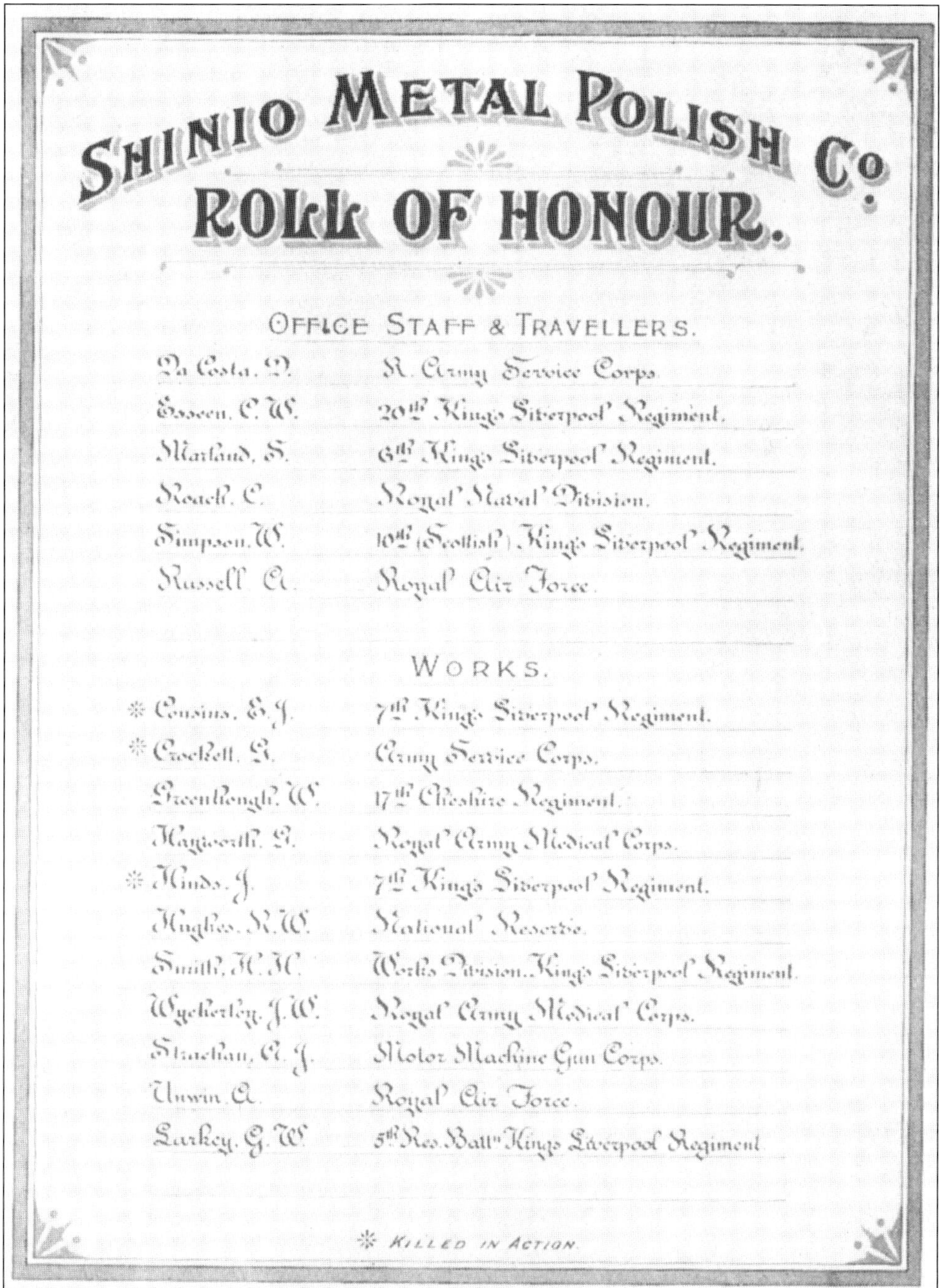

SHINIO METAL POLISH Co
ROLL OF HONOUR.

OFFICE STAFF & TRAVELLERS.

Da Costa, D.	R. Army Service Corps
Esseen, C. W.	20th Kings Liverpool Regiment.
Marland, S.	6th Kings Liverpool Regiment.
Roach, C.	Royal Naval Division.
Simpson, W.	10th (Scottish) Kings Liverpool Regiment.
Russell, A.	Royal Air Force.

WORKS.

* Cousins, E. J.	7th Kings Liverpool Regiment.
* Crockett, G.	Army Service Corps.
Greenhough, W.	17th Cheshire Regiment.
Hayworth, G.	Royal Army Medical Corps.
* Hinds, J.	7th Kings Liverpool Regiment.
Hughes, R. W.	National Reserve.
Smith, H. H.	Works Division. Kings Liverpool Regiment.
Wycherley, J. W.	Royal Army Medical Corps.
Strachan, A. J.	Motor Machine Gun Corps.
Unwin, A.	Royal Air Force.
Larkey, G. W.	5th Res. Battn Kings Liverpool Regiment

* KILLED IN ACTION.

Roll of Honour Tablet of the Shinio Polish Co.

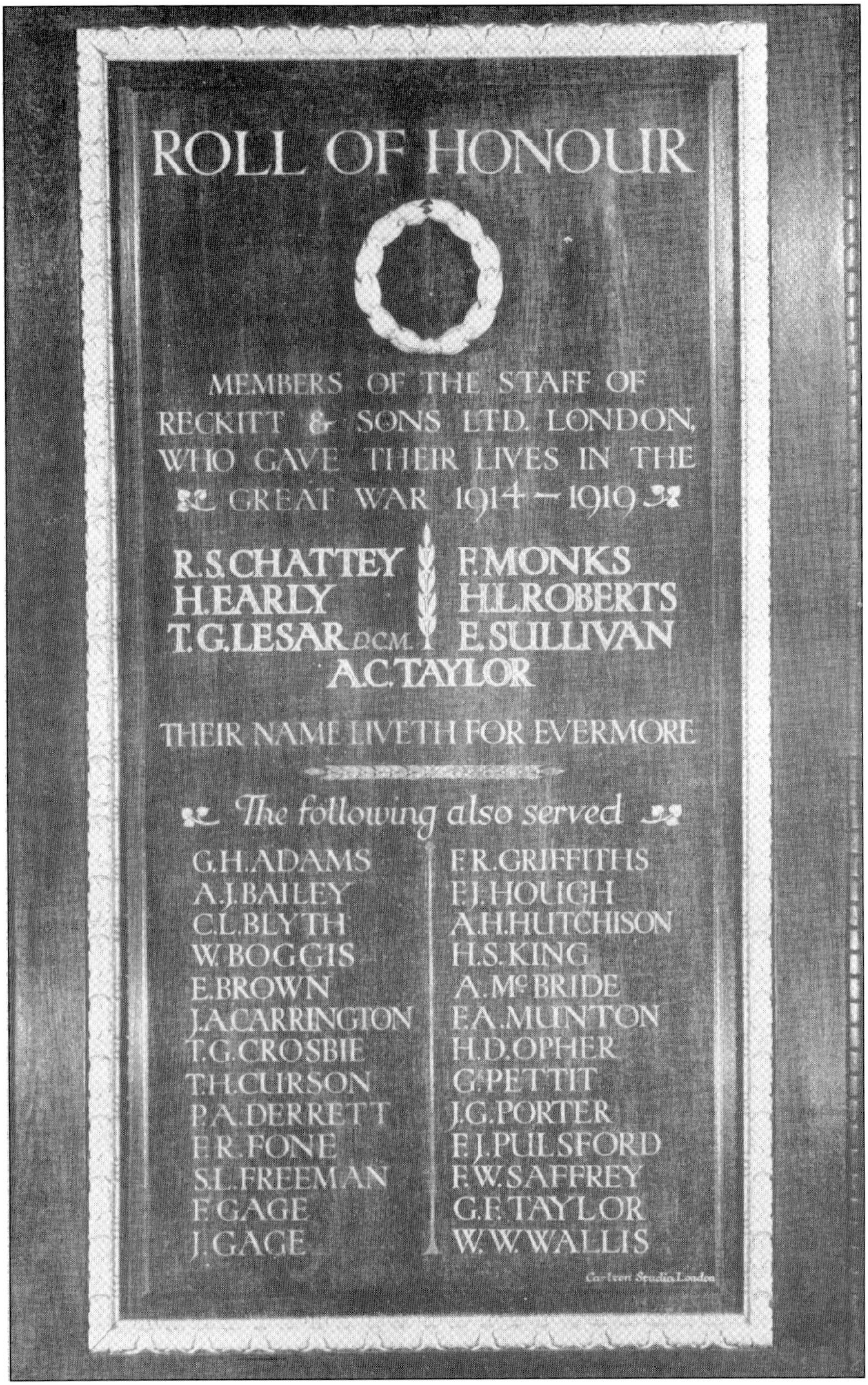

ROLL OF HONOUR
MEMBERS OF THE STAFF OF
RECKITT & SONS LTD. LONDON,
WHO GAVE THEIR LIVES IN THE
GREAT WAR 1914 – 1919
R.S.CHATTEY
H.EARLY
T.G.LESAR D.C.M.
F.MONKS
H.L.ROBERTS
E.SULLIVAN
A.C.TAYLOR
THEIR NAME LIVETH FOR EVERMORE
The following also served
G.H.ADAMS
A.J.BAILEY
C.L.BLYTH
W.BOGGIS
E.BROWN
J.A.CARRINGTON
T.G.CROSBIE
T.H.CURSON
P.A.DERRETT
F.R.FONE
S.L.FREEMAN
F.GAGE
J.GAGE
F.R.GRIFFITHS
F.J.HOUGH
A.H.HUTCHISON
H.S.KING
A.McBRIDE
F.A.MUNTON
H.D.OPHER
G.PETTIT
J.G.PORTER
F.J.PULSFORD
F.W.SAFFREY
G.F.TAYLOR
W.W.WALLIS
Carlton Studio London

Roll of Honour in memory of Members of Reckitt's Boys' Club.

Anderson, C.
Baxter, A.
Beckett, G.
Borrill, E.
Bowden, R.
Bryan, H.
Carver, A.
Cobb, H.
Cooper, C.
Cronk, T.
Dalton, P.
Dalton, T.
Dawson, W.
Dean, A.
Dodsworth, A.
Emerson, H.
Gall, H.
Hill, R.
Holland, H.
Hunter, S.
Jarratt, H.
Jubb, C.
Mace, H.
Magson, W.
Miller, F.
Millington, R.
Nasby, P.
Woodmancy, S.
Neal, H.
Peterson, G.
Robinson, W.
Scott, G.
Sellers, H.
Shields, L.
Simpson, H.
Smales, B.
Spires, G.
Thackery, H.
Thurloe, G.
Veal, A.
Walton, M.
Wharam, W.

During the War, officials of the Boys' Club kept in touch with members in various ways. At Christmas parcels were sent out to them, and at intervals circular letters were written to all. In addition individual correspondence was carried on with about a hundred of the boys.

The Reckitt's Memorial Fountain

General View of the Memorial Fountain

Major General Sir Peter S Wilkinson unveiling the Monument

Memorial Fountain

Representatives of Departments laying Wreaths around the Memorial.

The central figure represents "Sacrifice." The dead youth at her feet and the inverted torch are emblematic of the sacrifice made by Humanity in the Great War.

At the corners of the Fountain are cherubs holding dolphins, from whose mouth the water pours into the basin below:
The inscription reads:-

> "Erected by Reckitt and Sons Ltd., to the memory of those in the service of the company who gave their lives in the Great War 1914-1918,"

On the opposite side are the words:-

> "Great deeds cannot die, they with the sun and moon renew their light, for ever blessing those that look on them."
>
> Tennyson

'OURS' - 1920

War Memorial

Unveiling and Dedication

It was a great disappointment that the day appointed for the ceremony should open in cloud and rain, and so continue till the appointed hour, though fortunately the rain ceased during the service. The ceremony was impressive and touching from the opening, the grand old hymn "O God our Help in ages past." To the close when, after the hymn "Peace, perfect Peace" with its tender message of faith, came the procession of employees, some war disabled, bearing wreaths, appointed by their various Departments, and the relatives of the fallen with pathetic tributes "full of hope and yet of heart break."

After the ceremony a continuous procession of the public passed round the statue until long after dark, when the falling water of the fountain was illuminated by electric light, and the interest being maintained during following days. Manifold were the expressions of admiration both of the statue and of the scores of floral offerings which were placed around the coping of the fountain. Beautiful indeed it is, standing in grace and majesty with its invocatory arm raised over the dead glory of youth's life: a moment of anguished tear, but of holy triumph. Worthy the statue is of proud place in City Square or crowded public haunt, but let it not be said that it is lost amid its present setting. It rises in its beauty straight from the heart of factory buildings, an inspiration and an ideal to multitudes of men and women workers whose hurrying feet shall pass it by, but who, in years unborn and now, shall fail not to catch something of its message: as also it is a dedicated shrine where our honoured dead shall be remembered.

Scenes that will live long in the history of East Hull were witnessed at the Company's works in Dansom Lane on November 3, when a massive and artistic monument to the memory of the 153 employees of the Firm who made the supreme sacrifice during the late war was unveiled by Major-General Sir Percy S Wilkinson, K.G.M.G., C.B., and dedicated by the Bishop of Hull (Dr Gurdon).

The monument, which ranks as one of the finest examples of the sculptor's art in the city, has been erected on a most suitably ornamental piece of land adjoining the Francis Reckitt Institute.

The main inscription on it is as follows:

Wm. Aumonier, Head of the Studios of W. Aumonier & Son, London, designers and executants of the War Memorial Foundation is of French Huguenot descent and follows a long line of famous craftsmen settled in England. Mr Aumonier is Hon. Sec. Of The Master Carvers' Association. Member Of the Architectural Association and of The Art Workers' Guild, London

"Erected by Reckitt and Sons, Ltd., in memory of those who gave their lives in the Great War. Great deeds cannot die."

The central figure in the monument represents the symbol of sacrifice, a woman with a youth at her feet clasping a laurel wreath in his right hand. One arm of the central figure is raised on high at the supreme moment of her pride and anguish – pride that her sons should have so gallantly laid down their lives in the defence of their country, and anguish at all her broken dreams represented by the dead youth at her feet.

At the four corners of the central pedestal, or base, are cherubs, symbolising the promise of early life, and they are holding dolphins, from which water is emitted into the ornamental pond with its tessellated base, which encircles the whole monument, while surrounding the whole is an artistic arrangement of treillage work.

The Directors of the Firm present at the ceremony were the Right Hon. T R Ferens, P.C., J.P, Mr A B Reckitt, Mr Harold J Reckitt,

Mr Philip B Reckitt, Mr Arnold Reckitt, Mr A L Reckitt, Mr W H Slack, J.P., Major W H Willatt, J.P., and Mr C H Hardy. Others present included Mr William Aumonier, the designer of the monument, of the well known firm of Aumonier and Son, London, the Lord Mayor of Hull (Alderman T Beecroft Atkinson), the Sheriff (Councillor J W Locking), the Town Clerk (Mr H A Learoyd, L.L.B.), Col. Grant, J.P. (East Riding Territorial Force Association), and Councillor A Shepherd (President of the Hull Branch of the British Legion).

Every available space in the immediate vicinity of the monument was occupied by the employees of the Firm and relatives of the fallen.

The weather was not auspicious for the occasion, but happily rain did not fall while the ceremony was in progress. The proceedings were of a most impressive nature.

The windows of the Francis Reckitt Institute and the General Officer which the site adjoins were thrown open, and employees who could not find room in the actual enclosure viewed the proceedings therefrom, while others stood on roofs, or sat on walls, and high up in one of the towers of the main building could be seen people participating in the solemn service which the Bishop conducted.

The hymns, which were impressively sung by the large congregation, were accompanied by the Newland Orphan Homes' Band.

At the conclusion of the ceremony the "Last Post" and the "Reveille" were sounded by Mr A V Coates and Mr C Ogden. There was a touching scene when many wreaths of beautiful flowers and evergreens were laid with all reverence at the foot of the imposing representation of sacrifice – tokens from every Department of the Firm, from the Directors and the various administrative staffs down to the girls in the workrooms, who paid their heartfelt tributes. "In affectionate remembrance of our dear boys."

The staffs of the Firm in various centres other than Hull also sent wreaths, and there was a beautiful token composed of French poppies, similar to those which are going to be sold on Armistice Day, from the Hull Branch of the British Legion.

Major-General Sir Percy S Wilkinson, after unveiling the monument by releasing the cord which held the national colours in position over the central figure, said:

"The record of the Firm of Reckitt and Sons, Ltd., during the war has been a great and glorious one. No fewer than 1108 men from the Firm went to the war, and 153 of those men made the supreme sacrifice, whilst nearly 50 per cent of the remainder are either wounded or disabled, which is truly a great record."

"On November 1st All Saints Day it is the custom in France and Belguim to lay flowers on the graves of those whom one has loved, and you can be quite sure that last Tuesday there were flowers laid on the graves of all those soldiers who died in France and Flanders. It is quite impossible for most of you to visit the graves of your fallen comrades who lay on the battle fields of France, Flanders, Palestine and Mesopotamia, and all those other battlefronts of the great war, but just as the tomb of the unknown British warrior in Westminster Abbey is the tribute of the nation to its unnumbered dead so is the memorial the symbol to you of the graves of your fallen comrades. It is placed where you can go on certain anniversaries such as Armistice Day and think for a few moments of all your pals lying out there and of all they were to you, and where as you choose, you can leave wreaths as a tribute to their memory.

That is one of the great values of the Memorial. Two years ago, when unveiling a war memorial, I said I did not think that a memorial was necessary to remind the people of this generation of all they owed to those who had fallen and all those others who had been fighting alongside of them, but who were spared to return, but I was wrong. To our shame and our sorrow we have seen many employers of labour, many trade unions, many people in this country in a position to help, who are doing little or nothing for those who fought for them.

Some say it is not their job. Others talk a great deal about helping, and do nothing. Some are even hostile to those who served. It is, therefore, a particularly great pleasure to me this day to be associated with this great firm who proved their patriotism throughout the war, and who since have indeed shown gratitude to those men who went out and fought for their country.

This memorial is the emblem of sacrifice. During the past two years this country has been through very difficult times, and those difficult times are still with us. I think the only way we can meet and overcome them is by sacrifice; not the sacrifice of a few, or certain classes, but by the sacrifices of all classes in the country. We must drop all selfishness, and all must pull together for the common good. If we can only make a fraction of the wartime sacrifices which all made, in times of peace, I feel quite convinced that in a short time we shall make this country once more a united and prosperous country fit to live in, and those whose memory you are here to honour, those who made the supreme sacrifice for their country, have shown you how to make sacrifices."

The Bishop of Hull on the conclusion of the service paid a fitting tribute to the sculptor in the following words:

"I desire to express thanks and congratulations to the artist, Mr Aumonier, who has designed for you this beautiful picture and symbol of sacrifice. It stands among you, and you will see and understand the beauty of its significance. It seems at first sight as though Sacrifice symbolised a wasted life, and yet after all it is not so. In that sculpture the young man has lain down his life, apparently wasted, but he has already found life, and is clasping in his hand a laurel wreath, the crown of victory. It shows that the real power in every life is not in what it gets for itself, but what it proves in giving.

In her hand the figure of Sacrifice has a torch that she may hand it on to those who are left: that with the torch of sacrifice we may take on that race which they who have fallen have run so nobly to the goal, and may do our bit in our generation, and that we may hand on the torch to the generations who are to come.

In conclusion, I wish to say that we owe our best thanks to him who has given us this inspiration."

Wreaths were sent from the following Staffs, Departments, etc.:

KINGSTON

The Directors:	"In Remembrance"
The British Legion	"Memory's loving tribute."
Office and Social Staff	"In Memory of our fallen Comrades"
The Officers of the Boys' Club	"In remembrance"
The Birmingham Staff	"In loving memory of our comrades"

Starch Works:	"In affectionate memory of S,Snow, E.Pearson and H Sedman
Forewoman and Girls of No 1	"A token of remembrance in honour of our brave boys"
Starch Crystal	
The Blue Mill	
Miss Dunlin's Girls	"With deepest sympathy"
Square Blue and Tint Rooms	"In loving and honoured memory"
Girls of Bag Blue Room 22	"In affectionate remembrance of our dear boys"
Forewoman, Helper and Girls	"In affectionate remembrance of our gallant boys"
Of Bag Blue Room 23	
Girls of Bag Blue Room 63	"In loving memory"
Lead Paste Department	"In affectionate remembrance of our brave boys"
Zebo Department	"In remembrance of our gallant boys"
Block Lead Department (Girls)	"In affectionate remembrance"
Brasso Works	"A tribute in memory of A Adams, A Dodsworth, H Emmerson, E Jackson, J Markham, M Neal,
Department 24 (Men) Card Board	
Preparation	"To our fallen comrades"
Department 24 (Girls) Card Board	"In loving memory of the boys who have fallen"
Preparation	

Directors' Welcome to Ex-Service Employees: 1920

Approximately six hundred demobilised soldiers and sailors sat down to a tea in the Francis Reckitt Institute on 8th January at the invitation of the Directors. After tea the Company adjourned to the Concert Hall.

Mr Arthur B Reckitt was in the chair and was supported by the Right Hon. T R Ferens, J.P., Mr P B Reckitt, J.P., O.B.E., Capt. Arnold Reckitt, Mr Albert Reckitt, Mr W H Slack, J.P., Major W H Willatt, J.P., Mr C. M. Hardy and Mr A R Cleminson.

A list of our fallen was read by the Chairman whilst the whole company stood in silence.

Mr H Addision (Office Staff) proposed a vote of thanks to the Directors for their kind generosity in having made the recent gift to the ex-service men, also the allowances while on service, and parcels of food sent to the prisoners of war, one of whom he had happened to be. Mr H Lundy, M.M., seconded the vote which was supported by mr W Moor, M.M.
A musical programme and humorous recitals were rendered by an able concert party.

Mr Ferens presented to Sergeant-Major C Streat the Distinguished Conduct Medal, and referred to other employees who had gained distinctions.

Chapter 7

Reckitt's Employees Who Served

Walter Edward Smith

Born 28 April 1885, at the Blue-Bell Inn, 118 Witham, Hull. His father was the landlord here from 1883 to 1891. The family of 3 adults and 6 children left here in 1891 to live at 9 St Mark's Street.

Mrs Smith died on 4th August 1897, at the age of 28. Walter began work at the age of 13 years as a rivet boy in one of Hull's ship yards. In 1902 his father walked out and was never seen again, both of Walter's older sisters were working by this time, their combined wages kept the family together. In 1905 Walter got a new and better paid job at Reckitts, Dansom Lane, working in the Zebra Manufacturing Dept. It was here he met a dark eyed young woman called Gertrude Abbey, who was the assistant forewoman of the packing room. They married on June 24th 1911, at St Paul's Church, Sculcoates and in 1912 moved into a Reckitt's house at 3 The Grove, Garden Village.

The Great War came along and Walter enlisted on March 15th 1915, serving as 13846: Shoeing Smith, Royal Field Artillery, 32nd Division Ammunition Column. Here is an entry from his diary, 9th August 1918;

"On iron rations, waiting orders in Field, crossed no-man's land, entered Domart 2 am, water and feed. Plenty of German dead laid about, 5 am off again, - crossing battle-field, nasty sights, planes, tanks, horses and bits of dead. German had gone out of his head, confronted Canadian Sgt, hit on head and bayoneted."

Walter was demobilized on February 23rd 1919, he returned to Reckitts but found the life too claustrophobic after the army. He then gained employment with the Hull Tramways as a conductor and later as a driver.

His daughter Edith died of pneumonia, aged 13 years, on February 27th 1927.

Walter retired in April 1951 continuing an active life. His grandson wrote of him;
"I remember Grandad as a frail old man who walked with a stick and played with the toys he made for us."

He moved into a retirement home in 1968 and died on 29th November 1969, aged 83 years.

Robert Henry West was born on October 7th 1893 at 86 Rutland Street, Grimsby. He died at Castle Hill Hospital, Cottingham on April 20th, 1973.

Robert joined the firm on February 3rd 1908 aged 14 years and worked in the Accounts and Overseas Office. He enlisted in the 4th Battalion East Yorkshire Regiment on August 31st 1914.

The Reckitts boys enlist, Hull 1914.
Rober Henry West is second from right (standing)

In the Great War he saw action on the Ypres Salient, 2nd Battle of the Somme, Martinpuich, Contalmaison and High Wood. While on leave in 1917 he married Elsie May Todd at the Bethesda Chapel, Hull

Robert Henry West and Elsie May Todd on their Wedding Day, August 4th 1917.

Elsie May Todd was born on August 11th 1892 and joined Reckitts upon leaving school at the age of 14 at the Dansom Lane Works. She worked at Reckitts until marrying and died at Castle Hill Hospital on March 2nd 1975.

Robert's military service ended in January 1918 when he was invalided out suffering from peritonitis. After the war he returned to the Wages Department at Reckitts, he stayed with the firm until his retirement in 1958.

Robert and Elsie West had two children, Betty, who died at 6 months, and Joan, who later worked at Reckitts in the Office.

In 'OURS', the Reckitt's magazine of Spring 1959, the following tribute was featured concerning Robert:

"He was a pal, one of the best, always very even in temperament. A man of very high principles, obscured by his laugh and a joke and a sense of humour in a measure possessed by so few as they go through life."

Harold Elvin joined the firm of Reckitts on 8th February 1908 and worked in the packing room of the Kingston Works.

Before the war he was in the Territorial Force and served throughout the conflict with the R.A.M.C. 3rd N.F. Ambulance. In 1919 he returned to the firm, retiring in 1960. Florence and Harold lived at St Mark's Street for a while after their marriage and then moved to 36 Laburnum Avenue where they stayed.

Harold was born on March 9th 1895 and died in Hull in 1976 at the age of 81.

Miss Florence Tiplady worked on the catering staff of the V.A.D. hospital and lived at St Mark's Street, Dansom Lane. In 1919 she was introduced by a friend to Harold Elvin, a Reckitts worker, and they married in 1921, Florence then left the firm. She was born on 4th December 1895 and died in Hull in 1980 at the age of 85.

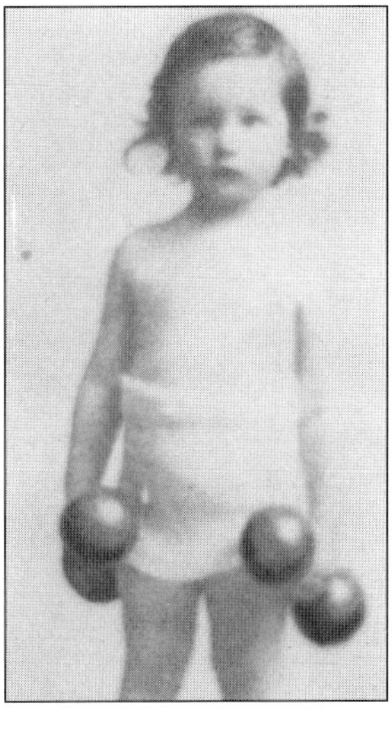

Basil Drake Arnold (age 2 years) Training for Kitchener's Army Published in 'OURS' – 1915

The Photograph above shows G. Hamshire (Canister Works), a prisoner of war in Germany, and three other prisoners representing the Belgian, Russian and French nations.

Herbert Squires was born on 24th April 1899 in Hull, and joined Reckitts factory on April 6th 1914 working on the office staff.

In the Great War he served with the Royal Engineers Signal Coy – attached to the Highland Division.

Herbert survived the war and returned to Reckitts, he lived at 16 Day Street, Anlaby Road, Hull and retired from the firm in 1964.

Herbert Squires died on 25th November 1989.

Cpt Cecil M Slack M.C. 1/4th Battalion East Yorkshire Regiment, was the eldest son of Mr W H Slack J.P. a Director at Reckitts Factory, Dansom Lane, Hull. He joined the firm in September1911 and worked in the General Office.

Cpt Slack served on the Western Front from April 1915 to April 1918, when he was taken prisoner: he was posted missing in the Hull Daily Mail on April 23rd and 24th 1918.

The following letter was published in Reckitt's magazine in 1916 regarding the Second Battle of Ypres 1915, in which Cpt Slack was wounded:

"A few days ago I witnessed a scene which I shall not forget – it was so grand and British. The Division on our right had to occupy a German trench which was believed to have been vacated. They had to walk across 500 yards of battlefield. At the given time in the afternoon they got out of their trench and commenced to walk, just as if they were strolling across a field in England. There was no excitement, some of the men had their rifles slung on their shoulders, some had their hands in their pockets, some were smoking, and an officer was carrying his coat over his arm.

The Boche put up a barrage at once, and men began to fall, but the troops went on through the shells without taking the slightest notice of anything except their line of advance and so into the Boche trench. Perhaps you will wonder why they walked. If they had hurried they would not have had the strength to charge had the line been held. It is only what any Division would do and has done, but it was a glorious sight."

Cecil Slack's home address was Wilton House, Holderness Road, Hull.

A Full List of Reckitts Men who survived the war.

Gives Name, Rank, Regiment, Department at which employed and Date of Commencement of Employment at Reckitts.

Morley Street Works

Name	Rank	Regiment	Unit	Department in which employed	Date joined the firm
Acklam, George Ernest	Sapper	R.E.		Morley Street	16.7.14
Arksey , Arthur	Pte	E Yorks		do	7.2.07
Bayes, George	Corpl	R.E.	ERFC	do	30.9.12
Borrill, Clive	Sapper	R.E.		do	5.7.11
Bratley, C (junr)	Pte	Labour Corps		do	25.10.09
Brown, J	Sapper	ERY		do	3.4.96
Brown, J E	Pte	MGC		do	1.2.99
Burkitt, H	Pte	RAMC		do	22.11.16
Chapman, W H		Royal Navy		do	21.9.11
Charlton, Thomas	Pte	E Yorks	3rd Batt	do	00.8.04
Church, Robert	L/Corpl	E Yorks		do	21.9.14
Clark, Walter	Pte	S. Lancs	15th Batt	do	00.3.04
Cole, Thomas Hadlin	A.B	Royal Navy		do	5.5.10
Curtis, Albert	Q.M.S	RAMC	9th Co	do	00.7.90
D'Arcy, john H	Sgt-Ins	RFA	213th Brigade	do	27.3.07
Deighton, F	Pte	E Yorks		do	19.8.12
Fenton, John Edward	Pte	E Yorks		do	15.9.15
Foster, Robert Fredrick	Gunner	RGA	152nd H B	do	7.11.11
Franklin, George Trooper	MGC Cvly	'C' Squadron		do	28.2.09
Gregg, Fred	Pte	RAMC	103rd Field Amb	do	10.8.10
Hanson, Hans	Pte	RAMC	No 1 Co	do	00.3.08
Hartley, H (junr)	Pte	E Yorks		do	25.7.03
Hodgson, Cecil	Pte	E Yorks	11th Batt	do	00.8.14
Holdsworth, John	2/Corpl	RE	1/1st ER Fld Co	do	18.10.06
Hopper, E	Gunner	RGA		do	13.8.14
Hutchinson, Hohn Henry	Driver	RASC	No 1 AHT	do	23.9.14
Lilley, Herbert	Pte	E Yorks	3rd Batt	do	29.12.09
Long, Francis Tom	Sapper	RE	IWT	do	00.9.14
Markham, Arthur	Pte	RAMC	28th Field Amb	do	00.5.03
Mawer, George	Gunner	RFA	92nd Battery	do	8.7.10
Noble, Harold Capt	R Artillery			do	26.5.96
Officer, Harold	Corpl	DLI	27th Bat	do	27.7.10
Palmer, Maurice Player	Gunner	RGA	Corps Troops	do	11.11.04
Peers, William Andrew	Pte	E Yorks	12th Batt	do	00.3.07
Pullon, Roger	Pte	E Yorks	6th Batt	do	22.2.98
Reed, George B	Pte	R. Sussex		do	26.4.16
Reed J	Pte	RAMC		do	21.10.10
Reed William James	Bmbdr	RFA	250th Brigade	do	00.11.06
Rodmell A	RND	Hawk Battn		do	24.2.13

Morley Street Works

Name	Rank	Regiment	Unit	Department in which employed	Date joined the firm
Scargill E	Pte	E Yorks		do	12.5.04
Seymour John Robert	Driver	RGA	146th HB	do	18.8.10
Shaw William	S/Sergt	RAMC	48th Gen Hosp	do	22.9.19
Sinderson George	Sapper	RE	ERFC	do	00.7.13
Smelt Fredrick	Pte	E Yorks	1/4th Batt	do	8.4.97
Smelt John Henry	Corpl	RE	Searchlight Sect	do	12.12.07
Smith E	Corpl	E Yorks	Cyclists	do	31.3.10
Smith John William	Gunner	Rga		do	21.6.12
Snailham John Henry	Pte	E Yorks		do	14.9.15
Spavin James William	Gunner	RFA	2nd Nthbn Bde	do	8.7.02
Sutton Francis	Gunner	RGA	177th H B	do	25.1.04
Terry E	Pte	York&Lanc		do	15.12.08
Thacker Arthur	Pte	E Yorks		do	26.8.14
Thompson John	Pte	RMLI	Portsmouth Div	do	00.10.06
Tindall E	Stoker	RNR	Minesweep-ing	do	12.12.11
Ward George Edward	Pte	N. Fus		do	00.6.97
Wharf W R	Sergt	RAMC	1/3rd NFA	do	21.8.11
Whitehead Herbert	Pte	D of W	3rd Batt	do	24.8.14
Wilson Alfred	Pte	E Yorks	4th Batt	do	00.6.15
Wood Thomas	Pte	E Yorks	3rd Batt	do	00.8.11

Canister Works

Name	Rank	Regiment	Unit	Department in which employed	Date joined the firm
Adams George William	L/Corpl	RAMC	Police	Brasso No 1	00.10.06
Alport Arthur	3rd A/M	RAF	OSRAP	Artists Dept	21.10.07
Anderson Arthur	Pte	RAMC	3rd Field Amb	Bricklayers	00.6.05
Andrews Norman	Driver	RFA	D/235 Brigade	Packers	00.9.09
Atkin Herbert	Pte	R Muster F	2nd Batt	Fancy Box	17.4.11
Atkinson John William	Pte	Lincolnshire	2nd Batt	Brasso No 1	15.4.16
Atkinson Sydney	Pte	N.Fus	2/7th Batt	Canister	2.3.10
Bartlett Frederick Robert	Pte	N.Fus	4th Batt	Electricians	00.10.08
Bell William Albert	2nd A/M	RAF	No 2 School	Canister	00.7.12
Bennett Sidney	Pte	N. Fus	7th Batt	Printing	15.5.12
Birch Arthur	Corpl	RAMC	No 1 Co	Fitting	00.6.12
Birks Donald	Pte	E. Yorks	4th Batt	Old Mill	29.11.13
Black Philip	Sergt	Yorkshire	2nd Batt	Canister	21.10.07
Booth William	Pte	E. Yorks	MGC Lab Corps	Brasso No 2	10.8.14
Bowden Benjamin	Pte	E. Yorks	7th Batt	Canister	28.4.14
Bradley Arthur	Pte	RAMC		Canister	19.4.10
Branton Frederick	Pte	D.of W	2nd Batt	Tin Stores	1.9.14
Bricklebank Thomas	Corpl	York & Lanc	2nd Batt	Brasso No 1	00.3.15
Briggs James Lewis	Bdr	RFA		Packers	21.10.07
Broadley James	Corpl	RGA	E Riding	Printing	21.10.07
Brock John Henry	Pte	R. Warwick	1/6 Batt	Plumbers	8.1.10
Brown Sydney	Pte	22nd Mtd Bde	No 5 Sec, MGS	Canister	26.2.08
Bryan William Henry	Pte	E, Yorks	11th Batt	Packers	21.10.07
Burniston John	Pte	E. Yorks	3rd Batt	Canister	3.4.16
Burns John Gregory	Gunner	RFA	4th Res	Canister Brigade	2.3.15
Buxton Harold	3rd A/M	RAF	84th Squadron	Mechanics	00.4.12
Caborn Frank	Corpl	E Yorks	11th Batt	Old Mill	9.1.11
Carrington Robert	Pte	AEC	258th Co	Canister	22.10.07
Chapman Robert George	Pte	RAF	9th AA Co	Joiners	11.3.14
Chapman Walter Hastings	3rd A/M	RAF		Joiners	15.3.16
Churlton Walter	Sergt	RE		Canister	6.1.08
Chatterton Walter	Cadet	RAF	No 2 SOA	Artists	00.7.16
Cheesebrough Henry	Pte	DLI	15th Batt	Canister	00.10.15

Canister Works

Name	Rank	Regiment	Unit	Department in which employed	Date joined the Firm
Cherry Albert	Pte	RAMC	88th Field Amb	Weigh Office	7.6.14
Clarke Bernard O	Corpl	RE	550th GFC (RE)	Artists	00.9.10
Coates Harold	Pte	York & Lanc	2/4th Batt	Canister	21.10.07
Colby Harold Colby	Gunner	RGA	E Riding	Printing	20.2.08
Colby Stephen	Pte	E Yorks	6th Batt	Fitting	21.10.07
Connaughton Thomas	Corpl	RE		Canister	9.8.09
Copeland Harold	Pte	MGC	6th Batt	Artists	00.8.13
Cracknell Albert	Pte	Lincolnshire	1/8th Batt	Canister	27.4.14
Crane Harold	3rd A/M	RAF		Canister	19.7.14
Crawforth Harry	Pte	E Yorks	3rd Batt	Old Mill	20.2.15
Dawson George Harold	Pte	E Yorks	11th Batt	Fancy Box	00.3.08
Decker Edward	Sapper	RE	529th Field Co	Canister	9.5.10
Derrick Arthur	Pte	E Yorks	4th Batt	Canister	12.8.14
Dick George Alfred	Gunner	RGA	4th E Riding	Canister	1.1.05
Douthwaite Fred	AB	Royal Navy	H.M. Minesweeper	Fitting	8.12.10
Downs Herbert	Pte	Bedford	4th Batt	Brasso No 3	00.9.09
Downs Walter	Pte	KOYLI		Canister	17.2.10
Dunwell John	Pte	RASC	MT	Canister	00.8.14
Ellis Thomas	Pte	DLI	29th Batt	Canister	28.10.07
Empson Charles Duncan	Sergt	RAMC		Stores	00.12.07
Farr Ernest Edward	Pte	RAMC	Provisional	Recovery	21.10.07
Fawcett Ernest Henry	Sapper	RE	240th AW Co	Litho	00.11.12
Featherstone Randolph	Pte	RMLI		Old Mill	11.1.11
Fulcher Arthur	Pte	E Yorks	1/4th Batt	Brasso No2	21.10.07
Gardner Arthur	Pte	ER Yeo	2/1st Batt	Office	16.1.16
Garrett Sydney	Sergt	ER Yeo	2/1st Batt	Gen Office	3.2.13
Gibson Raymond	Pte	Scot Horse	2/2nd Cyc Batt	Brasso No 3	00.1.17
Gill A	A/M TE	RAF		Canister	10.6.10
Gill Walter	Pte	E Yorks	1st Batt	Canister	18.5.08
Graves Arthur	Pte	RAF	Wireless School	Canister	22.9.16
Greasley Thomas E	L/Corpl	E Yorks	3rd Batt	Canister	14.5.12
Hailstone Harold	Pte	RAMC	138th Field	Joiners Field Amb	27.10.10

Canister Works

Name	Rank	Regiment	Unit	Department in which employed	Date joined the Firm
Hampshire George	Pte	E Yorks	4th Batt	Fancy Box	00.6.09
Hardy Joseph William	Gunner	RFA	174th Brigade	Brasso No 1	00.1.14
Hare Anthony William	Pte	E Yorks	2/4th Batt	Brasso No 2	21.10.07
Harrison Arthur	Pte	Sher For		Scrap Tin	00.1.08
Higgs Charles John	CMS	Rifle Brigade	12th Batt	Canister	22.2.11
Higham WilliamEdwin	2nd A/M	RNAS	42nd Squadron	Drawing Off	12.1.14
Holden Albert	Ldg Can	RAF		Joiners	2.6.08
Horn George	1st Wmn	Royal Navy		Canister	21.10.07
Hornby Percy Smith	Pte	E Yorks	4th Batt	Canister	12.3.09
Horner Frank	Sergt	RASC	3rd Divi Train	Litho	00.2.13
Howarth John	Corpl	MGC	2nd Batt	Brasso No 1	4.3.11
Hudson Herbert	Sapper	RE	W Riding	Printing	00.11.10
Hussey Henry Wilfred	Pte	RAMC	48th Co	Canister	21.10.07
Hutty Charles T	Pte	Labour Corps	41st Co	Canister	28.2.16
Huxford William Henry	AB	RNR	ML82	Litho	00.11.15
Irwin William Alfred	L/Corpl	RASCMT	4th Bridging Trn	Joiners	21.3.11
Johnson Walter	Pte	E Yorks	4th Batt	Scrap	20.6.10
Kell George	Corpl	RGA	146th H H Batty	Canister	21.10.07
King Reginald Delmore	Gunner	RGA	301st Siege Batty	Canister	8.3.15
Leathley Norman J	Pte	E Yorks	4th Batt	Canister	00.5.14
Littlewood Albert	Sig	E Yorks	1st Batt	Printing	25.7.11
Lowe Ernest William	Pte	E Yorks	4th Batt	Printing	00.12.14
Macdonald Walter	Sapper	RE	122nd Field Co	Canister	6.12.09
McDonald Henry Thomas	Pte	KOYLI	5th Batt	Mechanics	11.10.15
Markham John Henry	2nd A/M	RAF		Mechanics	00.4.15
Maude Fred	Pte	E Yorks	10th Batt	Brasso No 1	7.6.09
Maxwell Clarence William	Fitter	RFA	190th Brigade	Mechanics	00.2.14
Morton Percy	Pte	DLI	7th Batt	Printing	00.5.14
May Albert	Pte	E Yorks	14th Batt	Canister	3.7.08
Moy Edward	Pte	E Yorks	4th Batt	Canister	5.7.11

Canister Works

Name	Rank	Regiment	Unit	Department in which employed	Date joined the firm
Nicholson Harry	Pte	DLI	12th Batt	Old Mill	00.8.03
Oaten Walter	Pte	DLI		Canister	10.12.14
Parker Alfred	Sapper	RE		Canister	11.7.13
Pearson Alfred	Pte	RAMC	No 1 Co	Cook	20.8.08
Penman David Calder	Sergt	RGA	12th Siege Batty	Mechanics'	0.8.12
Petch Alfred Bernard	Pte	E Yorks	4th Batt	Office	22.3.09
Phillips F L	Corpl	RAMC		Canister	15.7.13
Pickering George Arthur	2/Lt	RE	469th Field Co	Drawing office	0.6.10
Pickering Walter	3rd A/M	RAF	No 4 (C) ARD	Mechanics	6.2.11
Pike John	Pte	N. Fus	18th Batt	Scrap	8.7.15
Rastrick Ernest Kendall	Sergt	RAMC	72nd Gen Hosp	Canister	22.10.07
Renshaw Arthur	Sapper	RE	12th ER Co Fld	Litho	0.7.09
Ricketts Harry	Gunner	RGA	105th AA Sect	Litho	0.2.15
Roberts Henry	Pte	RASCMT	HC 2 Co	Canister	21.10.07
Robinson H	Pte	KOYLI	2nd Batt	Canister	2.7.13
Rundle Charles Robert	Pte	RASC	7th Divl M T Co	Varnish	6.1.08
Rundle Joseph James	Corpl	RE	456th Field Co	Printing	21.10.07
Rutledge Harry	L/Corpt	E Yorks	1st Batt	Canister	17.6.14
Rylett George	Pte	E Yorks	1st Batt	Canister	14.9.14
Savage Ernest	Pte	E Yorks	4th Batt	Recovery 1	20.6.10
Sharpless Denis Joseph	Pte	E Yorks	11th Batt	Brasso No 3	21.10.07
Shenton John	Pte	DLI	27th Batt	Canister	30.5.13
Slide H E	Sapper	RE	31st Batt	Canister	11.7.14
Smelt George Henry	Pte	E Yorks	3rd Batt	Canister	20.9.15
Snowden Walter Groves	Pte	N.Fus		Canister	0.9.14
Spavin Thomas	Pte	Scot Rifles	2/5th Batt	Tin	21.10.07
Stainforth Edward	Driver	RE	448th Field Co	Fancy Box	0.8.06
Stathers Albert	Pte	Sher For	11th Batt	Canister	22.6.14
Stathers Joseph	Pte	RAMC	138th Field	Printing	8.12.14
Stead Robert William	Cyclist	Cyclist	4th Batt	Canister	3.5.13
Stephenson George Henry	Gunner	RGA	AAS	Brasso No 2	21.10.07

Canister Works

Name	Rank	Regiment	Unit	Department in which employed	Date joined the firm
Stephenson Harry	Sergt	E Yorks	4th Batt	Canister	0.9.11
Stevens Thomas Edward	L/Corpl	E Yorks	7th Batt	Canister	01.10
Sutton Thomas Hedley	Corpl	E Yorks	4th Batt	Litho	19.8.09
Sykes James	Pte	RDC	167th Protn Co	Canister	0.2.15
Taylor Alfred	Sapper	RE		Canister	22.6.13
Tether Robert	Corpl	E Yorks	4th Batt	Canister	1.5.13
Thickett Thomas	Pte	ASC	Labour Co	Brasso No 3	21.10.07
Thompson Cyril	Sapper	RE	431st Field Co	Canister	2.6.13
Thompson Wilfred Edmund	Sergt	RE	529th Field Co	Joiners	20.1.08
Tiede William	Pte	RAMC	2/3rd NFA	Brasso No 3	20.11.13
Turner Herbert William	Sergt	RASC(HT)	40th Divl Train	Office	21.10.07
Turner Joseph Henry	Gunner	RFA	14th Brigade	Printing	17.8.08
Turner Thomas Chistopher	Driver	RFA		Canister	0.3.13
Wadsworth Albert	Pte	RASCMT	19th Corps TMT	Mechanics	0.9.13
Walker John Edward	Pte	Yorkshire	18th Batt	Painters	0.7.05
Wallis James	1stA/C	RAF		Printing	21.10.07
Walsh Arthur	Bdr	RGA	164th Siege Batty	Old Mill	0.10.07
Warriner James	Pte	Labour Corps	360th Emp Co	Canister	12.4.15
Weaver Frank Ernest	Pte	E Yorks	1/4th Batt	Canister	17.3.10
Westoby James F W	Sergt	E Yorks	4th Batt	Printing	23.2.11
Wilkinson John	Bdr	RFA	Y21 TMB	Brasso No 1	0.2.14
Wilkinson Lewis Canister Works	L/Corpl	RE	W Riding	Litho	0.10.07
Wilson George	Pte	RDC	8th Batt	Canister	13.7.14
Wolfe Samuel	Pte	E Yorks	1st Batt	Packers	0.8.14
Wood Harry	Corpl	RE		Canister	2.7.08
Wride Frederick Albert	Pte	W Yorks	10th Batt	Hoist	26.2.11

Kingston Works

Name	Rank	Regiment	Unit	Department in which employed	Date joined the Firm
Abbey Alfred Maude	Bdr	RGA	124th Hy Bty	Pckg Room	30.10.11
Abbey John	Sapper	RE	233rd Fld Co	Eng Dept	7.12.08
Allison Arthur	Slg	RFA	251st Bde	Brasso	8.9.13
Anderson Ernest Alfred	Pte		53rd Labour Co	Cardboard Pl	0.7.05
Andrews James Hodgson	Gunner	RFA	2nd Nthumbrn Brigade	Engineering	0.8.07
Armstrong Harold	Pte	Sherwd For		Tin Stores	23.10.12
Askew Frederick	Pte	E Yorks & DLI	10th & 7th & 2/7th	Starch	9.9.14
Atherton Andrew	Corpl	E Yorks	4th Batt (T)	Robin Starch	23.7.08
Atkinson Albert	Pte	RAMC	88 San Sect EEF	Card Box Room 19	6.4.01
Atkinson George	Pte	RAMC	3rd Nthmbrn Field Amb	Hoists	30.4.09
Atkinson George Reginald	L/Corpl	E. Yorks	13th	Starch	8.6.05
Atkinson James Stanley	Sergt	RE	Tyne Electl Eng	Electrical	18.6.06
Ayre Frank Percival	Driver	ERRE	448 Fld Co	Eng. Dept	0.4.08
Ayre Thos	Pte	N. Fuse		KW Box Shop	27.1.15
Bacon James	Pte	E Yorks		K W Fitters	24.9.17
Bannister Albert Edward	Pte	RAMC	34th Co	Brasso Mixing Dept	4.8.04
Barker James William	Pte	MGC	148 Bde	Weigh Office	6.8.07
Barley Albert	Sapper	RE		K W Garage	22.12.10
Barmby Leonard	L/Corpl	RE	448 (N) Fld Co	Pkg Rm off	9.2.11
Barmby Walter	Pte	Tank Corps	2nd Batt	Painters Shop	0.5.06
Barnes Clarence	Pte	RAMC	77 Fld Amb	Hoists	0.12.08
Barrett Robert	Pte	RAMC	1/3n Fld Amb (T)	Hoists	25.11.07
Barratt Alfred	Pte	Labour Co		K W Sawmill	29.11.16
Baxter James	Corpl	APC		Pkg Rm Off	22.9.06
Baxter James	Pte	RAF	100th Squadron	Engineers	21.11.03
Beadleson John Edward	Gunner	ERRGA		Mepo Mixing Dept	0.9.97
Beeston Frank	Gunner	RGA	Hull Hvy Batty	Export Dept	31.3.02
Bell Arthur	Driver	RFA		KW Hoists	13.9.09
Bell Edgar S	Pte	E Yorks	3rd Batt	Starch	0.2.15
Bell Richard	Sapper	RE	459 Fld Co	Eng Shop	21.1.07

Kingston Works

Name	Rank	Regiment	Unit	Department in which employed	Date joined the Firm
Benson Albert William	Pte	E. Yorks	1st and 4th	Hoists	29.12.09
Benson Sydney	Pte	DLI	51st	Brasso (Social Hall)	20.6.14
Billham William Henry	Pte	Labour Co	46th	Starch	8.4.05
Binnington Walter	Sapper	RE	ERFRE	Eng. Dept	0.11.07
Black William Henry	Pte	E Yorks	13th Batt	Morley Street	25.9.91
Blashill Lewis	Pte	RAF		Cdbd. Prep	0.10.08
Blexhill C		RME		Lead	11.9.17
Blyth George	1st Pte	Indt Air F	100th Squadron	Cdbd. Dept	0.10.14
Boland Vincent J	Pte	E Yorks		Bricklayers	12.11.14
Bradley Walter H	Sapper	ERRE	1/1st Fld Co	Fitting Shop	24.1.12
Bolder Charles	L/Corpl	RAMC	9th Co	Sawmill	0.9.97
Bower Lancelot	Pte	E Yorks	4th	Packing	25.11.03
Bowes Wm Johnson	Pte	RASCMT		Tin Stores	6.11.16
Boynton Harold	Pte	RASCMT	12th HSBC	'C' Whouse	4.7.98
Brady John Francis	Pte	E Yorks	10th	Sawmill	0.1.07
Brett Albert	Pte	RAMC	3rd Nthmbn FA	Hoists	2.5.11
Brock William Edmund	3rd A/M	RAF		Gen Pkg Rm	26.10.14
Brock George Robert	3rd Clerk	RAF	No 2 AD	Packing Rm	0.10.91
Brocklesby William Henry	Pte	E Yorks	3rd	Brasso	0.4.16
Brown Arthur Henry	CQMS	RE	Tyne Elect Eng	Eng Dept	15.8.10
Brown Benjamin	L/Corpl	RAMC	80th San Co	Box Shop Wirebound	16.11.98
Brown E L	Fireman	NR		Brasso	3.12.14
Brown George	Pte	RAMC		Lead	12.2.15
Brown Harry	Pte	N. Fus	36th Batt	Packing Rm	9.4.02
Brown Walter	Pte	RAMC		Packing Rm	11.9.01
Bubbings Henry	Sapper	RE	IW and DRE	Starch	21.5.06
Burn Gilbert	Pte	Sh For	1st Batt	Box Shop	7.7.13
Busby Thomas	Pte	E Yorks	1/4th	'C' Whouse	29.7.07
Butler Alfred	Pte	Labour Corps	315 Wks Co	Dept 24 Card Prep	1.7.08
Cavill Robert William	2/Corpl	RE	Sig Service	Box Shop Wirebound	22.11.95
Chapman George James	Pte	KOYLI	2/4th	Cdbd Rm 24	0.3.04
Chapman John	Pte	Leicester	1st Batt	Hoists	0.2.09
Charlesworth Malcolm	Pte	RASCMT	1st SBAC	Tin Stores	6.3.11
Clark Arthur	Sergt	E Yorks	4th	Brasso	1.8.10
Claxton Duncan John	Pte	RAMC	No 6 Fld	Packing Room Amb	17.1.11

Kingston Works

Name	Rank	Regiment	Unit	Department in which employed	Date joined the Firm
Clayton Harold	Pte	RAMC	1/3rd N Fld Amb	Hoists	0.11.08
Clinton David	Pte	E Yorks		Hoists	10.5.12
Clipson Albert Edward	Pte	E Yorks	13th Batt	Starch	5.5.13
Clubley Walter	Pte	RAMC	3rd Batt	Packing Room	12.10.03
Coates John Henry	3rd A/M	RAF	8 TDS	Engineers	1.12.13
Cobb George William	Pte	RE	305th Co	Hoists	11.11.08
Cockerill Harold	Pte	RAF	No 8 Balloon sct	Sawmill	0.6.99
Cockerill Herbert	Pte	DLI	52nd	Wirebound	13.5.14
Cockerill John William	Sapper	RE	East Riding	No 2 Sawmill	22.9.00
Cockill John	Pte	E Yorks	4th Batt	Hoists	14.12.08
Codd Sidney Walter	Sapper	ER(F)RE	Elec Light Co	Plumbers	24.5.12
Coe Thomas Drewery	Corpl	RAMC	133rd Brit Gen Hosp	No1 sawmill	0.7.11
Coggin George	Rflmn	KRR	25th Batt	Blue Works	5.4.98
Coggin Fred	Pte	N.Fus	1/5th	Hoists	0.1.15
Coggin James	Pte	E Yorks	2/4th Res Batt	C Whouse	13.12.06
Collier George William	Pte	Border	8th	Cardbox	5.4.11
Collingwood G	Pte	E Yorks		Packing Rm	20.2.05
Collins Alfred	Pte	Nthld Fus	9th	Packing Rm	26.2.00
Collins Charles Bernard	Pte	KOYLI	1/4th	C Whouse	20.2.14
Collins John Henry	Pte	E Yorks		Sawmill	6.12.10
Conlon J	Pte	RAMC		Sawmill	0.5.94
Connaughton H	Pte	E Yorks		Lead	29.10.12
Cooper George	Pte	RASC	Remounts	Gen Pkg Dept	0.9.01
Cooper John William	Driver	RFA		Blue	3.11.10
Coulson Walter	Pte	Tank Corps	4thBatt	Eng Dept	17.1.11
Coverdale James	PteqRAMC		Starch	17.5.15	
Cox John Stanley	Pte	W Yorks		Brasso	4.9.14
Craven Joe	Pte	Lancs Fus	2nd Lancs	Robin Starch	7.6.16
Crawford Thomas Arthur	Pte	Labour Corps		Rice Works	4.4.15
Crosher George H	Sapper	RE		Drawing Office	
Curtin Charles	L/Corpl	E Yorks	4th	Joiners	24.2.00
Curtis Benjamin	Gunner	RFA	2nd Nthmbn Bde	Starch Works Tunnel Stoves	26.7.19
Curtis Charles Blanchard	Pte	RAMC	No 5 MPC	No 1 Sawmill	14.4.04
Danby George	Pte	E Yorks	4th Batt	Hoists	3.10.10
Davis Arthur	Pte	E Yorks		Lead	23.7.15
Dawson Fred	Pte	E Yorks	3rd Batt	Builders	17.7.79
Deans David	Bdr	RFA	47th Brigade	Cdbd Prep	1.1.09
Dearnley Ernest	Gunner	RFA	1st Batty	Packing Dept	22.12.99

Kingston Works

Name	Rank	Regiment	Unit	Department in which employed	Date joined the Firm
Dempsey Arthur	Pte	Lincoln	7th	Wirebound	27.7.99
Denman Fred	Sig	RFA	251st Brig	Packing Rm	24.8.08
Denton Alfred	Seaman	Royal Navy		Packing	28.1.15
Dinsdale Walter	Pte	N Fus	1st Batt	Mepo Mixing Dpt	20.6.15
Dockerill William	Bdsmn	Ox & Bucks L Infantry	2/4 Batt	Starch	0.5.15
Donovan James	Pte	Bedfordshire	12th Labour	C Whouse	2.7.03
Dresser Walter	Pte	RAOC		Packing Rm	20.2.14
Drinkall Richard James	L/Corpl	RAMC	1/3rd N. Fld A	Sawmill	0.10.08
Drum Christopher	Pte	E Yorks		Brasso	5.10.09
Drum Frank		Navy		Packing Rm	16.2.14
Drury S	Gunner	RGA		Box Shop	16.8.06
Dyble Ernest R	Pte	E Yorks		C Whouse	4.1.15
Easter Frank	3rd A/M	RAF	No 2 Trg Sqdn	Laboratory	0.11.14
Edwards Oliver Joseph	Bdr	RFA	69th Div	Packing Rm	26.9.00
Egglestone Thomas	Pte	RAF		Hoists	0.5.15
Ellis Tom	L/Corpl	E Yorks	4th Batt	Box Shop	12.2.12
Ellis Herbert	Pte	W Yorks		Tinners	21.7.15
Elsworth John	Pte	RAF	Regent Pk Depot	Pkg Rm Off	29.7.90
Elvin Harold	Pte	RAMC	3rd N F Amb	Packing Rm	8.2.08
Emmerson John Richard	L/Corpl	N. Fus	1st Batt	Cdbd Dept	0.10.15
Enderby George Edward	L/Bdr	RGA	163 & 111SB	KW	9.10.99
Enderby Herbert	Pte	E Yorks	5th © Batt	Packing Room	5.7.09
Fenton J H	Pte	Labour Corps		Sawmill	31.7.99
Fenten Robert	Pte	KOYLI	1/4th Batt	Box shop wirebound	24.9.06
Finon John	A.B	Royal Navy		Starch	30.10.14
Firth Fredk Arthur	Boy	Royal Navy		Sawmill	8.4.13
Fitzgerald J T	Sapper	RE	IWT	Tin Stores	10.6.15
Fletcher George Horsman	Pte	RAMC		Gen Pkg Rm	7.10.05
Flowers George	Pte	RE	29th AA Search Light Section(T	Fitting Shop	17.10.00
Foulger Arthur	Pte	RE	London Elec Eng	Brasso (Expt	0.10.15
Fox A	Pte	RASCMT		Box Shop	18.9.01
Fox Charles Henry	Pte	MGC	25th Div	Fitters	7.3.09
Frow Herbert	Pte	R. Berks	1st Batt	Box Shop	0.4.13
Fuller Fred	Pte	Gren. Gds		Electricians	31.3.16
Fullerton Arthur	Pte	Trg Batt		Lead	23.2.15

Kingston Works

Name	Rank	Regiment	Unit	Department in which employed	Date joined the Firm
Fullerton R	Pte	E Yorks		KW	1.8.11
Gardham Henry	Pte	Labour Corps	22nd Labour Co	Starch	8.4.08
Garfitt Walter	Pte	HLI	3rd Batt	Starch	10.9.14
Garry Harry	Sig	E Yorks		Starch	31.5.20
Gettings William Edgar	Driver	RFA	136th Batty	Cdbd Prep	0.11.04
Gibson Frederick	Pte	MGC	57th Batt	Packing Rm	0.9.99
Gislingham Alexander Henry	Cadet-Pilot	RAF	50th N F Sqdn	Engineering	14.10.13
Gleadle Frederick William	Pte	Yorks	1st Res	Case Making	14.2.91
Gleadle Joseph	Pte	RAF	3rd A C Depot	Pkt Rm Off	20.8.89
Gleadhill William Henry	Pte	E Yorks	4th Batt	Sawmill No 1	0.6.04
Glenton Frederick	Sergt	RAMC	Nasrich Hospital	Packing Rm	21.1.07
Glew Alfred	Sergt	E Yorks	4thBatt	Sawmill	0.1.11
Gold James	Pte	RAMC		Hoists23.9.14	
Goldspink Samuel James	Pte	RM		Starch	
Gooding Harry	Sapper	RE	1st E Riding	Sawmill	0.3.98
Govier John	Pte	E Yorks	7th Batt	Export Dept	21.1.02
Grainger Amos	Boy	Royal Navy		Box Shop	20.5.14
Green Harold	Pte	Border		Sawmill	23.10.11
Greenwood John Chas	Pte	Labour Corps	Labour Batt	Box Shop	25.10.09
Hardy Frank	2nd Air-crftsmn	RAF	NSDP Benton	Packing Rm	20.11.89
Harper J	Pte	Labour Corps		Sawmill	27.10.14
Harris Frank	Boy	Royal Navy		Box Shop	25.9.13
Harrison F R	Sergt	RE		Social Dpt	0.10.04
Harris Walter	Pte	RASC		Packing Rm	20.10.11
Harrison George	Pte	Labour Corps	40th Labour Batt	Packing Rm	9.4.02
Harrison Herbert Henry	Corpl	RE	1stLondon Res Field Co	Eng Dept	1.12.08
Harrison John	Pte	E Yorks	4th Batt	Box Shop	11.7.11
Harrison R	Pte	E Yorks		Packing	2.11.04
Harrison Robert Reed	Pte	E Yorks	4th Batt	Packing Rm	20.1.10
Hawkes Laurence	3rd A/M	RAF	No2 FG	Joiners	0.7.14
Hebb Louis Vernon	Pte	E Yorks	4th Batt	Packing Rm	6.5.08
Hedges Francis Ernest	L/Corp	E Yorks	2nd Batt	Starch	
Hewson Thomas Henry	Pte	AVC	22nd Vet Hosp	CB Plant	20.1.00
Hill Henry Ellis	Capt	RE	84th Field Co & 20th Divl HQ	Management	1.9.14

Kingston Works

Name	Rank	Regiment	Unit	Department in which employed	Date joined the Firm
Hobbins Harry	Pte	Worcester	1st Batt	Weigh Off	10.11.12
Hodges Fred	Gunner	RFA		Brasso	3.11.13
Hodgson George	Pte	E Yorks	4th Batt	Packing Rm	17.12.06
Hodson Wm P	Pte	DLI		Card Prep	3.9.14
Holden Thomas				Packing	2.9.14
Holdsworth George	Driver	RFA	38th DAC	Tin dept	0.11.93
Holdsworth Jesse	Pte	E Yorks		Hoists	11.4.08
Holdsworth Joseph	Gunner	RGA		Packing Rm	8.5.05
Holtby Alfred	CSM	W Yorks	10th Batt	Watchman	0.10.09
Hoodless George Steven	Gunner	RFA	55th Brigade	Fitting Shop	28.8.14
Hopkinson James	Pte	E Yorks	Hoists	18.3.10	
Hopper Charles	Sapper	RE	1st E Riding	Sawmill	0.1.00
Hopper Thomas	Pioneer	RE		Social	4.10.02
Hough William Arthur	Driver	Lahore Divl Artillery	83rd Battery	Cdbd Prep	11.9.10
Houghton John William	Stoker 1st Cl	Royal Navy		Packing Rm	11.4.04
Housley W	Pte	EYorks		Lead	22.10.03
Howard Thomas	Gunner	RGA	ER	Hoists	16.5.04
Howes George William	Pte	E Yorks	3rd Batt	Starch	13.10.13
Hoyle Henry	Corpl	E Yorks	5th Batt	Pkg Rm Off	3.2.11
Hudson Albert	Driver	RFA	$3/2^{nd}$ Ntmbn B	'C' Whouse	16.4.10
Hudson Harry	Corpl	RE		Pkg Rm Off	27.3.07
Hudson Herbert	Pte	Scots Rifles	2nd Batt	Packing Rm	7.4.13
Hudson Herbert	Sergt	RAMC	No 8 Co	Plumbers	14.1.04
Hunt William John	2/Corpl	ER (F)RE	Signals	Elect Dept	19.1.20
Hunter G H	Sapper	RE		Laboratory	31.5.16
Hunter John	Pte	E Yorks	4th Batt	Hoists	0.10.08
Hutchinson John	Pte	DLI	27th Service Batt	Joiners	24.8.14
Hutchinson John T	Pte	RASCMT		Hoists	
19.6.16Jefferson Fred	Pte	E Yorks	11th Batt	Starch	28.8.14
Jeffrey Fred	Serg	E Yorks		Lead	9.3.15
Jensen George	Pte	E Yorks	11th Batt	Box Shop	20.6.94
Johnson Arthur	Pte	E Yorks	2nd Batt	Weigh Office	6.7.03
Johnson William E	Pte	RAMC		Lead	18.8.15
Jones Alfred	Corpl	E Yorks		Lead	19.1.11
Jones Alf	Pte	E Yorks		Hoists	19.6.06
Joy Neville Holt	Capt	E Yorks	4th Batt	Management	0.11.11
Kean Chas	Driver	RFA	No 35		
3.12.12					
Keech I	Pte	E Yorks		Hoists	1.11.15
Keogh Joseph	Pte	E Yorks		W Box	3.11.04

Kingston Works

Name	Rank	Regiment	Unit	Department in which employed	Date joined the Firm
Kerbyson George Andrew	L/Corpl	E Yorks	3rd Bat	Eng Dept	30.12.05
Key Ernest	Gunner	RGA		Pkg (on scales)	14.12.05
Kirk George	Bdr	RGA	119th AAS	Box Shop	15.6.96
Kirk Joseph H	Sapper	ER (F)RE		Electricians	17.8.11
Kirk William	Sapper	RE	Elect Light Co	Elect Dept	20.11.06
Kitching Albert	Pte	Sher For		Box Shop	15.1.12
Landen Thomas	Sergt	RE	Elect Light Co	Electrical	0.5.06
Lang Donald	Pte	E Yorks	4th Batt	Hoists	17.2.19
Large Edward	Pte	Lancs Fus	15th Batt	Sawmill No 1	8.9.14
Large William	Pte	E Yorks	1/4th Batt	Packing Room	19.10.06
Leggott Thomas George	Capt	Tank Corps	HQ Tanks BEF	Planning Dept	0.11.07
Lester Harold	Pte	RAMC		Starch	28.8.14
Livingston John Alexander	Sapper	RE	Searchlight Co	Eng Dept	24.2.02
Lott Harry	Pte	E Yorks	4th Batt	Brasso	22.4.12
Lott John	Pte	Labour Corps	780 Artisan Works Co	Dept 24 Cdbd Prep	24.5.10
Lowery Ernest Boston	1st A/M	Australian Flying Corps		Fitting Shop	28.5.06
Lowsley John	Pte	Lincolnshire	Labour Co	Tin Stores	2.5.04
Lundie Henry	Serg	RGA	236th Siege Batty	Packing Room	0.5.11
Lyon Albert	Sapper	RE	ER (Fld Co)	Fitters Shop	0.6.06
Lyon E	Pte	E Yorks		Sawmill	8.9.08
Lyon Henry	AB	Royal Navy		Brasso	0.11.12
Lyon William	Pte	Scottish	Labour Batt	Starch	12.10.00
Maxwell Ernest	Pte	MGC	35th Batt	Packing Room	3.9.04
Maxwell Martin	Pte	RAMC	No9 Egyptian Gen Hosp POW	Packing Room	18.1.00
McAllister Arthur	Pte	RAMC	67th Gen Hosp BSF	Works' Dept	15.5.11
McCoy Charles Sidney	2nd A/M	RAF	30th TDS	Eng Dept	1.9.13
McDonald Arthur	Pte	Labour Corps	49th Batt	Cdbd Prep	18.10.15
McDonald John William	Pte	Sher For	1st Garr Batt	Hoists	1.2.06
McDonald William Arthur	Driver	RFA	317th Brigade	Paper Stores	31.10.10
Mace H	Sapper	ER (F) RE		Painters	3.12.08
Maggs J H		Ayre & Lanark Yeo		Packing	11.10.07
Mansell George Henry	Sergt	E Yorks	13th Batt	Packing Room	20.2.10
Mapes H	Pte	E Yorks		Packing	11.10.17
Mates J W	Pte	Training Res		Packing	13.6.03
Marriott G	Pte	Coldstream Guards		'C' Whouse	1.2.07

Kingston Works

Name	Rank	Regiment	Unit	Department in which employed	Date joined the Firm
Marsden Harry	Pte	E Yorks		Stores	23.10.11
Mearns George Reynolds	Pte	RASC	26th Co	Packing Room	5.5.15
Metcalfe George Frederick	Pte	E Yorks	4th Batt	Sawmill No2	0.9.07
Midwood Harold	Pte	RASC		Brasso	0.10.14
Midwood Walter	Pte	E Yorks	4th Batt	Brasso	17.6.11
Miles Arthur	Pte	E Yorks		Lead	9.6.11
Miller Dan	Pte	N. Fus	1/3rd Batt	Sawmill	26.6.88
Miller G W	Pte	RAMC		Sawmill	19.2.07
Millington Alfred	Gunner	RGA		Packing Room	13.8.06
Millington Joseph	Stoker	Royal Navy	Channel Patrol	Starch	5.3.06
Mills John William	Corpl	Labour Corps	305thWks Co	Packing Room	26.9.98
Milner George	Sergt	RAMC	3rd Nthmbn FA	'C' Warehouse	9.5.05
Milner Paul William	Sergt	E Yorks	1st Batt	Wirebnd Cases	19.9.99
Moore William	Corpl	E Yorks	4th Batt	Joiners	29.6.11
Moirod Walter	Pte	Lincolnshire	52nd Labour Co	Brasso	0.10.07
Mulligan H	Pte	RAM		Lead	28.9.98
Musson John Charles Percy	L/Corpl	RE	4th Field Survey	Planning Dept	0.10.05
Nasby Lawrence	Pte	Sher For	11th Batt	Blue Mill	0.2.15
Naylor George Henry	Pte	RAM		Box Shop	10.11.01
Naylor William Henry	Sergt	W Yorks		Brasso	22.5.16
Neave Henry James	Sergt	RE	Tyne Elec Eng	Eng Dept	12.8.12
Neave Herbert Marriage	Sapper	RE	Signals	Electrical	6.5.12
Ness John	Pte	Labour Corps	611th Argl Co	Export Dept	5.6.15
Newton Alfred	Pte	E Yorks	4th Batt	Builders	1.7.11
Nicholson Arthur	Pte	RAF	MT Section	Timekeeper	9.5.98
Nixon James Robert	L/Corpl	Labour Corps	35th Lab Gr HQ	Brasso	19.9.06
Nolan Herbert	Pte	DLI	19th Batt	Packing Room	16.11.11
Norman Andrew	Pte	N. Fus	8th Batt	Joiners	14.12.05
Ogden Charles	Sergt	Yorkshire	19th Batt	KW	20.3.11
Omer John H	Pte	RAF	57th Wing	Starch	2.1.99
Osbourne William George	Pte	RAMC	18th Co	Card Box Dept 24	4.2.98
Ostler William Henry	Stoker	Royal Navy	HMS Royal Sovereign	Fitting Shop	0.8.03
Parker John Cuzes	Petty Off	RAF		Export Dept	13.4.16
Parkinson Alfred	Pte	E Yorks		Joiners	14.8.15

Kingston Works

Name	Rank	Regiment	Unit	Department in which employed	Date joined the Firm
Parkinson Edward	Pte	E Yorks		Starch	14.8.15
Paton Thomas	L/CorpL	RE	1st BBA Co	Fitters Shop	30.1.11
Paulson Arthur	Pte	E Yorks	3rd Batt	Box Shop	4.12.99
Paulson George	Driver	RE	1/1st ERRE	Hoists	27.6.10
Paulson Harry	Pte	RAMC	36th&59th FA	Box Shop	12.10.04
Payne George William	Pte	W Yorks	5th Batt	Brasso (Expt)	0.9.09
Peacock John Henry	Pte	Lincolnshire	3rd Batt	Sawmill	0.7.98
Pearson John Richard	Pte	Labour Corps		Sawmill	23.3.11
Peck Francis Henry	Lt IOM	RAOC	Ordnance College	Planning Dept	0.2.13
Pickering Cecil Charles Macdonald	Sig	N Fus	51st Batt	Drawing Off	9.8.15
Pickering George Barnes	Pte	E Yorks	4th Batt	Cdbd Prep	17.9.11
Pickering Henry Tinegate	Pte	KOYLI	52nd Batt	Packing Room	20.2.14
Pipes Edward	2/Pte	RAF		Box Shop	1.10.14
Pipes John	Seaman	Royal Navy		Blue	16.11.11
Pittock Arthur	Gunner	RND	63rd Div	Wirebnd Cases	13.4.11
Pittock James Alfred	Pte	E Yorks	4th Batt	Brasso	10.5.06
Pixton William S	Driver	RFA	117th Brigade	Brasso	0.8.10
Pizer Clarence	Sapper	RE	ER(F)	Fitters	18.3.07
Pizer Tom Spence	Pte	Queens R W Surrey	11th Batt	Brasso	28.4.13
Pockley Harold	Pte	RAMC	29th CCS	Tin Dept	10.5.05
Polley Alfred Cook	Bmbdr	RFA	A/251 Brigade	Work Office	0.4.11
Pollock David	Pte	E Yorks	1/4th Batt	Starch	23.11.14
Pollock John	Pte	Labour Corps	492 Labour Co	Starch	13.4.12
Porter Harold	Pte	RASCMT	4th Corps Troops MT Co	Packing Dept	26.6.04
Potter Fredk	Pte	E Yorks	4th Batt	Hoists	26.10.10
Poulson Harry	Gunner	RGA	MPP	Boxshop	3.8.91
Priestley John	Pte	E Yorks	7th Batt	Boxshop	1.5.00
Priestley Joseph	Corpl	E Yorks	4th Batt	Packing Room	3.2.06
Proctor Joseph	Gunner	RFA	31st Remt	Starch	3.10.15
Proundley Frederick	Pte	E Yorks	Depot	Lead	6.9.15
Pullon Charles	Pte	Labour Corps	838 Labour Co	Sawmill	6.7.98
Purdy Richard James	Pte	E Yorks	11th Batt	Starch	3.9.14
Ranby Samuel	Gunner	RFA		Boxshop	8.11.13
Reckitt Arnold	Capt	E Yorks	4th Batt	Director (Works)	0.0.00

Kingston Works

Name	Rank	Regiment	Unit	Department in which employed	Date joined the Firm
Redfern George	Pte	Yorkshire	4th Batt	Builders	17.3.19
Redfern Robert	Pte	E Yorks	4th Batt	Tin Stores	0.4.06
Reed Thomas Henry	Corpl	E Yorks	4th Batt	Sawmill	27.7.10
Reeson George Ernest	Pte	DLI		Boxshop	28.3.16
Renshaw Arthur	Pte	RAOC		Packing	7.5.00
Reynolds Albert Ernest	Pte	Nthld Fus	3rd Batt	Sawmill	0.2.00
Richards Frederick Charles	Pte	E York		Lead mill	20.12.09
Richards Robert William	AB	Royal Navy		Paste Filling	0.8.05
Richardson Alfred	Pte	E Yorks	8th Batt	Brasso	0.9.14
Riches Fred	Sapper	ERY		Lead	17.11.13
Rickles Arthur	Pte	E Yorks	4th Batt	Tin Stores	0.9.11
Ridley Alfred	Sergt	E Yorks	4th Bat	Export Dept	22.4.12
Robinson George	Sapper	RE		Fitters	29.1.11
Robinson Thomas	ACI	RAF		Eng Dept	6.9.05
Ror Charles Edward	Pte	E Yorks	14th Batt	'C' Whouse	3.9.14
Rowse Eric William	Deck hd	RNRT		Brasso	6.7.13
Russell William	Pte	E Riding Yks Yeo	2/1st Batt	Brasso	0.3.11
Rymer Donovan William	Sapper	RE	Special Bridging Batt	Planning Dept	0.6.09
Sanderson Arthur Spence	Pte	D of W WR	2nd Batt	Packing Room	1.11.15
Scott Walter	Pte	Nthld Fus	7th Batt	Box Shop Wirebound	16.10.96
Seaton Harold	Pte	E Yorks	4th Batt	Blue Mill	9.5.12
Seaton Walter	Pte	City of London	30th Batt	Hoists	22.2.09
Seeley Herbert D	Pte	Shrwood For		Export	3.6.15
Sellers James Edwin	L/Corpl	AOC	Detachment	Gen Pkg Dept	0.8.04
Senior Harold	Sapper	RE	1/1st E Riding	Sawmill	3.6.08
Shaw Charles	L/Corpl	RAOC	10thCoy	Dept 24 Cdbd Prep	0.1.14
Shaw Harry	Pte	Sherwood For		Packing Room	5.1.12
Shelton George	Bmbdr	Rga	ER	Hoists	0.12.06
Siddle Thomas	AM	RAF		Box Shop	15.2.15
Siddle Thomas	Pte	Yorkshire	13th Batt	Expt Pkg Dept	7.7.13
Sidwell Harry	2/Corpl	RE	22nd A A Co	Fitting Shop	0.5.07
Silvery J	Pte	E Yorks		Lead	7.10.91
Simpson George Cooper	Pte	RASC	Remounts	Packing Room	26.5.03
Smales James Edwin 2.2.05	Pte	York & Lanc	1st Bat		Starch
Smith Charles	2/Corpl	RE	ER (Fortress)	Engineering	19.4.99

Kingston Works

Name	Rank	Regiment	Unit	Department in which employed	Date joined the Firm
Smith E J	Sergt	RAMC		Blue	14.5.90
Smith John	L/Corpl	E Yorks		Lead	13.1.15
Smith John Arthur	Pte	Eyorks	4th Batt	Packing Room	22.11.04
Smith Joseph	Pte	Labour Corps		Tin Stores	8.5.13
Smith Walter Edward	Driver	DAC		Lead	22.9.05
Smith William	Corpl	E Yorks	MGC	Packing Room	21.3.11
Smith William Bernard	Flt/Cdt	RAF		Wirebound Box Shop	1.6.16
Snowden Charles William	Pte	RAMC	19th Coy	Hoists	9.1.15
Speckman Francis William	Pte	E Yorks		Packing Room	27.11.1
Stanley H	Gunner	RFA		Starch Pkg	25.10.99
Stanley J E	Driver	RAF		Lead	19.8.12
Stark Ernest	Driver	DAC		Starch	12.6.19
Stather James	Gunner	RGA	AA	Packing Rm	11.11.14
Stephenson Ernest	Pte	Yorkshire	15th Batt	Blue Mill	9.6.15
Stephenson George	Pte	E Yorkshire		'C' Whouse	23.3.15
Stephenson Walter	Pte	Nthld Fus	35th Batt	Eng dept	7.10.12
Stone John	Pte	E Yorkshire		Box shop	23.10.09
Storey Thomas	Pte	DLI	51st Batt	Sawmill	13.3.14
Stow Walter	Sapper	RE	London Elect. Eng	Hoists	20.6.16
Strachan Ernest Ewart	Pte	Artists Rifles	OTC	Management	10.5.00
Stubley Hoseph William	Pte	3/7 N.Fuss	35th Batt	Boxshop	21.5.00
Suddaby Harry	Pte	E Yorkshire		Brasso	8.5.13
Sumpton William	Pte	RASCMT		Sawmill	0.9.02
Swales Benjamin James	Pte	E Yorkshire	4th Batt	Starch	5.11.94
Swatmar George	Pte	Canadian Inf	1st Batt	Hoists	20.12.08
Sykes E	Pte	E Yorkshire		Room 24	14.1.08
Taylor Charles	Sergt	MGC	34th Batt	Hoists	22.10.19
Taylor John	Sapper	RE	529 Field Co	Eng Dept	16.8.10
Taylor John Robert	Pte	E Yorkshire	2nd Batt	Builders	6.12.10
Teasdale Benjamin Shillito	Pte	E Yorkshire	7th Batt	Gen Packing Rm	25.1.15
Tebb George	Pte	RAMC		Brasso	22.5.16
Thackery W	Gunner	RAF		Tin	11.11.07
Thirsk Fred	Pte	RAMC	64th Field AMB	Wirebound	4.8.01
Thirsk Herbert	Sergt	Queens Own	2nd Batt Cam Hldrs	Dept 24 Crdbd Prep	0.6.10
Thompson Robert	GDSMN	Welsh Guards	1st Batt	Eng Dept	15.8.17
Thorley William	Telegt	Royal Navy		Brasso	0.2.16
Thurlow Henry Frederick	Pte	RASCMT		Packing Rm	6.4.10
Tindall George Henry	AB	Royal Navy		Dept 24 Cdbd Prep Cdbd Prep	0.10.12

Kingston Works

Name	Rank	Regiment	Unit	Department in which employed	Date joined the Firm
Todd John Thomas	Pte	RAMC	12/35th Co	Dept 24 Cdbd Prep	9.3.99
Tong George	Pte	E Yorkshire		Cardbox	19.8.10
Towers F	Pte	APC		General	8.2.15
Trevor Harold D	Pte	Wiltshire	6th Batt	Packing Rm	6.9.03
Trotter Edmund	Pte	E Yorkshire	4th Batt	Boxshop	13.12.01
Trotter George Ernest	Pte	RAF		Rm 19 Cdbox	12.2.98
Trotter Thomas	Sapper	RE		Wirebound	10.9.93
Trowell Frank	Sapper	RE	483 Field Co	Fitters Shop	1.6.10
Turner John William	Pte	RAF		Tin Stores	6.12.15
Turner N	Pte	Trng Res		Brasso	28.12.14
Turner W	Gunner	RFA		Packing	9.10.14
Vasey Frederick Robert	L/Corpl	RE	Elect Light Co	Electrical	19.9.08
Walsh Albert Edward	CSM	RGA	E Riding	Engineers	3.9.00
Walsh Harold	Pte	E Yorks	4th Batt	Sawmill	0.9.11
Walters G	Corpl	E Yorks		Fitters	4.6.08
Walton H	Pte	KOYLI		Joiners	19.3.08
Ward Edward Brant	Boy	Royal Navy		Sawmill	12.2.12
Ward Fred	Pte	RASCMT	1028 Co	Wbd Dept	9.9.02
Warrener Walter Herbert	AB	Royal Navy	HMS Barham	Hoist	0.6.10
Waters Clement	Pte	E Yorks	4th Batt	Hoists	26.2.12
Watson Bruce	Pte	Labour Corps	483rd Labour Corps	Blue Dept	15.8.10
Webster C	Pte	RFA		General	30.3.05
Weekes Frederick James	Pte	E Yorks	14th Batt	Packing Rm	14.12.14
Weissenborn Charles	Sapper	RE		Joiners	29.5.11
Welburn Christopher	Sergt	RAMC	3rd Nthbn FA	Packing Rm	15.12.05
Wheatley P	Pte	RAMC		Sawmill	27.3.08
Wheldale Horace William	Pte	RAMC	3rd Nthbn FA	Packing Rm	1.7.98
Whileblood John Marshall	Pte	E Yorks	11th Batt	Blue Dept	4.2.06
Whitaker Robert John	Corpl	RE	Special Brigade	Laboratory	23.11.03
Whitelock James Edward	Pte	RAMC/RAOC		Joiners	4.3.88
Whittle A	Pte	E Yorks		Lead	11.2.14
Whittle J	Sapper	RE	ER (F)	Fitters	26.11.12
Whitworth Daniel	L/Corpl	E Yorks		Hoists	17.1.10
Willatt William Henry	Major	RE		Director (works)	0.0.01
Wiles Chas H	Pte	S Staffs		Packing Rm	3.9.14
Wiles George Leaf	Corpl	RGA	E Riding	Paper stores	14.1.0
Wilkinson E	Pte	Nthld Fus		Starch	30.3.16
Wilson Arthur J	Pte	HLI	1/6th Batt	Cdbd Prep sweeping	0.7.13

Kingston Works

Name	Rank	Regiment	Unit	Department in which employed	Date joined the Firm
Wilson John	1st Egmn	RNR	T. Mine-Sweeping	Engineering	7.7.13
Wilson Joseph	Pte	Norfolk	2/6th Batt	Brasso	27.6.16
Wilson Robert	Bmbdr	RGA		Packing Rm	22.4.12
Winship George	Pte	Gloucester	1st Batt	Wirebound	19.1.14
Withernwick Charles	Sergt	DLI	2nd Batt	Hoists	18.1.10
Woollons Charles H	Pte	RAMC (T)	1/3rd N F AmB	Box shop	3.10.11
Woollias Harry	CorplRGA	E Riding		Brasso	25.5.08

General Office

Name	Rank	Regiment	Unit	Department in which employed	Date joined the Firm
Addison Harry	L/Corpl	E Yorks	4th Batt	General Office	0.8.06
Allen Wilfred Smith	CQMS	KRR	21st Batt	General Office	1.4.09
Archer Arthur Stanley	Pte	Labour Corps		General Office	24.8.05
Arnold Arthur	Pte	RAMC	Military Hosp	General Office	1.7.04
Arrowsmith Arthur France	2/Writer	RNAS	Airship Sect	General Office	23.3.14
Ashton ThomaS	Pte	RAMC	31st B Sty Hsp	General Office	5.11.10
Baker Ernest	Pte	E Yorks	4th Batt	General Office	23.8.05
Batty Marshall	Gnr Sig	RGA		General Office	14.5.00
Baxter George Percy	SB Att	Royal Navy		General Office	12.11.00
Bays Arthur	Corpl	RAMC	42nd CCS	General Office	0.8.13
Bayston Arthur Stanley	Pte	E Yorks	4th Batt	General Office	29.3.09
Bell John William	Pte	RAF	'E' Squadron	General Office	15.3.97
Beynon Gwilym	Lieut	Indian Army	Supply & Trans	General Office	5.8.02
Brown William	Pte	E Yorks	10th Batt	General Office	10.03.13
Butler William R C	Corpl	RAOC		General Office	11.12.99
Campion Frederick William	CMS	RGA	E Riding	General Office	8.8.99
Cape John Arthur	Pte	E Yorks	3rd Batt	General Office	17.4.00
Christie John Charles	Pte	ACC	51st Batt	General Office	30.4.01
Clark Henry	Sergt	Y&L RAF		General Office	16.5.04
Cleminson Arnold Russell	Capt	RASC		General Office	0.11.98
Coates Albert Victor	Corpl.	E Yorks	4th Batt	General Office	0.1.06
Coates Frank William	L/Corpl	E Yorks	4th & 7th Batt	General Office	0.7.11.
Cooper Harold Hill	Lieut	KORL	3rd Batt	General Office	0.5.11
Cowl Richard Charlton	Lieut	E Yorks &	10th Batt & 141st Squad	General Office	0.4.12
Crawford George Henry	Pte	E Yorks	1/4th Batt	General Office	9.2.05
Crowder Charles William	Fl/Cadet	RAF	39th TDS	General Office	14.8.16
Dewick George H	Pte	E Yorks	10th Batt	General Office	18.4.10
Easterbrook George William	Corpl	APC	Trans. RE	General Office	1.2.97
Fairclough Herbert	Pte	E Yorks	4th Batt	General Office	17.4.99
Ford Ernest Henry	2/Lieut	RGA		General Office	7.9.03
Foster William Gordon	Corpl	APC		General Office	9.12.03
Fox Sydney Thomas	Pte	E Yorks	3rd & 8th Batt	General Office	0.4.15
Glover H W	Lieut	TMB		General Office	10.2.08
Grundy William	Pte	RASC	MT,HQ Staff	General Office	19.11.17

General Office

Name	Rank	Regiment	Unit	Department in which employed	Date joined the Firm
Holdsworth Harold	S/Sergt	E Yorks	10th Batt	General Office	0.7.08
Howlett Harold	Pte	RAMC RASC & APC		General Office	27.7.08
Hunter Percy	Pte	E Yorks	5th (Cyc. Batt)	General Office	4.6.09
Jackson Arthur William	Pte	E. Yorks	14th Res Batt	General Office	14.8.11
Johnson Frank Ernest	Gunner	RGA	57th AA Co	General Office	22.7.07
Johnson Ralph Helman	Sergt	RAMC	No 27 Gen Hosp	General Office	21.3.04
Jones John William	B.S.M	RGA	E. Riding	General Office	24.11.00
Jubb Henry Martin	Driver	RASC	21st Res M.T Co	General Office	8.9.14
Knee Henry Leslie	Lieut	RGA	286th Siege Bat	General Office	1.9.14
Leech Percival	L/corpl	RAMC		General Office	0.0.06
Longley Edgar Percy	Corpl	APC	No 1 Det York	General Office	8.6.03
Loten B Stewart	Sig	RGA RE	346th Siege Batt	General Office	23.4.00
Macadie George William	Pte	E. Yorks	4th Batt	General Office	0.3.00
Machin Bakewell John	2/Lt	QRWS	3rd Batt	General Office	0.4.14
Martin Frederick	Pta	Dorset	3rd Batt	General Office	0.6.15
Mason John	Sergt	RAMC	47th Field Amb	General Office	0.7.08
Morris Ernest Oswald	SQMS	Worc. Yeo		General Office	10.8.08
Musson Bertie	Pte	2/1st ERY	7th Cyc Brigade	General Office	2.12.14
Neale Eric Audas	A/Sergt	RGA	E Riding	General Office	0.7.09
Nicholson Thomas	A/S/Sgt	RFA	28th Batt	General Office	3.6.05
Niven Frederick					
Cecil Watson	Corpl	E Yorks	10th Batt	General Office	0.3.09
Parkinson Ernest V	Corpl	Labour Corps	42nd POW Co	General Office	29.3.09
Platt James Richard	Corpl	APC		General Office	25.4.04
Pollard Edward James	Lieut	Yorkshire	12th Batt	General Office	5.8.99
Porter Ernest	Sergt	E Yorkshire	4th Batt	General Office	2.11.96
Powell W L	Sergt	RAMC		General Office	27.2.11
Proctor Donald James	Pte	APC	York No 2	General Office	16.6.13
Reynolds William	Pte	RASC	163rd BSS	General Office	12.8.12
Rimmington William Frederick	Pte	DLI	15th Batt	General Office	12.4.03
Robinson Samuel Bolton	Pte	E Yorks	1/4th Batt	General Office	20.3.03

General Office

Name	Rank	Regiment	Unit	Department in which employed	Date joined the Firm
Rooms Harold	Lieut	RGA	E Riding	General Office	0.11.06
Rust Thomas Ernest	Corpl	E Yorks	10th Bat	General Office	19.2.06
Sallabank James	3rd Clerk	E Yorks		General Office	30.7.98
Sanderson James Thornton	L/Corpl	E Yorks	4th Batt	General Office	21.4.10
Saunders John Edward	Pte	RASC	530th HT Co	General Office	9.7.06
Sawyer Frederick Charles	Lieut	E Yorks	4th Batt	General Office	21.8.11
Shaw Ernest	Gunner	RGA	256th Siege Batt	General Office	6.6.09
Sheppard Walter	Corpl	E Yorks	10th Batt	General Office	19.9.07
Slack Cecil Moorhouse	Capt	E Yorks	4th Batt	General Office	0.9.11
Squires Herbert	Sapper	RE	Signal Service	General Office	6.4.14
Stabler William	2/Lieut	KOYLI	9th Batt	General Office	21.10.01
Stead A E	Sergt	E Yorks		General Office	0.5.10
Stokell Charles	Corpl	E Yorks	11th Batt	General Office	17.3.13
Streat Clifford	A/CSM	E Yorks	10th Batt	General Office	26.10.08
Stuffins Clarence	2/Lieut	Hunts	1st Cyc Batt	General Office	29.5.11
Sumpton John	Corpl	APC		General Office	9.5.11
Taylor Arthur Banfield	L/Corp	KRR	20th Batt	General Office	18.11.12
Timmons Charles Basil	AB	Royal Navy	HMS Colossus & Queen	General Office	0.9.14
Upton Alfred James Neville	Pte	E Yorks	11th Batt	General Office	12.7.10
Vicors Roy	Pte	E Yorks	3rd Batt	General Office	5.8.12
Vincent Thomas	RSM	RAMC	2/1st NF Amb	General Office	22.12.99
Wallis Walter James	Pte	E Yorks	10th Batt	General Office	16.12.12
Webster Edward Wilson	Pte	E Yorks	10th Batt	General Office	3.4.11
Wheelhouse Stanley Emerson	Pte	R Berks	1st Batt	General Office	9.12.12
Wilby Walter Arnold	2/Lieut	Tank Corps		General Office	14.3.13
Willis Eric Samuel	2/Lieut	RAF	5th TDS	General Office	15.2.09
Warfolk Ralph	Sergt	RAMC	61st Field Amb	General Office	0.3.09
Watson Harry	2/Lieut	ACC		General Office	0.2.09
West Robert	L/Corp	E Yorks	4th Batt	General Office	3.2.08

Outside Staff

Name	Rank	Regiment	Unit	Department in which employed	Date joined the Firm
Ainsworth Arthur Ogdon	Pte	Nthmptshire	Depot Staff	Representative	21.2.11
Allen Frank Leslie	1st Pte	RAF	No 5 TDS	Representative	5.4.09
Anderson Harry	Corpl	QRWS	16th Batt	Representative	0.3.10
Arnold Sydney	S/Sergt	RASC	EFC	Representative	2.4.06
Austin Arthur Warburton	CQMS	DLI	18th Batt	Representative	0.9.11
Backhouse Laurence Henry	Sergt	RGA	326th Siege Batt	Representative	27.2.11
Baines Joshua	Pte	Sher For	16th Batt	Renovator	0.9.10
Bell James	Pte	RASC	1st BMTD	Representative	8.9.13
Bramhill John Henry	Pte	RAF		Representative	10.6.87
Bromby Thomas Alfred	Capt & Adjt	KRR & Indian Army	21st Batt & 2/5th Light Infy	Representative	4.5.14
Brown Cecil James	Pte	R.Fus	20th Batt	Representative	0.2.12
Burrows Francis Cecil	L/Corpl	RASC	MT	Representative	0.6.01
Cassie James Harvey	B Wdn	RASC		Representative	0.5.05
Charles Percy Victor	Corpl	London	Batt 1/18th	Representative	20.7.08
Clements T A	RQMS	N.Fus	2nd Batt	Representative	16.10.16
Clemes Thomas George	Sergt	RGA	262nd Siege Batt	Representative	4.11.12
Cogdon G B	2/Lieut	RGA		Representative	24.5.14
Connor Francis Joseph	Lieut	RAOC		Representative	0.9.09
Cook George	Pte	RAVC		Representative	22.2.04
Davidson James	BQMS	RGA	121st Siege Batt	Representative	15.8.10
Davis Walter John	2/Clerk	RAF	34th Trg DS	Representative	6.11.99
Dawson George Henry	CPO	Royal Navy		Renovator	16.10.10
Eastwood Francis	2/Lieut	D of W	3rd W Riding	Representative	13.10.13
Elliott Walter John Lester	Pte	RASC	MT	Representative	25.3.06
Ellis Albert Ernest	Pioneer	RE	RTE	Representative	7.7.19
Emment Thomas Clifford	Sergt	RASC		Representative	1.3.12
Evans Richard Booth	Pte	RASC	MT	Representative	27.3.11
Farrell Herbert	Corpl	Kings L'pool	17th Batt	Representative	0.5.10
Fisher Joseph	Driver	RFA	466th Batty	Representative	14.6.14
Fookes Edward Sidney	Gunner	RGA		Representative	19.1099
Forsyth Herbert French	L/Corpl	APC	Perth Office	Representative	0.7.05
Gates John	Sergt	R Warwicks	15th Batt	Representative	18.4.07
Greaves Walter	Pte	W Yorks	18th Batt	Representative	25.6.14
Giffiths Fred Richard	2/Lieut	E Kent	1st Batt	Representative	0.6.00
Hayward Raymond Joseph	Pte	APC	Preston No 2	Representative	0.4.13
Hodgkinson Arthur James	Corpl	RAF	1st AP	Representative	1.1.08
Hodgson John	Pte	RASC	MT	Renovator	0.11.11
Homer Frederick George	Gunner	RGA		Representative	11.5.00

Outside Staff

Name	Rank	Regiment	Unit	Department in which employed	Date joined the Firm
Hook Arthur John	Clerk	RAF	No 4 AAP	Representative	25.3.01
Hughes Walter Marmaduke	1/Pte	RAF	E Fortune	Representative	0.1.11
Jagoe Allen Wilson	Lieut	MGC	4th Batt	Representative	15.5.11
Jefferson George Herbert	Pte	E Yorks	4th Batt	Representative	0.2.12
Jenkins Richard John	Bdr	RGA	321st Siege Batt	Representative	29.3.10
Jones Benjamin William	Bdr	RFA	3A Res Brig	Representative	0.5.13
Jones Edward	Pte	RAF	58th Wing	Representative	24.11.13
Jones Trevor	Sig	RFA	52nd Army Bde	Representative	0.6.01
Jones William Eyton	Corpl	RWF	2nd Batt	Representative	3.6.12
Knight George	Pte	RASC	MT	Representative	0.6.13
Laming Samuel Asa	Lieut	28th L.Cav	IAR of Offs	Representative	12.11.12
Lawson William Henry	1 A/C	RNAS	Mullion	Renovator	27.3.99
Lawton Howard	Sergt	R W Kent	4th Batt	Representative	30.8.09
Lewis Thomas Henry	Pte	RASC	MT	Representative	1.9.99
Lincoln Joseph Thomas	Pte	London	15th Batt	Representative	0.10.09
Martin William Henry Bennett		Lieut	MGC	Representative	0.7.13
Merrifield Arthur Henry	Pte	Norfolk	12th Batt Yeo	Representative	0.6.08
Morris Lewis Edward	Pte	E Lancs	3rd Batt	Representative	4.8.04
Parsons Stanley Shortland	L/Corpl	Wiltshire	1/4th Batt	Representative	0.7.13
Pegler Henry Vizer	Pte	W Yorks	6th Batt PWO	Representative	5.11.06
Piper Reginald	A/C2	RNAS	HMS President	Representative	7.6.14
Plaster Frederick Seymour	Gunner	RGA	35th Fire Comd	Representative	7.10.07
Portbury Edward James	L/Corpl	SLI	11th Batt	Representative	0.6.09
Poulton John	Pte	RAVC	Lowland Divl	Representative	2.6.08
Price Edmund Rupert	Pte	RASC	MT	Representative	12.10.05
Rogers Frank Webb	Corpl	RGA	194th Siege Batt	Representative	0.3.06
Routledge T	L/Corpl	York & Lanc	1st Batt	Renovator	0.1.13
Sargent Archibald	Pte	RAF		Representative	0.3.16
Sharp William Charles	A/Bdr	RGA	No 1 Mobile Bde	Renovator	0.5.13
Shute Percy Clifford	Lieut	Middlesex	2nd Batt	Representative	0.8.14
Smith John Herbert	Pte	R Fus	Frontiersmen	Representative	10.6.01
Soutar Walter Smith	RSN	RAMC	2/1st Hld CC	Representative	7.2.14
Southey Clarence Victor	LAC	RNAS	Head quarters	Representative	1.7.00
Stephenson Arthur George	L/Corpl	York and Lanc	4th Batt	Representative	1.7.99
Temperton Wilfred	Sergt	RASC	1009th MT	Representative	7.3.10

Outside Staff

Name	Rank	Regiment	Unit	Department in which employed	Date joined the Firm
Taylor George Thomas	2/Lieut	Suffolk	12th Batt	Representative	0.7.14
Temperton Wilfred	Sergt Co	RAMC	1009th MT Co	Representative	7.6.09
Tilley William Henry	L/Corpl	RME	I Group	Representative	7.6.09
Wallgate L S	Lieut	Yorks	5th Batt	Representative	17.3.13
Wardle Georg	2/Clerk	RAF	Head Quarters	Representative	0.3.06
Wentworth William	CQMS	RASC	880thMT Co	Representative	31.8.99
Witteridge Albert E	L/Corpl	RE	146th IB Signals	Representative	0.1.12
Williams Bruce	Pte	KOYLI	10thBatt	Renovator	9.7.03
Williams Thomas Francis	Sergt	R Fus	26th Batt	Representative	0.10.10
Winn Frederick Arnold	WO	RASC	HQ MT	Representative	27.4.08
Wyer Ronald George	Lieut	RASC	MT	Representative	0.6.06
Wyllie Frederick	Pte	RASC	Remounts	Renovator	21.3.10
Yuill Frederick Charles	Corpl	KOSB	3rd Bat	Representative	7.1.07

Bluebell House

Name	Rank	Regiment	Unit	Department in which employed	Date joined the Firm
Brown George John	Pte	R Berks	4th Batt	Die Setter	0.1.10
Buchan Frank	Pte	Middlesex	1st Bat	Office	16.10.13
Cates Frederick Edward	A/C 1	RAF	5th Strs Dist Pk	Bluebell	0.7.16
Clack Arthur	Pte	RE	Cons Wks Camp	Packing	0.11.17
Clare Arthur Stanhope	Pte	Middlesex	4th Batt	Office	15.9.09
Davison Henry Thomas	Pte	RASC	381st Co	Bluebell	16.5.16
Evans George William	Gunner	RFA	177th Brigade	Bluebell	7.11.07
Garling George Thomas	Gunner	RFA		Handy Man	0.9.13
Hutchison Francis Samuel	Pte	N Staffs	2/6th Batt	Bluebell	28.10.07
McDonald Andrew Joseph	Driver	RFA	112th Brigade	Yard Lab	0.9.13
Metcalf Albert Osbourne	L/Corpl	R Fus	Depot	Representative	2.11.07
Middlemiss William Thomas	Gunner	RGA	No 12 Fire Comd	Tin Canister	19.10.16
Munton Frederick Albert	Corpl	London	2/20th Bat	Representative	0.11.10
Pincott Alfred Ernest	L/Serg	E Surrey	7th Batt	Motor Driver	0.4.15
Porter John Alfred Graham	Gunner	RFA	285th Brigade	Representative	1.1.12
Prigg William Henry	2/Lieut	Devonshire	3rd Batt	Bluebell	18.6.14
Slater Robert	Pte	N Staffs	13th Batt	Stoker	0.2.09
Smith Ernest	Gunner	RGA		Representative	1.7.07
Stannett Edward	Pte	RME	Mech Unit	Fitters	23.2.16
Steel Thomas	Pte	Tank Corps		Blubell	0.11.10
Stiles Francis Walter	Sapper	RE	2/3rd Field Co	Storekeeper	0.10.07
Sturrock Thomas	Pte	R Scots	2/10th Batt	Office	16.9.12
Thorpe Wallace	A/M	RAF		Bluebell	12.1.07
Turner Walter Spencer	Pte	QORWK	4th Res Batt	Tin Making	0.9.15

London House

Name	Rank	Regiment	Unit	Department in which employed	Date joined the Firm
Adams George Henry	Pte	RASC		M Lorry Dr	4.12.99
Bailey Arthur John	Rfn	Rifle Brigade	3rd Batt	Office	29.2.04
Blyth Charles Leonard	A/Sergt	RAMC	No 9 Co	Office	9.5.06
Boggis W	Mech	RAF		London	5.3.00
Brown Edward	SQMS	London	2/4th Batt	Introducer	19.2.12
Carrington Julius Augustus	S B Att	RNSR	Devonport Depot	Office	18.3.01
Crosby Thomas Gordon	Pte	RAVC	11th D Sqdn	Stableman	0.0.00
Curson Thomas Henry	Gunner	RFA	50th Brigade	Warehouse	9.5.04
Derrett Percy Alfred	Capt	RFA	90th Batty	Introducer	11.4.10
Fone F R	Pte	Essex		London	4.11.12
Freeman Stanley Leonard	Pte	RASC	69th Aux St Co	M Lorry Dr	26.2.08
Gage Frank Albert	Corpl	RAOC	63rd Co	Warehouse	29.6.03
Gage Josiah	Pte	RE	Signals	Carman	3.10.99
Hough Frederick James	Sapper	RE	3rd Fld Sur Co	Warehouse	11.3.12
Hutchison Arthur Henry	Corpl	RASC	EFC	Office	6.5.12
King Harry Storey	RFN	QWR	16th London Batt	Office	21.4.03
McBride Arthur	A/C2	RNAS	HMS President II	Office	27.12.03
Opher Hubert Douglas	A/M	RAF	63rd Squadron	Introducer	3.12.06
Pettit George	Pte	RNE	Chatham Div	Warehouse	0.8.92
Pulsford Frederick James	Pte	E Surrey	8th Batt	Office	4.11.12
Seffrey Frederick William	Pte	RASC	MT	M Lorry Dr	11.2.02
Shoosmith Henry Francis	Pte	RAMC	8th Co	Stableman	31.10.16
Taylor George Frederick	Pte	Middlesex	2nd Batt	Renovator	18.11.01
Wallis Walter William	L/Corpl	RE	IW & L	Advt Inspector	

2.6.96

Liverpool House

Name	Rank	Regiment	Unit	Department in which employed	Date joined the Firm
DaCosta David	Capt	RASC	512th MT Co	Representative	9.10.03
Brooks Lewis	Pioneer	RE	IWT	Warehouseman	0.1.14
Esseen Carl Wilhelm	Pte	Kings L'Pool	12th Batt	Office	0.1.08
Evans Edwin	Pte	Kings L'Pool	9th Batt	Labourer	0.9.15
Greenhough Walter	Pte	Cheshire	17th Batt	Packer	0.5.02
Hayworth George	Pte	RAMC		Labourer	6.10.13
Hughes Roger Wm	Pte	Kings L'Pool	3rd Batt	Gen Repairs	0.10.11
Hulton Harry Rainford	Pte	R Irish Fus	1st Batt	Mechanic	0.11.14
Larkey George Woolley	L/Corpl	Kings L'Pool	5th Res Batt	Joinery	14.12.15
Marland Sydney	Pte	MGC	128th Co	Office	0.3.14
Roach Christopher	Tele	RNVR	HMM Clacton Belle	Office	0.10.06
Russell Arthur	L/A	RAF	No 2 (N) ARD	Shinio	0.1.13
Simpson William	Pte	L'Pool Scots		Representative	0.1.00
Smith Herbert Henry	Pte	Kings L'Pool	4th Batt	Joiners	0.6.10
Strachan Arthur James	Pte	MMGC		Engineer	0.0.00
Unwin Arthur	2A/M	RAF	251st Sqdn	Fitting Shop	11.2.16

Plymouth House

Name	Rank	Regiment	Unit	Department in which employed	Date joined the Firm
Ackland Walter James	Sapper	RE	1st Brdg batt	Printing	1.2.11
Delafield Richard Henry	Driver	RASC	Horse Transport	Printing	26.8.10
Fifield George Robert	Pte	Devon	1/6th Batt	Blue Dept	0.11.95
Hamlyn Henry	Gunner	RGA		Plymouth	0.0.96
Helson John Richard	Pte	Dorset	2nd Batt	Starch Dept	27.4.93
Hole Ernest Alfred	Sapper	RE	356th E & M Co	Blacklead	3.2.11
Hole William Henry Stanley	Sapper	RE	356th E & M Co	Starch	4.8.09
Hunter Edward George	Pte	Leicester	11th Batt	Starch	26.8.04
King Frederick John	2/OS	Royal Navy		Printing	0.10.15
Lavers Reginald Lewis	Pte	S Staffs		Starch	27.4.02
Watkins John Charles	L/Corpl	Devonshire	5th Batt	Warehouse	19.4.11
Westcott George Frayne	Pte	RASC	954th MT Co	Blue	6.3.05

Dublin House

Name	Rank	Regiment	Unit	Department in which employed	Date joined the Firm
Fletcher	Pte	RGA		Vanman	4.2.14

Australian House

Name	Rank	Regiment	Unit	Department in which employed	Date joined the Firm
Alanson Harry Godwin	Pte	AAMC	11th Fld Amb	Office	00.1.12
Bingham George Alexander	Pte	AIF	18th Batt	Sydney	0.8.13
Jackson Andrew James	Driver	AIF	11th Batt	Storeman	18.3.13
Phillips John Edwin	YMCA Rep	AIF		Office	1.3.97
Steel George	Sergt	AIF	25th AASC	Representative	0.0.03

New Zealand House

Name	Rank	Regiment	Unit	Department in which employed	Date joined the Firm
Crewes William Ewart	Gunner	NZFA	NZEF	Traveller	13.9.09
Forsythe William George	Sergt	NZFA	NZEF	Office	20.12.11
Jackson George Winchester	Sergt	AMC	NZEf	Traveller	9.2.14

South African House

Name	Rank	Regiment	Unit	Department in which employed	Date joined the Firm
Fradd Ernest	Corpl	SAFA		Office	0.6.13

New York House

Name	Rank	Regiment	Unit	Department in which employed	Date joined the Firm
Fuller Matthew	2/PO	Navy	SS Gargoyle	Office	20.3.16
Jayne Edward I	3/PO	Navy	Battleship Delaware	Office	18.7.07
McGuire Edmond A	CPO	Navy	Shore Duty	Office	4.4.13
Meyer William A	SM	US Army	Training Camp	Office	7.7.13
Shanley Michael P	1/PO	Navy	Training Camp	Office	9.4.17
Steward Francis S	CPO	Navy	Shore Duty	Office	28.8.16

Paris House

Name	Rank	Regiment	Unit	Department in which employed	Date joined the Firm
Barbereau Pierre	Soldat de lere Classe	Infanterie		Paris	0.5.14
Bellissant					
Blanquet Camille	Sergt	Infanterie		Paris	2.11.13
Bouhours Maurice				Paris	2.3.14
Brochet Constant Jean Marie	2/Class	Singalese Sharpshooters		Warehouse	0.0.10
Brunelliere				France	
Brazant Gaston	Brigadier	182 Regt d'Artillerie	Traveller	1.4.08	
Courtier				Paris	5.1.14
Delezy Charles				Paris	29.5.14
Degraeve Francis	2 eme Lt			Paris	24.2.13
Depla Henri	Caporal	ENE		Introducer	20.4.14
Duminy Rene				Paris	29.11.09
Dupont Ernest				Paris	6.3.11
Fournier Theo	Sergent Mitrailleus	Infanterie		Paris	25.1.13
Francois Robert	1st Class	165 Infanterie		Introducer	6.10.13
Goudeau E	Caporal	18 Division		Paris	24.2.13
Guerin				Paris	
Hallez Marcel	Infanterie			Introducer	2.6.13
Hanstete Frederic	Soldat de 2e Cl	Infanterie		Traveller	0.0.10
Harris T J	Gunner	RGA		Paris	30.3.08

Paris House

Name	Rank	Regiment	Unit	Department in which employed	Date joined the Firm
Jullian A				Paris	4.11.12
Leber Georges	Adjudant	24e Regt d'Infanterie	Introducer	1.4.10	
Legave Pierre	2e Canonier Servant	20 Regt d'Artillerie		Paris	15.2.13
Marchal Paul				Paris	17.4.11
Mercier Georges				Paris	15.9.12
Morin Andre	Soldat 2e Classe	Infanterie		Traveller	1.5.07
Morin Leon	Brigadier			Traveller	18.8.09
Morton Ernest Charles	2/Lieut	3rd Batt		Paris	0.2.12
Royer				Paris	27.4.14
Simbault				Paris	11.5.14
Thurneyssen Lucien Georges				Paris	5.11.13
Vanderbergh Camille	Infanterie			Traveller	29.9.10
Veyres Robert	Sergt			Paris	27.2.11

Belguim House

Name	Rank	Regiment	Unit	Department in which employed	Date joined the Firm
Claeijs J	Cav Sergt M	Transport Corps		Introducer	19.1.11
De Belva M A	1st SM	5th Lancers		Introducer	15.4.12
Gaudinne F E G	Pte	Amb Column Ad Corps		Traveller	
Petit H H	Capt	Belgian Line		Introducer	

Chapter 8

The Dansom Lane Shrine

The Dansom Lane Shrine features a list of the men who served from Pennington Street, Pemberton Street, Wilton Street, Wilde Street, Upton Street, Montrose Street and Dansom Lane. In the center, surrounded by a black border, is the list of the 'Fallen'.

No names were added to the Dansom Lane shrine after 1916. This accounts for the small number of dead within the black border. Many more men were killed from this area than are recorded here. And many of the men listed as serving were killed later in the war.

The shrine in its original position on the factory wall. It was removed in early 2001 as the old buildings are to be demolished.

The 'Great War' brought with it among the populace an enthusiasm for 'Street Shrines', this was not slow to catch on in Hull and soon took deep root in the Hessle Road district. On Saturday 23rd September 1916, striking scenes were witnessed, that would soon be repeated all over the city, in Walker Street, Wheeler Street, Marmaduke Street and Waterloo Street.

Each house down every street was decorated across its front or in its windows with flags and photographs of men serving at the front. The Hull Daily Mail described the scene on September 26th:

> "May Terrace in Walker Street is quite a show place, for the residents put out in a line down the center, tables containing photos adorned with glasses of flowers and coloured cloth, and there was a homely and pathetic touch furnished by memorial cards of relatives who have lost their lives. A cigar box stood on a table in this terrace and the hundreds of visitors on Saturday evening and again on Sunday were invited to contribute a copper for our sailors and soldiers tabacco. Faith Terrace was another that was elaborately adorned in honour of their menfolk serving their 'King and Country".

The shrine in Walker Street featured over 300 names, many of whom had made the ultimate sacrifice, this object of remembrance has long since vanished. The business of designing and making these monuments boomed in the city as this custom spread rapidly, craftsmen advertised in the local papers as the demand grew. The following item was printed in the Hull Daily Mail on September 26th, 1916:

> "Designs and estimates for Street Shrines and Rolls of Honour - Mark Taylor and Sons, Lithographers and printers, Chapel Lane, Hull."

In Dansom Lane a committee was formed by women who had either lost a son or who had sons serving at the front to raise funds for their own Street Shrine. The shrine was unveiled at a ceremony on 21st October 1916 by Mr W H Slack, who was on the Board of Directors at Reckitts, he spoke of the "self-sacrifice and loyalty of the men who had gone forward to fight.

A notable address was given by the reverend E J Harvey and Alderman Scott, Councillor Morrill also addressed the gathering. Large numbers of people crowded into Dansom Lane for the ceremony which took place on a Saturday afternoon at 3 o'clock. The shrine occupied a prominent position in Dansom

W H Slack

Lane and was liberally decorated with flags and flowers, as was the whole area. This fine piece of craftsmanship could be seen in the original position until only recently. In the Hull Daily Mail it stated:

"This is one of the most artistic shrines to be seen In the city and the number of men it shows to be serving does great credit to the locality."
The thoughts of the whole gathering that day went out to loved ones now overseas, there were others present for whom the event held only memories.

Reckitt's girls leaving work - on the left can be seen 'Subscription Mill', Dansom Lane, at the turn of the century.

When the ceremony was completed the 'East Hull Silver Band' played the National Anthem and marched past the platform where the dignitaries took the salute. A detachment of 'Boy Scouts' had also paraded for the occasion and the whole 'Lane' was decorated with patriotic flags and bunting.

The following letter to the Editor of the Hull Daily Mail was published on 24th October, 1916:

"Sir, kindly allow the undernamed committee of the Dansom Lane Shrine to express our sincere thanks to Philip B Reckitt who generously provided the decorations for the street. Also to Mr W H Slack who presided at the unveiling ceremony and who was supported by Alderman Scott, Councillor Morrill, Mr John Wright, the Reverend J Handy and the Reverend E J W Harvey, M A.

P B Reckitt

"Our thanks are also due to the members of the East Hull Silver Band and St Marks Troop of Boy Scouts and to the following ladies who rendered solos – Mrs Wells Miss F Bell Miss Leake and Miss Alice McDonald.

We also desire to thank very gratefully all who contributed towards the cost. We are, Sir etc".

Signed.

Mrs S Myers   Mrs J F McDonald   Mrs M Golden   Mrs A Cooper

The following list of 'The Fallen' is from the Dansom Lane Shrine, all of the men on it I have been able to trace in the 'official records' or in the Hull Daily Mail. Much information has been passed on to me by Mr M K Mann, who has been very generous in sharing his work on this subject as he continues his mammoth task of cataloguing all of Hull's Rolls of Honour. The Commonwealth War Graves Commission has kindly sent me the final resting places of those men who could be traced and the Cemetery Records Office, Chanterlands Avenue, Hull, was very helpful in passing on details of soldiers buried in Hull. A few of the names recorded here originally had little information with them and some of them can be seen in the Reckitts magazine – 'OURS'.

Between the World Wars these shrines were kept vibrant with fresh flowers and flags as the city kept alive the memory of its fallen sons. With the passing of time all but a handful have disappeared, as the nation all too soon forgets the sacrifice of that generation and most who stop to view the remaining monuments see with uncomprehending eyes the names surrounded with a black border, the hell they endured was real enough at that time and we should not forget their sacrifices.

Dansom Lane Shrine
The Fallen

Pte John Woodliff Barton, 2nd Battalion East Yorkshire Regiment, Reg No 11310, was born in Hull and enlisted in Hull. He was killed in action on May 5th 1915, his body was never found but his name is recorded on the Menin Gate, Ypres, Belgium, panels 21 and 31 (MR29).

Pte Barton appears in the Hull Daily Mail Roll of Honour on May 4th 1917.

Bombardier George Arthur Beacock, 37821, 'A' Battery, 107th Brigade, Royal Field Artillery. Killed in action 3rd September 1916. He has no known grave but is commemorated on the Thiepval memorial. Pier and face 1A and 8A (MR 21 PT 3). His name appears in the Hull Daily Mail Roll of Honour of 17th November 1916 and 3rd September 1917 – in memoriam.

Pte George Wilson Beckitt, 8th Battalion East Yorkshire Regiment, Reg No 21953, joined the firm on 27th February 1911. He was born in Hull and enlisted in Hull and was killed in action on June 13th 1916 at the age of 20. He is buried at Ridgewood Military Cemetery, Voormezeele, Belgium. Plot 2, Row T, grave 6. (B 37).

George Wilson Beckitt was the son of John and A E Beckitt of 264 Dansom Lane, Hull. His photograph can be seen in the 1916 chapter.

Pte William Arthur Binns, 8th Battalion East Yorkshire Regiment, Reg No 13554, was born in Hull and enlisted in Hull. He died of wounds on November 6th 1915 at the age of 21 years. He was the son of Margaret and Arthur Binns of 24 Pemberton Street, Hull. His name appears in the Hull Daily Mail 'In Memoriam' on10th November 1915.

Pte Binns is buried at Baileul Communal Cemetery extension, France. Plot 1, row F grave 192 (FR 285).

Pte James Blain, 12th Battalion East Yorkshire Regiment (3rd Hull Pals), Reg no 12/904, was born in Hull and enlisted at the Hull City Hall in September 1914. He went to Egypt in 1915 and was sent to France with his unit in March 1916, to prepare for the Somme Offensive. Pte Blain was wounded during the latter part of the Somme Campaign and succumbed to his wounds on August 11th 1916, at the age of 41. He is buried at St. Vaast Post Military Cemetery, Richebourg L'Avolie, France, Plot 3, row Q, grave 17. (FR 631).

He was the son of Mrs Emily Horne of Hull and left a widow, Gertrude Blain, and five children, who lived at 6 Holborn Mount, Holborn Street, Hull. Pte Blain's name appears in the Hull Daily Mail Roll of Honour on 12th September 1916.

On the Dansom Lane Shrine the following is recorded;

L/Cpl G Brocklesby, East Yorkshire Regiment; this man is not in the official records of the East Yorks. In the Hull Daily Mail he is reported to have served with Kings Own Yorks. Light Infantry. He was killed serving with the latter on 8th May 1915, aged 18. He was the son of Charles and Sarah Ann Brocklesby of 1 Wenlock Terrace, Rustenburg Street, Newbridge Road, Hull. His name is commemorated on the Menin Gate Memorial, Ypres. He has no know grave. His home address was Dairy Farm, Dansom Lane, Hull.

Cpl George Dent, 13th Battalion East Yorkshie Regiment, (4th Hull Pals) Reg No 13/427, was born in Hull and enlisted in Hull in September 1914 at the City Hall. His unit was sent to Egypt in 1915 and France in March 1916 to take part in the Somme Offensive. He was killed by shellfire during the latter stages of the Somme Campaign on 21st August 1916 and is buried at St Vaast Post Military Cemetery, Richebourg L'Avolie, France. Plot 3, row R, grave 11. (FR 631).

Cpl Dent was the son of Mr Dent, coal merchant, of Elm Tree House, Sutton Bank, Chapman Street, Hull. Cpl Dent's name appears in the Hull Daily Mail on 6th, 17th and 18th September 1916 and on 28th August 1917 'In Memoriam'.

Pte Walter Evans, 1/4th Battalion East Yorkshire Regiment, Reg No 2782, was born in Hull and enlisted in Hull. He was killed in action on 16th April 1916 and is buried at Lindenhock Chalet Military Cemetery, Kemmel, Belgium. Plot 1, row 1, grave 12. (B79). Walter Evans was the husband of Mrs A Evans, 6 Princess Walk, Craven Street, Hull: Late of 6 Cloverlly Avenue, Upton Street, Dansom Lane.

Pte John Percy Jacklin, Yorks and Lancs., reg No 34382, died of wounds on Septmeber 30th1916, at the age of 36,and is recorded in the Hull Daily Mail Roll of Honour for 16/17th October 1916. His home address was 15 Pemberton Street, Hull. He is buried at Dernancourt Communal Cemetery Extension, Somme, France. 111 B 4.

Pte J W Jagger, East Yorkshire Regiment. The only suitable Jagger in the official records of the East Yorks. is William, 1st Battalion, Reg No 8241, born Hull, enlisted Beverley. Killed in action on 10th July 1915, and buried at la Brique Military Cemetery . No home address given.

Sapper William Thomas Kemp 138432 Inland Water Transport. Royal Engineers. Enlisted in Hull. Died 3rd may 1916. He is buried in Gravesend Cemetery Kent.

Pte M Lockwood CD. This small amount of information recorded on the shrine was very confusing. CD should be CG - Coldstream Guards. Pte Mark Lockwood was killed serving with the 3rd Battalion Coldstream Guards on September 9th 1914, at the age or 23 years. He was the son of Issac and Eliza Lockwood of Hull and is buried in Boitron Churchyard. Seine-et-Marne. France.

Pte Thomas Macaulay 7th Bn East Yorkshire Rgt. Reg No 11119, was born in Hull and enlisted in Hull. He was killed in action on the first day of the Somme Battle. 1st July 1916 aged 26 years and was the husband of Ann Macaulay of 7 Hessle Avenue, Dansom Lane, Hull. Thomas is buried in Fricourt New Military Cemetery, France. Row C grave 18 (Fr 373).

Sgt Charles Edward Myers (Cpl. in the official records), 1st Battalion East Yorkshire Regiment, Reg. No. 9790, was born at Gravesend, Kent, and enlisted in Hull before the war as a regular. This young soldier was killed in action at the 1st Battle for Ypres, on 28th October, 1914. He is buried in the Canadian Cemetery No 2, Neuville – St Vaast, France. Plot 20, row B, grave 8. (Fr 1896)

Pte George William Myers, 1st Battalion East Yorkshire Regiment, Reg No 3/6112, was born at Chatham and enlisted in Hull. He was killed in action during the opening stages of the Somme Campaign on July 23rd 1916, and his body was never found, his name is recorded on the 'The Thiepval Memorial', France. Pier 2, face C. (MR21)

Pte Albert Needham 1/4th Bn East Yorkshire Regiment. (not recorded in soldiers died) Reg No 2816. Died of consumption at the age of 18 years on 29th April 1915. He was buried in Hedon Road Cemetery, Hull, on 3rd May 1915. He was the son of G H Needham of 5 Railway Cottages, Sutton Bank, Hull.

Able Seaman Albert Reed, Royal Naval Reserve, was killed in action in the North Sea on April 27th, 1916, at the age of 24. His home address was 25 Hume Street, Hull. He served on MMR HMS Killingholme. Albert's name is recorded on the Plymouth Naval Memorial.

Pte Herbert Sellers, 1/4th Battalion East Yorkshire Regiment, Reg No 4715, was born in Hull and enlisted in Hull. He died of wounds on September 19th 1916, and is buried at St Sever Cemetery, Rouen, France. Plot B, Row 22, grave 27. (FR145, PT2). His photograph and other details can be seen in the 1916 Chapter.

Pte George Spires, 1st Battalion Coldstream Guards, was killed in action at the age of 22 years on December 22nd 1914. His photograph and other details can be seen in the 1916 Chapter. He has no known grave but is commemorated on the Le Touret Memorial, France. Panels 2 and 3. (MR 22 PT8)

Pte G W Thurnell WYR. Recorded as William Thurnell in Soldiers Died and by the War Grave Commission. He was born in Hull and enlisted in Leeds into the 11th Battalion West Yorkshire Regiment. William was killed serving with that unit on 2nd April 1916 and is buried in Lievin Communal Cemetery Extension. France.

11024. Pte Edgar Winson, 10th Bn West Yorkshire Regiment. Edgar was born in Spurn, Linc's resided and enlisted in Hull and was killed in action on December 11th 1915. He has no known grave but his life is commemorated on the Menin Gate Memorial to the missing. Belgium.

Pte Harry Edmund Wolfe, 2/4th Battalion East Yorkshire Regiment, Reg No 2463, was born in Hull and enlisted in Hull. He died at home on 23rd March 1916, and was buried in Hedon Road Cemetery, Hull, at the age of 20. Plot 134, grave 91 (Yorks 1)

Pte Wolfe was the son of Samuel and Martha Wolfe of 12 Woolaton Avenue, Dansom Lane, Hull.

The following is a list of the men who served as recorded on the Dansom Lane Shrine. It may be remembered that it was completed in 1916, so any man who enlisted in late 1916, 1917 or 1918 will not be included. Some of those listed were killed after 1916 and are marked with an asterix, I am sure that more men were killed than I have been able to trace. Many of those on this list would have been badly maimed, wounded or taken prisoner.
There are many mistakes on this list. Some units are incorrect. First initials can in some cases be confusing and ranks are often wrong.

Dansom Lane

J H Acey
Pte E M Adams
Pte K Allison EYR
Pte J Barker EYR
Pte G W Bell EYR
Pte J Benson EYR
Gnr A Bill RGA
Pte H Bilton EYR*
Pte A W Brown RF
PteJ Brown EYR*
Pte W Coates CSG
Pte G H Cracknell EYR*
A Dawson HMS
Pte A Deyes EYR (Discharged)
Pte H Easterby RFA
Pte R Edkins EYR
Gnr G Tanton RFA
Pte G W Fieldhouse RAMC
Pte L Fieldhouse RMLI
Pte F Fuller G Guards
Sgt T R Gascoine EYR
Gnr M Golder RFA
Pte A Gorbert EY
Pte J Gorbert RE
Pte W Gray EYR
Pte G W Harrison EYR
Gnr W Holt RGA
Pte J Kendrick EYR
J Langan RN

Cpl G Acey CSG
J Alexanader Transport
Pte R Arksey EYR
S Bee Minesweeper
Cpl H Benson NF
Sgt G Benstead RAMC
Pte A Bilton GH
Gnr F Boylan RGA
Pte J H Brown EYR*
Pte W Brown MGC
Pte J H S Cooper MGC
Gnr J W Daddy RFA*
Pte F Deyes EYR
Gnr F Denman RFA
Gnr G R Edkins RGA
Pte J R Edkins EYR
L/Cpl H Farrow EYR*
Pte J Fieldhouse RGA
Pte J W Frankland
Pte G H Galloway EYR
Pte W Grenville EYR
Pte J Goodyear MGC
Pte G Gorbert EYR*
Pte H B Gray EYR
Sgt H Gregory EYR
Pte J Haylock EYR
Sgt A Hotchkin AFA
Gnr C Kershaw RGA
G Lord Minesweeper

Pte A Lurrimar EYR
Pte G Lowery EYR
Pte A Macdonald EYR
Pte G R Mcdonald EYR
Cpl GA Marshall MGC
J Mayes RN
Pte G W Mills NF
Pte C Mitchell EYR
Pte H Moore EYR
Pte G Needham NF*
Gnr H Nock RGA*
Gnr W Overton RFA
Pte J Ovington EYR
L/Copl G Pattison ERFRE
Pte A Pexton ASC
Pte H Pickering ASC
Pte C T Purkiss RFA
Pte A Reed Transport*
Pte P Revell CAMC
F Richardson Minesweeper
Pte C Rothery Minesweeper
Pte W Scott EYR
Pte G F Shaw KRR
Pte R Shaw KRR
H T Skelton RN
Cpl G Starkey
Pte J Tranmer EYR
Pte W Tranmer EYR
Gnr J W Whittan RFA
Pte F Wright RFA*
Pte F Young EYR
Pte J V Lorrimar RG
Cpl H Macauley EYR
L/Cpl I Macdonald
Gnr A W Marshall AAC*
Pte J Mayes EYR*
T Melady Coastguard
Pte G C Milner RGA
Pte R N Moore BE
Pte F Myers EYR
Pte W Needham NF*
G W Overton HMS
Pte A Ovington EYR
Driver G Pattison RFA
L/Cpl H Pearson Hussars*
Cpl C H Pickering ASC*
Driver E H Pickering ASC
Pte E Purkiss WYR*
Pte J Revell WYR*
R P Revell CAMC
Pte H Richardson CS*
Pte L Scott EYR*
Rifleman G F Shaw KRR
Rifleman R Shaw KRR
Pte C Simpson AC
Pte A Sleight DLI
Pte J Sumpton RETS
Pte A Tranmer EYR
Pte J R Wallis EYR
Chief P O Jesse Wood RN
Pte S Wright EYR

Pennington Street

A Berridge RE*
W H Briglin RFA
A E Everett EY
Cyclist J Everett EY
Trooper H Fox ERY
S Berridge EYR
Cpl J Clayton EYR*
Cyclist J O Everett EY
Cyclist W T Everett EY
Pte S L Fox

Gnr J Frow RFA
Sgt J W Horn EY
Pte C W Ladigus RAMC
Gnr S Osgerby RGA
Gnr J Osgerby RGA
Pte J Sellers EYR
Pte W Spires CSG
CC Wetherell RFA
Pte H Higginson EYR
Pte S Irwin EYR
Pte B Osgerby ASC
Gnr T Osgerby RFA
Pte C Sellers EYR
Pte J E Sellers ACC
Gnr G Thurnwell RFA

Pemberton Street

Driver A Armstrong RFA
A Eastwood Transport
Bugler A Elvin RE
Pte F R Elvin ASC
Pte H Elvin RAMC
Pte A W Gaunt KOYLI
Spr J Jacklin NDRE*
Pte C F Nunn NF
Spr H Scott RE
Pte A P Thurwell EYR
Sto D Ward RFR
Pte E Drewery EYR
Pte J F Eastwood EYR
App F Elvin Transport
Sub Lieut G Elvin RNR
Pte S Eyre EYR
Gnr S C Huffee RFA
Spr F Milestone ER
Pte B Robinson EYR
W Scott Transport
Pte A R Thurnell EYR*
Spr W J Waring

Wilton Street

H W G Eglan RN
A Firth RN
Sgt G E Mitchell Hamps Reg
Pte J G Willey ERYY
Sub Lieut W Wright RNR
J W Eglan RN
Sgt P Goodare EYR*
Gnr C M Rounding RGA
Charles Wright Minesweeper

Wilde Street

Pte F Crompton EYR
Pte S Ducker EYR
Pte C W Glenton RAMC
F Gordon RN
Driver C F Lingard RFA
Pte F Watson EYR
Pte W Crompton CSG
Bdr H Glenton RFA
Pte F Glenton RAMC
Pte W H Hall TMB
Pte C Roginson ASC
Pte G W Watson RGA

Nurse Hilda Wright Army SE
Nurse Lily Wright Red Cross
E Wilburn RN

Upton Street

Pte J W Bays RGA
Gnr L Binns RGA
Pte G J Chapman EYR*
Pte H Claxton EYR*
S B Cracknwll HMS
Cpl F Fenton EYR
Spr F Fenton RE
Pte R Fenwick NF
Spr G Flowers RE
Pte F Grimbleby EYR
Pte S A Hay EYR
Pte J Hunter RFA
Gnr LA Hunter EYR*
Pte H Jewitt KOYLI
Pte P Tigg EYR
Driver A Keightley RHA
Pte D Kirby EYR
Pte A Lockwood RFA
Pte C Lockwood NF
J Marrow HMS
Sgt C W Nicholson RFA
Pte R Scotney EYR
Pte R Redfern EYR
A E Shephard EYR*
R Smith RN
Pte H Stevens ASC*
Pte C Whitely NF

Montrose Street

L/Cpl J Barron
L/Cpl H Baxter CSG
Gnr A Bell RGA
Pte F Binns CSG
Spr W Binns RE
Pte W H Clark TR
Pte A Daviss EYR
Pte G French NF
Pte J French CSG
Driver C R Gothard RFA
Driver C Grantham RFA
Pte H Hammond LR
Sgt Major J Jackson EYR
Trumpeter D Johnson RFA
Driver M F Milner RFA
L/Cpl A Rowntree EYR
L/Cpl F Sampson EYR
Gnr A W Winters RGA

The ties that link the city of Hull with Reckitt's Factory and the Great War might be looser than before, but they would never be severed so long as people lived that remembered, even if they had never served in that distant conflict. Those individuals would be numerous until three full decades after the Second Great War had ended. The men who returned to Reckitts' Factory in 1919 and 1920 met formally to rekindle that grand spirit forged in adversity, but the ties were also in the safe keeping of the old men who preferred to join no organization but lived their lives tending their gardens, having the occasional pint at their local or playing on the bowling green in the hot summer. Their middle-aged children knew their tales about the Great War off by heart, for they too had lived that time through sympathetic participation in another's experience. The grandchildren also knew of those far off times, introduced in infancy to the tradition by the old men with an informal but very deliberate laying on of hands. A minority of these younger people, like this author, the last generation to inherit the traditions of empire, would also pass on the tablets and so ensure that continuity was assured.

In Holy Trinity Church, hanging high above the congregation, are the Great War standards of Hull's Territorial Battalion, the 1/4th East Yorkshire Regiment, now tattered and torn. The standards of the 1st and 2nd Hull Pals are in the same church, now so fragile and faded they have had to be framed behind Perspex to preserve them. I asked the people at the church whose standards they were and received a puzzled look and a shrug of the shoulders. These once proud mementoes of great events are now only fading objects of interest.

The street shrines of Hull have dwindled to a handful over the years. Many were lost in the Blitz, others were thrown away during the mass demolition of the 60's or when old churches were closed down. Others were of such poor quality they gradually deteriorated over the years until information recorded on them was illegible. The demolitions in Hull continue today as new roads are built and more modern buildings are needed. The Dansom Lane Shrine was taken down early in 2001 and now sits in a factory storeroom awaiting its final fate. There it sits on the concrete floor, dusty and so unkempt that it is virtually impossible to read the names recorded because of the dirty glass.

This record of human suffering and service recorded upon this small memorial freezes in time the harsh history of life and death in wartime. Decades after the Great War we now see the remaining street shrines obscurely or with a hurried glance. During and after the war they would have been highly visible

and arresting to all. This little monument commemorates not only individuals but is a celebration of an unprecedented response to the call to arms. Calling them "Street Shrines' gives immediate religious echoes blending well with the view of the war as a conflict between the forces of darkness and the forces of light.
The Reckitts factory memorial and garden of remembrance have been beautifully kept since 1920, new memorial plaques, featuring the men of both world wars who lost their lives, have been cast in bronze and it is hard to imagine anyone being unimpressed when viewing this magnificent and moving memorial. The central figure of sacrifice and her fallen son reaffirm the nobility of the warrior by appealing to an ancient tradition expressed in a romanticized form; highlighting the soldiers sacrifice and the civilian debt. This example of monumental art provided a focus for the people of Reckitts' factory in their ceremonies of remembrance and public mourning which began in the decade following the Armistice and which continue to this day.

Families in Hull were torn apart by the Great War as people looked out onto a world where individuals and groups of individuals once present were present no more. The stress of bereavement was inflicted in massive and concentrated quantities on the community. Most of the Reckitts' boys killed have no known grave, many of their families hoped they were taken prisoner or were still lying on the battlefield unfound. Eventually hope faded; these men are now commemorated on the great memorials to the 'Missing' which can be found in all theatres of war. The rest lie in the ground they once contested or in the large cemeteries where the hospitals and casualty clearing stations once stood. The last resting places of the Reckitts' men, and of all the other men who fell in the Great War, are silent and beautifully kept by the War Graves Commission. The land that once echoed to the sound of armies in combat and the agonies they suffered now stands enveloped by a profound silence. Visitors still come to pay their respects and on the summer breeze only the sweetness of birdsong high above can be heard.

The Reckitts men, like so many others, were rudely torn away from the joys of life and remembrance is only one step in acknowledging the sacrifice made by so many. However, I would suggest that we all owe them a continuing duty to preserve these monuments of war that commemorate them as a permanent record of the role they have played in our heritage and history.

Conclusion

Remembrance 1991

The Industrial Chaplain, Mr C Percy stands before the War Memorial in the Reckitt's Garden of Remembrance, November, 1991.
To the rear on the grass – left and right – can be seen the new rolls of honour featuring men of both Great Wars who gave their lives.

Every year since the end of the first 'Great War' Reckitts employees and officials have gathered in the Garden of Remembrance, Dansom Lane, to pay their respects to the 'Fallen' and remember the men who gave all for their country. New rolls of honour have recently been made and now stand behind the statue of sacrifice, cast in bronze and mounted on stone blocks. In November, 1991, I gained permission to attend one of these gatherings.

At 10 o'clock I arrived at the factory reception lounge with my camera not knowing what to expect. As I sat there the room began slowly to fill with people, old soldiers bedecked with medals and wearing proudly their regimental badges on their berets stood smartly about chatting and laughing. The civilians present greeted each other in a way that only people with one purpose and with one mind could do.

At this point I felt the whole atmosphere to change to one of a united body with a solemn task. Boxes were brought into the room and beautiful wreaths of poppies taken out, each with its own inscription. Trays of poppies were handed round and an air of expectation filled the gathering.

The old soldiers left the room first followed by the others, I waited till nearly the last and was told I could stand anywhere so long as I kept out of the way.

As I stepped outside – the first thing I saw was the veterans wearing white gloves and carrying their standards. The morning was cold with brilliant sunshine befitting such an event. The white memorial stood out magnificently in the morning sun and was in sharp contrast to the green of the smartly cut grass and red brick of the buildings. The civilians stood in a crescent facing the memorial with Mr C Percy, Chaplain, at their head. On the grass in front of each person was a white wooden cross with a poppy at its center, the standard bearers marched to their positions and the service began.

Mr Percy's words rang out loud and clear on that cold morning when no wind disturbed the colourful standards, an old soldier stood to one side and read out Binyon's immortal opening lines:

> **"They shall not grow old as we that are left grow old, age shall not weary them nor the years condemn.**
> **At the going down of the sun and in the morning we will remember them."**

At 11 am the whole gathering stood in silence as the ex-soldiers lowered their standards and the last post was sounded. Nothing stirred as the shrill bugle call cut through the still morning air. This was an emotional moment and one I shall never forget, the faces of the 'Fallen' flitted before my mind's eye as the thoughts of the whole gathering were focused upon their sacrifice, a poignant tribute to the sufferings of these fine young men.

As the service progressed the Company Directors and representatives approached the memorial in pairs and with due respect laid their wreaths around the fountain, pausing each time to bow their heads and think of the 'Fallen' before turning and taking their places once again in the crescent. The massed red poppies of remembrance gave added meaning to this beautifully kept memorial and when the last wreath was laid, the final words said, the gathering slowly filed back into the factory reception lounge.

Mr P Wade and Mr I Stewart - standing before the monument.
Outer Crescent: From left to right
Mr D Clark Mr B McLean, Trainee, Mr C Percy - Industrial Chaplain, Mr T Parker Mr F Beckett Mr M Kay Mr N Varey, Two employees.

The old soldiers stood outside folding away their standards and chatting, I paused to talk to them a while. Such events for men who have experienced battle must be very important as in their minds the 'Fallen' will never age and the act of remembrance is paramount. After the event I met Jane Lister who told me of the new rolls of honour in the gardens and allowed me to return at a later date to photograph them.

The Reckitt's men who fought in the World Wars and who gave their lives are still buried in the ground they onc e contested. The cemeteries near the various battle areas are beautifully kept and have a sad beauty all of their own.
At 11 am on the 11th day of the 11th month 1918, the Armistace was signed and the 'Great War' came to an end. It felt good to be alive on that cold November morning as a strange stillness descended over the Western Front, a stillness that could be heard around the world. In 1919 the men returned home leaving behind them their comrades buried in massed graves. The Reckitt's men who returned can be found still in a special Remembrance issue of 'OURS' of 1919, many bore the scars of battle, many were badly maimed, most carried mental scars with them for the rest of their lives as they returned to a world greatly changed from the one they knew, a world not renewed.
Some men who returned to Reckitts never recovered from their war experience and during the early 1920's men still died as they succumbed to ailments and wounds received on active service.

The following minor mistakes have been made on the new Rolls of Honour:

The names of Charles Darling and Alfred Dean have been omitted; nor are they to be found in the Commemorative issue of 'OURS' –1919. However both can be seen in the 1916 Chapter.

Leek G A: initials should be G E
Marham L: initial should be J
Piercey A: initials should be W A
Wolfe R E: initials should be H E
Nasley:should be Nasbey

The names recorded here are not only of men who worked at the Hull works, those from other branches are as follows:

H Richard - Paris	F Natton - Paris	Lemoine - Paris
C Lauren - Paris	A Laurent – Paris	P Guermonpres – Paris
M Babault – Paris	A Dumez - Paris	P Pasnelle – Paris
V D James – Australia	H D Wyatt – New Zealand	

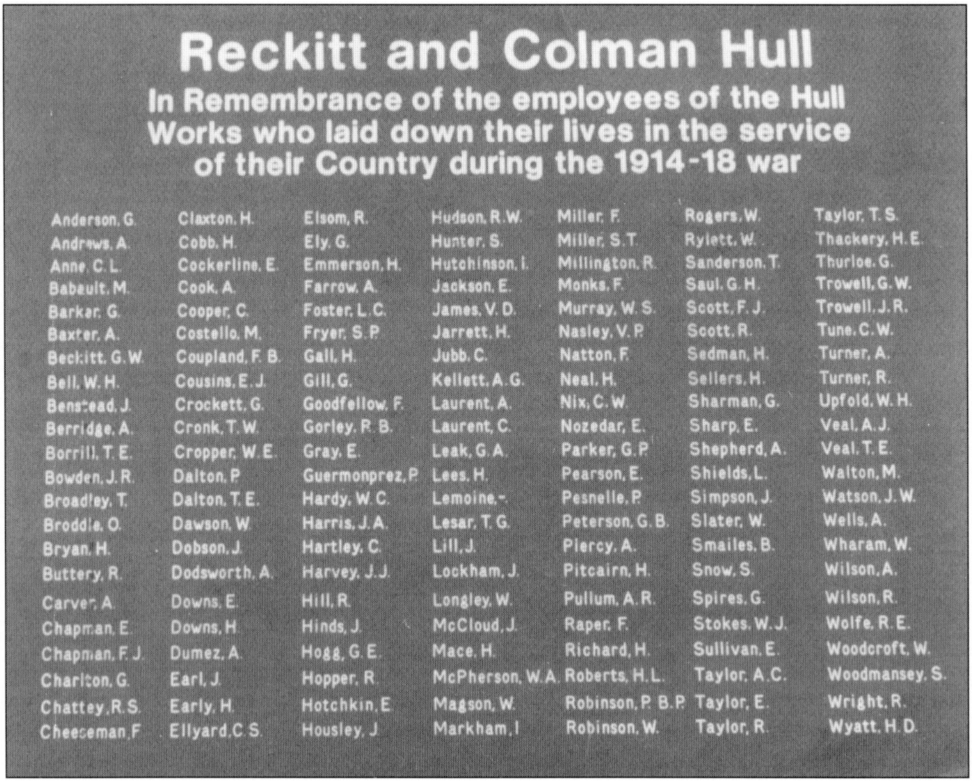
Reckitt and Colman Hull
In Remembrance of the employees of the Hull Works who laid down their lives in the service of their Country during the 1914-18 war
Anderson, G.
Andrews, A.
Anne, C.L.
Babault, M.
Barker, G.
Baxter, A.
Beckitt, G.W.
Bell, W.H.
Benstead, J.
Berridge, A.
Borrill, T.E.
Bowden, J.R.
Broadley, T.
Broddle, O.
Bryan, H.
Buttery, R.
Carver, A.
Chapman, E.
Chapman, F.J.
Charlton, G.
Chattey, R.S.
Cheeseman, F.
Claxton, H.
Cobb, H.
Cockerline, E.
Cook, A.
Cooper, C.
Costello, M.
Coupland, F.B.
Cousins, E.J.
Crockett, G.
Cronk, T.W.
Cropper, W.E.
Dalton, P.
Dalton, T.E.
Dawson, W.
Dobson, J.
Dodsworth, A.
Downs, E.
Downs, H.
Dumez, A.
Earl, J.
Early, H.
Ellyard, C.S.
Elsom, R.
Ely, G.
Emmerson, H.
Farrow, A.
Foster, L.C.
Fryer, S.P.
Gall, H.
Gill, G.
Goodfellow, F.
Gorley, R.B.
Gray, E.
Guermonprez, P.
Hardy, W.C.
Harris, J.A.
Hartley, C.
Harvey, J.J.
Hill, R.
Hinds, J.
Hogg, G.E.
Hopper, R.
Hotchkin, E.
Housley, J.
Hudson, R.W.
Hunter, S.
Hutchinson, I.
Jackson, E.
James, V.D.
Jarrett, H.
Jubb, C.
Kellett, A.G.
Laurent, A.
Laurent, C.
Leak, G.A.
Lees, H.
Lemoine, -
Lesar, T.G.
Lill, J.
Lockham, J.
Longley, W.
McCloud, J.
Mace, H.
McPherson, W.A.
Magson, W.
Markham, I
Miller, F.
Miller, S.T.
Millington, R.
Monks, F.
Murray, W.S.
Nasley, V.P.
Natton, F.
Neal, H.
Nix, C.W.
Nozedar, E.
Parker, G.P.
Pearson, E.
Pesnelle, P.
Peterson, G.B.
Piercy, A.
Pitcairn, H.
Pullum, A.R.
Raper, F.
Richard, H.
Roberts, H.L.
Robinson, P. B.P.
Robinson, W.
Rogers, W.
Rylett, W.
Sanderson, T.
Saul, G.H.
Scott, F.J.
Scott, R.
Sedman, H.
Sellers, H.
Sharman, G.
Sharp, E.
Shepherd, A.
Shields, L.
Simpson, J.
Slater, W.
Smailes, B.
Snow, S.
Spires, G.
Stokes, W.J.
Sullivan, E.
Taylor, A.C.
Taylor, E.
Taylor, R.
Taylor, T.S.
Thackery, H.E.
Thurloe, G.
Trowell, G.W.
Trowell, J.R.
Tune, C.W.
Turner, A.
Turner, R.
Upfold, W.H.
Veal, A.J.
Veal, T.E.
Walton, M.
Watson, J.W.
Wells, A.
Wharam, W.
Wilson, A.
Wilson, R.
Wolfe, R.E.
Woodcroft, W.
Woodmansey, S.
Wright, R.
Wyatt, H.D.

The New Memorial Plaque in the Reckitt's Garden of Remembrance.
For the men of that factory who gave their lives in the 'Great War'

Appendix 'A'

'OURS' 1920

We have pleasure in recording that Lieut. Allen W. Jagoe was summoned to attend at Buckingham Palace on June 11th to receive the award of the Military Cross.

Lieut. Jagoe was born in 1886. He entered our service in 1911, and enlisted when the War commenced, first serving in the ranks and winning the Military Medal. He afterwards received a commission. It is worthy of note that he is an Irishman who volunteered for service. He represented the Firm in the Cork district, and is now working for us in the Sheffield district.

"Ours" sends hearty congratulations to Lieut. Jagoe.

Appendix 'B'

'OURS' 1920

Mr T F Williams

We much regret to record the death of Mr Thomas F Williams, who worked as Introducer on Mr A S Elsworth's ground, taking the Ashton-under-Lyne district.

Mr Williams was born on March 9th 1886, and entered our service on October 30th 1910. He joined up early in the War and was badly wounded in 1918. He resumed his work as Introducer in July 1919, during which year he married, but unfortunately he broke down in February 1920, and although everything possible was done for him, he passed away on June 13th 1920.

Mr George Chapman

Another old employee who has passed on is Mr George James Chapman. He was at first employed in the Starch Works, where he started in 1904 at the age of eighteen. He joined up at the beginning of the War, but unfortunately contracted consumption during his military service. After his demobilization he was transferred to the Cardboard Preparation Plant in May 1919. His health, however, was unsatisfactory, and three months spent at the Cottingham Tuberculosis Hospital produced no permanent good. He was compelled to cease work finally in August of this year and died on November 1st. His Foreman, Mr G Curtis, speaks of him as a very good worker, steady, industrious and conscientious. To his widow we would convey our sympathy in the loss she has suffered.

George's home address was 4 Rosedale Avenue Upton Street, Hull. He was buried in Hedon Road Cemetery, Hull on 4th November 1920.

‘OURS’ 1921

We regret to note the death of Mr John F Brady (Sawmill) in his 29th Year. He commenced work in the Sawmill in 1907. During the War he served with the 10th East Yorks in France for a year and was held by the Germans as a prisoner of war for six months. He never appeared to recover fully from the effects of his imprisonment in Germany and went off work in February 1921. He was sent to Ilkley for a fortnight by the firm, but unfortunately no renewal of health followed. He died on June 27th. His father, who died 16 years ago, was also a sawyer with the firm.

His Foreman, Mr Curtis, speaks of him as a good conscientious worker. We would express our sympathy with his family in the loss they bear.

Appendix 'C'

HONOURS & AWARDS

Military Cross and Bar
C M Slack

Military Cross
H E Hill A W Jagoe W H B Martin

D.C.M.
T G Lesar C. Streat C Witherwick

Military Medal and Bar
A Clark W Moore A Walsh

Military Medal
J Baines T Bricklebank F Caborn J Gates W C Hardy A Harrison J Hopkinson A W Jagoe
N J Leathley H Lundie A Mills G Milner C W Nix Wm Smith Chas Taylor W R Wharf
T F Williams R Wilson H B Lees

Meritorious Service Medal
A W Austin Frank R Harrison T Nicholson A E Stead

Mentioned in Despatches
E Brown J H Cassie F J Connor S T Fox N H Joy (twice)
E O Morris F A Munton T Vincent W A Wilby

Croix De Guerre (France)
Pierre Legave Theo Fournier Georges Leber

Mentioned in Despatches (France)
Gaston Bruzant Andre Morin

Croix De Guerre (Belgium)
J Claeijs

Militaire Medal 2nd Class (Belgium)
J Claeijs

Arabian Decoration (Chevalier du Ouissam Alaouite)
Constant Jean Marie Brochet

Civil Decorations

Philip B Reckitt Order of the British Empire
Harold J Reckitt Reconnaisance Francaise, 2nd Class

Appendix 'D'

Letter from Mr W Aumonier - Memorial Sculptor

In the report of the Reckitt's Works Council meeting of 1920, it states that the name of Pte. Edward Jackson, 'D' Coy, 8th Battalion East Yorkshire Regiment, had been omitted from the list of the 'Fallen' as shown on the memorial tablets. The Council decided to act upon the sculptor's instructions, Mr Aumonier of London, and wait six months to allow time for other names to be added as well as the above. The following letter was sent to the Council regarding this matter:

"To the Secretary of the Works' Council

Dear Sir,

The omission of a name or two is a frequent occurrence on these memorials I find, and it is as well to leave it open for a time in case of further alterations. Such a large staff as Reckitts must, of necessity, make it very difficult to check the names, and you will I imagine sooner or later hear of others. Only recently I finished on with the names cut in marble, and it was discovered after that three of the names were living men who were very surprised to see their names amongst the fallen! In your case it will not be very difficult as you have plenty of room at the bottom. If it is only one name it can be centered between the two columns. You can't of course, get it alphabetical but no one notices that.

If you send me the name I will draw it out and your local man can do it quite alright from my drawing, as it is rather a long way to send from London just to do one name.

Yours faithfully

W. AUMONIER."

Appendix 'E'

'OURS - January, 1920

Gifts to Returned Service Men

On December 5th, a meeting took place between the Directors and the men who had served in H.M. Forces and returned to work.

The Meeting was first addressed by the Rt. Hon. T R Ferens, J.P., who stated how pleased the Directors were at the safe return of so many of the workers. He announced that it had been decided to distribute a sum of § 8,000 amongst them. Mr Ferens gave details of the method in which this would be shared out.

The particulars are as follows:-

> Resolved:- That § 8,000 be distributed amongst the Companys employees who have served in H.M. Forces during the Great War, and that it be divided so that men in the Company's employ on the 4th August, 1914, should receive 25 per cent more than those who were employed subsequent to that date."

This amount is sufficient to pay those employees with the firm prior to the 4th August, 1914, 5s. per month for each month's service, and those employees who joined the Firm after the 4th August, 4s. per month.

Qualifications:-

1. Employees must have been in the service of the Company on the 4thAugust, 1914, or

2. If employed since 4th August, 1914, they must have completed three months service with the Company prior to enlistment.

3. Allowance will be made for Widows or Children or Parents of men who have been killed in action, or who have died on service, or who are missing in action.

4. Allowance will be paid to those men who have signed on for further service with the colours, and will be paid to the date of re-enlistment..

5. No allowance will be made to men who have not returned to the Company's employ since their discharge from the Army etc.: nor to those who returned to the Company's employ and left prior to the 5th December, 1919.

He then called upon Mr W H Slack to say a few words, and in the course of Mr Slack's remarks he emphasised the interest which the Works Council had taken in the return of their fellow workers. This had lead to the Directors inviting members of the Works Council to be present with them that evening.

Mr Slack also stated that it was the intention of the Directors to have a Social Gathering somewhere between Christmas and the New Year, so that they might spend an evening together, but the date and particulars of this function would be announced later.

A vote of thanks was moved by Mr G Cooper, seconded by Captain T L Leggott, and carried with acclamation.

Mr Ferens called upon Mr Arthur B Reckitt to reply on behalf of the Directors, who expressed the pleasure that it gave the whole of the Directors to be able to meet the men, and stated that he hoped his son, Captain Geoffrey Reckitt, M.C., would be able to participate in the forthcoming event, the date of which has been fixed for January 8th.

Appendix 'F'

Record of Service by Men of Reckitts' Division
of
St John Ambulance Brigade

Prior to the formation of the Division on 27th July, 1912, Ambulance Classes had been held for many years and a large number of employees had qualified for First-Aid Certificates. The Division created a revival of interest amongst these Ambulance workers, and , at its inception, numbered 24 all ranks. All the uniforms and equipment were provided by the Firm.

Members turned out on numerous occasions on public duty connected with the Hull Corps, also at Reckitt's Sports, &c. In addition, valuable experience was gained in the treatment of accidents in the Works from time to time. Their records show that over 200 cases were treated during 1912/13.

On the outbreak of War, the strength of the Division had increased to 43, all of whom volunteered for service, and as the majority of the members were registered with the Home Hospital Reserve, the first draft of 18 N C O's and men were dispatched to the Military Hospitals at Aldershot, Colchester, and Woking, on 8th August, 1914. Further drafts were sent later to other Military Hospitals in response to calls from the War Office through the St John Brigade, and subsequently, nearly all ranks were absorbed in one or other of the Reserves administered through the Brigade.

Whilst serving in the Home Hospitals, many volunteered for service abroad, and were eventually transferred to France, Salonika, Mesopotamia, &c.

Three members of the Division who were not accepted for service with the Army, did creditable work in connection with local Air-Raids, and also V A D transport duties.

Appendix 'G'

Employees' Contributions

During the War voluntary weekly deductions were made from the wages of men and girls, for the provision of parcels of foodstuffs, sweets and cigarettes, sent out to fellow employees every six or seven weeks. To non-smokers and men in hospital an equivalent in cash was sent.

Prisoners of War were also adopted.

From November,1916, to April 1919, the employees contributed § 709 for parcels and cigarettes, and § 176 for parcels to Prisoners of War, a total of § 885.

The Christmas parcels sent out by the Company were packed by Forewomen and Helpers in their own time.

Lord Mayor of Hull s Fund for Blinded Soldiers, Sailors and Civilians

The total amount contributed by employees on behalf of the above Fund was § 581, being made up of § 443 from Kingston and Morley Street Works, and § 138 from Canister Works.

Girls Working Party

The Girls Working Party consisted of Forewomen, Helpers and several girls from various rooms, who worked very hard in providing comforts for the men at the Front. The credit of forming the organization was due to Miss M Jones, the Head Social Worker. The work which was done at home, commenced in September, 1914 and was carried on to the end of 1918. the following is the record of work done during this period: 3772 Sandbags, 1240 Socks, 370 Scarves, 200 Shirts, 87 Belts, 424 Mittons, 138 Cuffs or Gloves, 59 Helmets.

Special Constables and Volunteers
Hull

96 men who were exempted from military service on account of age or indispensability, served as Special Constables. From April 12th 1915 to August 5th 1918, there were 49 air raid calls and eight air raid attacks.

63 employees also enlisted in Local Volunteer regiments, the training for which was done during evenings and week-ends.

Appendix H

A Complete List of the Fallen

Name	Rank	Regiment	Branch of Works in which employed	Date joined the Firm		Date of Death
Anderson George	Pte	12th E Yorks	Canister	21.10.07	Killed	28.8.16
Andrews Albert	Pte	4th E Yorks	KW Brasso	28.1.07	Killed	16.7.16
Anne Charles Louis	Corpl	Infanterie	Paris House, Introducer	23.10.11	Killed	
Babault Maurice			Paris House	3.3.09	Killed	26.4.16
Barker G	Pte	18th KRR	Representative	9.2.14	Killed	6.8.17
Baxter Albert	Pte	4th E Yorks	KW Room 17	22.7.09	Killed	9.7.15
Beckitt George W	Pte	8th E Yorks	KW Hoists	27.2.11	Killed	13.6.16
Bell William Henry	Pte	8th E Yorks	KW WB Dept	20.3.11	Killed	3.5.17
Benstead J	Pte	Tank Corps	Morley St Wks	8.6.14	Died of wounds	23.10.18
Borrill Thomas Edgar	Pte	2/8th Sherwood	KW Electns	21.9.11	Killed	26.9.17
Bowden J R	Pte	4thE Yorks	KW S Mill	13.5.07	Killed	24.4.15
Broadley Thomas	Pte	4th E Yorks	Morley Street	25.8.14	Killed	26.4.15
Broddle O	Pte	13th Lincs	KW		Killed	22.4.17
Bryan Herbert	Pte	22nd DLI	KW Box Shop	6.2.13	Missing	26.3.18
Buttery Robert	L/Corp	7th E Yorks	Canister	3.2.15	Killed	12.5.17
Carver Arthur	Pte	4th E Yorks	KW Hoists	7.2.88	Killed	24.11.15
Chapman Edward	L/Corp	3rd E Yorks	Morley Street	22.8.10	Died (flu)	9.10.18
Chapman F J		4th E Yorks	Canister Wks	21.7.14	Killed	6.8.16
Charlton George	Pte	11th E Yorks	Morley Street	18.8.14	Killed	20.2.18
Chattey Robert S	Pte	2/24th London Regt	London	20.12.06	Killed	13.12.17
Cheeseman Fred	Pte	2/7th Man	Canister	1.6.09	Killed	
Claxton Henry	Pte	16th Notts & Derby	KW Packing	20.10.91	Killed	15.11.17
Cobb Harry	Pte	5th Bord' Regt	KW Export	6.2.11	Killed	30.9.16
Cockerline Ernest	Pte	1/6th W Yorks	Canister	18.4.16	Killed	11.10.18
Cook Albert	Pte	1st E Yorks	Canister	8.12.14	Killed	22.2.17
Cooper Clifford	Pte	4th E Yorks	KW Box Shop	12.10.09	Died (pneumonia)	16.8.18
Costello Mark	Pte	4th E Yorks	KW Sawmill	8.11.12	Died in Germany	2.6.18
Coupland Fred B	Pte	RAMC	Canister	7.9.14	Killed	17.10.17
Cousins Ernest J	Pte	7th King's L'pool Regt	Shinio Branch	21.8.13	Killed	28.6.16
Crockett George	Driver	RASC	Shinio Branch	22.5.13	Killed	21.3.18
Cronk Thomas	Pte	4th E Yorks	Canister	2.6.13	Killed	10.9.16

Name	Rank	Regiment	Branch of Works in which employed	Date joined the Firm		Date of Death
Cropper W E	Pte	1st E Yorks	KW Export	24.3.02	Killed	28.5.17
Dalton Perciva	Pte	4th E Yorks	Canister	14.3.10	Killed	24.4.15
Dalton T E	Pte	4th E Yorks	KW Fitters	11.3.07	Killed	6.5.15
Darling C	Sapper	Engineers	Bricklayer	0.0.05	Killed	9.5.16
Dawson Wilfre	Gunner	RFA	KW Hoists	1.9.14	Killed	22.8.18
Dobson James	Gunner	RGA	K Office	14.5.00	Killed	14.11.17
Dodsworth A	Gunner	RGA	KW Brasso	2.5.07	Killed	28.10.18
Downs Ernest	Pte	2/7th Man	Canister	1.3.08	Killed	21.3.18
Downs Harry	Pte	7th E Yorks	Canister	28.9.15	Killed	21.9.18
Dumez Andre	Sanitaire	Infanterie	ParisHouse, Introducer	27.3.11	Died of wounds	1.6.15
Dean Alfred	Stoker	Royal Navy			Killed	31.5.16
Earl John	Gunner	RGA	KW Joiners	17.1.00	Killed	15.7.18
Early Harold	Pte	18th RWF	London	20.3.11	Killed	13.11.16
Ellyard C S	Pte	4th E Yorks	Representative	3.2.13	Killed	6.8.15
Elsom Robert	L/Cpl	16th R Scots	Canister	1.7.14	Killed	22.3.18
Ely George	Sapper	ER (F) RE	KW Motor Driver	5.7.09	Killed	4.7.17
Emmerson Herbert	Pte	4th E Yorks	KW Rm 47	2.11.08	Killed	10.9.16
Farrow Arthur	Pte	1st E Yorks	Morley Street	17.9.14	Killed	9.4.17
Foster L C	Pte	2/8th Sherwd For	KO	3.3.13	Killed	7.4.17
Fryer S P	2/Lt	RFA	Representative	21.11.10	Killed	27.10.18
Gall Henry	Pte	4th E Yorks	Canister	11.12.11	Killed	20.4.18.
Gill George	Driver	RFA	Representative	23.6.13	Killed	3.9.17
Goodfellow Fred	Pte	12th E Yorks	Morley Street	27.8.14	Killed	13.11.16
Gorley R B	Pte	6th Shropshire	Representative	1.4.09	Killed	6.9.16
Gray Edwin	Pte	15th W Yorks	Canister	13.10.14	Killed	3.5.17
Guermonprez Paul	Caporal	Regiment de Zouaves	Paris House	14.11.10	Killed	20.9.14
Hardy Walter Charles MM	Pte	6th E Yorks	Canister	21.10.12	Killed	17.7.17
Hartley Charles	Sergt	7th Lincoln	Morley Street	22.11.06	Killed	27.7.18
Harvey John James	Pte	MGC	Canister	19.9.10	Killed	1.4.18
Hill Richard	Pte	5th Bord Rgt	KW packing room	4.1.12	Killed	1.10.16
Hinds John	Pte	7th Kings L'pool Regt	Shinio	10.5.11	Killed	26.11.15
Hogg George Edward	Cpl	11th E Yorks	KW lead	8.6.11	Killed	13.10.16
Hopper Richard	Pte	9th Scottish Rifles	KW packing	8.1.02	Killed	20.9.17
Hotchkin Ernes	tPte	12th E Yorks	KW Hoists	18.9.02	Killed	13.11.16
Hudson R W	Pte	E Yorks	Morley Street	13.8.14	Killed	11.3.19
Hunter Samuel	Pte	7th E York	Canister	2.9.14	Killed	12.5.17
Hutchinson Ivan	Lt	5th E Yorks	K Office	1.9.13	Killed	22.4.18

Name	Rank	Regiment	Branch of Works in which employed	Date joined the Firm		Date of Death
Jackson E	Pte	7th E Yorks			Killed	4.11.18
James Vernon D	L/Corpl	18th AIF	Sidney Office	0.5.06	Killed	1918
Jarrett Henry	Pte	10th W Yorks	Canister	6.12.09	Killed	23.4.17
Jubb Cecil William	Pte	9th W Yks	Canister paste dept	19.9.12	Killed	27.9.16
Kellett A G	Sergt	RFA	Representative	16.9.12	Killed	17.12.17
Laurent Andre		Infanterie	Paris House Introducer	27.6.14	Killed	
Laurent C			Paris House	3.7.14	Killed	
Leak G E	Pte	4th E Yorks	K W Lead	18.12.11	Killed	15.9.16
Lees Harold MM	Pte	2nd RWF	Caniste	20.5.14	Killed	20.7.16
LemoinE			Paris House	4.5.14	Killed	
Lesar Thos Geo DCM	Sergt	4th Royal Fus	London	18.3.12	Killed	23.8.18
Lill John	Trooper	20thHussars	Canister	26.2.12	Killed	26.6.15
Lockham John	Pte	7th E Yks	Canister	1.4.16	Killed	23.4.17
Longley W	Pte	1/5th Borders	K W Sawmill	18.3.07	Killed	1.10.16
McCloud John	Gunner	RFA	RW Lead Mill	3.10.13	Killed	24.10.17
Mace Herbert	Pte	4th E Yks	Morley Street	5.10.14	Killed	27.3.18
McPherson W A	L/Corpl	10th E Yks	K Office	2.11.03	Killed	5.6.16
Magson Walter	Pte	9th W Yks	K W Sawmill	20.9.12	Killed	31.7.18
Markham Joseph	Pte	1/7th EYks	K W B'layers	21.8.85	Killed	9.10.17
Miller Frank	Pte	4th E YkS	K W Hoists	8.5.08	Killed	13.10.15
Miller S	Pte	RMLI	Representative	17.5.09	Killed	22.8.18
Millington Raymond	Pte	RASC	Representative	15.9.13	Killed	1.9.17
Monks Frank	Pte	9th DLI	London	0.11.06	Killed	30.3.17
Murray W S	Pte	4th E Yks	K Office	4.4.00	Killed	11.6.15
Nasbey Valentine Percival	Pte	4th E Yks	Canister	19.6.11	Killed	17.6.16
Natton Francois	Soldat	Infanterie	Paris House Introducer	11.10.13	Killed	0.12.16
Neal H	Pte	4th E Yks	K W Brasso	28.2.07	Killed	8.11.16
Nix Charles W MM	Corpl	11th E Yks	Canister	21.10.07	Killed	29.9.18
Nozedar Edward	Pte	12th Suffolks	Canister	26.2.17	Killed	20.10.18
Parker Gerald P	Driver	ER(F)RE	K W Lead	27.2.11	Killed	28.3.18
Pearson Edwin	Pte	11th Yks	K W Starch	21.8.99	Killed	15.7.17
Pesnelle Pierre			Paris House	30.6.13	Died	
Peterson G B	2/Lt	4th E Yks	K Office	16.8.09	Killed	31.3.18
Piercy William A	Pte	21st Nth Fus	Morley Street	9.9.97	Died of wounds	25.4.17
Pitcairn Henry	Pte	Nthld Fus	Canister	12.1.15	Killed	16.6.17
Pullum Arthur Richard	Pte	EFC,RASC	Bluebell	1.11.04	Died of Dysentery	15.7.18
Raper Fred	Pte	11th E Yks	Morley Street	14.8.14	Killed	25.3.18
Richard Henri			Paris House	0.4.15	Died of Gas	0.7.19

Name	Rank	Regiment	Branch of Works in which employed	Date joined the Firm		Date of Death
Roberts Harold L	Pte	2/16th London Reg	London	24.2.13	Killed	31.10.17
Robinson P B P	2/Lt	8th KOYLI	K O	10.11.10	Killed	1.7.16
Robinson W	Pte	RAMC	KW Sawmill	16.1.98	Killed	27.10.16
Rogers William	Driver	RFA	Canister	27.2.08	Killed	14.7.16
Rylett William	Pte	4th E Yks	Canister	19.2.12	Killed	14.7.16
Sanderson Thomas	Pte	1/6th Nthld Fus	Canister	11.9.15	Killed	15.9.16
Saul George Henry	Gunner	RGA	Morley Street	25.1.12	Died of wounds	10.10.18
Scott Francis Joseph	Pte	4th E Yks	K W 35 Rm	24.5.09	Killed	4.8.16
Scott Robert	Pte	4th E Yks	Canister	11.12.12	Killed	25.5.16
Sedman H	Pte	7th E Yks	KW Starch	7.12.98	Killed	13.4.17
Sellars Herbert	Pte	4th E Yks	K W Sawmill	14.2.11	Killed	16.9.16
Sharman George	Pte	1st Gdn Hldrs	Canister	21.10.07	Killed	1.4.16
Sharp Edward	Pte	M/Gun Corps	KW Lead	20.10.10	Killed	28.6.18
Shepherd Albert Edward	Pte	1/4th E Yks	Canister	6.11.12	Killed	30.10.18
Shields Leonard	Pte	13th E Yks	K W Sawmill	17.2.11	Killed	18.11.16
Simpson John	Pte	15th DLI	K W Box Shop	6.7.14	Killed	29.3.18
Slater William	Gunner	RFA	K W Blue	16.9.14	Killed	30.6.17
Snow S	Pte	1st E Yks	K W Starch	26.7.00	Killed	1.7.16
Spires G	Pte	1st Coldstream Guards	K W Fitting Shop	26.4.07	Killed	22.12.14
Stokes William J	Stoker	HMS Derwent	Canister	5.2.08	Killed	2.5.17
Sullivan Edward	Pte	16th RWF	London	7.6.09	Killed	11.7.16
Taylor A C	Pte	7th Buffs	London	16.2.01	Killed	3.5.17
Taylor Eli	Stoker	Royal Navy	K W Fitters	16.10.08	Killed	20.5.15
Taylor Robert	Pte	4th E Yks	Canister	26.5.13	Killed	10.9.16
Taylor T S	Pte	2nd S W Brdrs	Morley Street	26.1.16	Killed	16.5.17
Thackery Herbert E	Pte	4th E Yks	K W Hoists	1.12.10	Killed	28.11.16
Thurloe George	Pte	11th E Yks	Morley Street	9.6.13	Killed	28.6.18
Trowell G W	Pte	4th E Yks	K W Sawmill	6.11.03	Killed	23.4.18
Trowell J R	Pte	4th N Fus	K W Packing	4.2.04	Killed	15.9.16
Tune C W	2/Lt	13th E Yks	K Office	29.3.10	Killed	23.11.17
Turner Albert	Pte	12th DLI	Canister	0.7.11	Killed	7.6.17
Turner Robert	Pte	4th E Yks	K W Packing	14.10.00	Killed	23.4.17
Upfold Wm Henry	Stoker 1st Class	Royal Navy	K W Fitter's Labourer	24.7.11	Killed on HMS Hawk	15.10.14
Veal Arthur Jubb	Pte	2/4th E Yks	Canister	14.5.13	Died on Service	3.10.18
Veal Thomas E	L/Corpl	E Yks	Morley Street	31.1.16	Killed	23.10.18
Walton Maurice	Pte	1st E Yks	K O	27.7.14	Killed	25.4.18
Watson J W	Pte	1st E Yks	Morley Street	12.8.09	Killed	11.7.17
Wells Albert	Pte	E Yks	Paper Stores	12.7.11	Killed	3.12.16
Wharam William	Pte	4th E Yks	Canister	17.8.15j	Killed	3.5.15

Name	Rank	Regiment	Branch of Works in which employed	Date joined the Firm		Date of Death
Wilson Albert	L/Corpl	4th E Yks	Canister	9.9.12	Since died of consumption	
Wilson Richard	Pte	Labour Corps	Morley Street	24.9.14	Died	27.4.18
Wolfe Harry Edmund	Pte	2/4th E Yks	Canister	25.1.11	Died on service	23.3.16
Woodcraft William	Pte	RASC	K W Packing	11.1.90	Died of TB	2.6.18
Woodmansey Sydney	Pte	1st E Yks	K Office	2.8.14	Killed	27.10.17
Wright Robert	Pte	18th Lan Fus	K W B'layers	2.11.14	Killed	26.3.18
Wyatt Herbert D	Gunner	NZFA	N. Z. Office	24.6.12	Died of wounds	15.6.17
Wadge Ernest	Lt	Canadian Rifles	Ontario Office		Killed	12.11.17

The following young men were listed as 'Missing in the commemorative issue of "OURS" –1919

Name	Rank	Regiment	Branch of Works in which employed	Date joined the Firm		Date of Death
Berridge A	Pte	1/4th E Yks	K W		Killed	23.4.17
Harris J A	Pte	10th E Yks	K W Packing	5.2.07	Killed	24.3.18
Housley J	Pte	1/4th E Yks	K W Packing	8.11.01	Killed	10.4.18
Smailes Benjamin	Pte	1st Bn E Yks		15.12.10	Killed	1.7.16

Appendix 'I'

The following is a list of the men who were killed during the war but were never featured in the magazine – 'OURS'

However they do feature in the special commemorative issue of 'OURS' published in 1919.

Rifleman G E Barker

18th Bn King's Royal Rifle Corps. Reg No.c/6068. Killed 6th August 1917. Commemorated on the Menin Gate Memorial. Belgium.

L/Cpl John Benstead Tank Corps

In 'OURS' he is listed as serving with the East Yorkshire Rgt: He was killed with the 10th Bn Tank Corps on 23rd October 1918. His Reg No was 92373. John was the son of Charles and Ellen Benstead of 9 William's Terrace, Holderness Road, Hull and is buried in Premont British Cemetery. France.

Pte Harry Bryan 79629 DLI

Listed in 'OURS' as serving with the Yeomanry: He was killed with the 22nd Bn Durham Light Infantry, on 26th March 1918 and is commemorated on the Pozieres Memorial. France.

L/Cpl Robert Buttery 24857 East Yorkshire Rgt

Was born and enlisted in Hull. He was killed serving with the 7th Bn East Yorkshire Rgt on 12th May 1917 and is commemorated on the Arras Memorial to the missing.

Pte Mark Costello 203768 East Yorkshire Rgt

Is listed in 'Soldiers Died' as being killed in action - France and Flanders, serving with the 1/4th Bn East Yorkshire Rgt. Mark was born in Hull and enlisted in Hull, but died a prisoner of war in Germany on 2nd June 1918. He is buried in Neiderz Wehren Cemetery. Germany.

Pte Fred Bartholemew Coupland 390518 Royal Medical Corps.

Was killed in action on 17th October 1917 aged 29 years. He was the son of Fred and Elizabeth Coupland of 13 Craven Street, Holderness Road, Hull and is buried in St Julien Dressing Station Cemetery. Langemark. Belgium.

Gunner Alfred Dodsworth 118602 Royal Garrison Artillery

Died at home on 28th October 1918 aged 27 years. He enlisted in Hull into the 3rd Riding Royal Garrision Artillery with the regimental number of 334. Alfred was the husband of Fanny Dodsworth of 14 Coral Grove, Grange Street, Hull and is buried in Hull Northern Cemetery.

Pte Harry Downs 11625 7th Bn East Yorkshire Regiment

Was killed on 21st September 1918 and is buried in Assevillers new British Cemetery. France.

Pte Henry Gall 2674 1/4th Bn East Yorkshire Regiment

Was born in Hull and enlisted in Hull. He was killed on 20th April 1918. This is given as 1916 in 'Soldiers Died'. Henry was the son of Mr J W and Mrs M H Gall of 92 De Grey Street, Hull and is buried in Lindenmoek Chalet Military Cemetery. Kemmel. Belgium.

Pte Edwin Gray 1G/181 15th Bn West Yorkshire Regiment

Killed on 3rd May 1917 and commemorated on the Arras Memorial to the missing.

Pte Fred Raper 21056 11th Bn East Yorkshire regiment (2nd Hull-Pals)

Was born in South Millford, Sheffield and enlisted in Hull. He was killed in action on 25th March 1918 aged 20 years. Fred was the son of Mr and Mrs Raper of Hull and is commemorated on the Arras Memorial to the missing.

Stoker 1st Class William Henry Upfold 35362 Royal Navy HMS Hawke

Was killed on 15th October 1914 aged 38 years. He was the son of William Henry and Maria Upfold of Hull and was the husband of Agnes Jane

McMullen (formerly Upfold) of 4 Southcoates Lane, Hull. William is commemorated on the Chatham Naval Memorial.

Pte Arthur Jubb Veal 203706 2/4thBn East Yorkshire Regiment

Was born in Wigan – Lancashire and enlisted in Hull. He died on 3rd October 1918 aged 20 years. Arthur was the son of George William and Georgina Veal of 81 Clarendon Street, Spring Bank, Hull and is buried in Somerset Military Burial Ground. Bermuda.

Pte Thomas E Veal 42042 9th Bn The Yorkshire Regiment

Was killed on 23rd October 1918 aged 20 years. He was the son of Thomas and Betsy Veal of 24 Burleigh Place, Providence Row, Hull and is buried in Pommereul British Cemetery. France.

Pte Arthur Berridge 201561 A COY 1/4th Bn East Yorkshire Regiment

Was born in Hull and enlisted in Hull. He was killed on 23rd April 1917 aged 20 years. Arthur was the son of Charles Thomas and Janet Berridge of 60 Alicia Street, Hull and is commemorated on the Arras Memorial to the missing.

Pte James Alfred Harris 28057 10th Bn East Yorkshire Regiment (Hull Commercials)

Was born in Hull and enlisted in Hull. He was killed on 24th March 1918 and is commemorated on the Arras Memorial to the missing.

Pte John Housley 220024 1/4th Bn East Yorkshire Regiment

Was born in Hull and enlisted in Hull. He was killed on 10th April 1918 and is buried in Trois Arbres Cemetery. Steenwerk. France.

Pte Ernest Cockerline 57231 1/5th Bn West Yorkshire Regiment

Was killed on 11th October 1918 and is commemorated on the Vis-en-Artois Memorial. France.

Pte Albert Edward Shepherd 200710 D COY 1/4th Bn East Yorkshire Regiment

Was born in Hull to William and Rose Shepherd and enlisted in Hull. He died on 30th October 1918 - 'Soldiers Died' gives his date of death as 31st - at the age of 27 years. Albert is commemorated on the Soissons Memorial. France.

Pte Edward Jackson 26574 7th Bn East Yorkshire Regiment

Was born in Hull and enlisted in Hull. He was killed on 4th November 1918 and is buried in Romeries Communal Cemetery Extension. France.

L/Cpl Albert Wilson

The information given on this man is that he served with the 1/4th Bn East Yorkshire Regiment and that he died of consumption. I can find no record of him in the Hull Cemeteries Register, in 'Soldiers Died', or in the Commonwealth War Graves Register - they record 113 by the name of Wells with the initial 'A'.

Pte Benjamin Smailes 3/6509 1st Bn East Yorkshire Regiment

Was born and enlisted in Hull. Killed in action 1stJuly 1916 at the age of 19 years. He has no known grave but is commemorated on the Thiepval Memorial to the missing. France.

Index

Name	*Rank*	*Page no.*
Adams, A		129
Adams, George H	Pte	111
Addison, H		130
Ainsworth, Arthur Ogden	Pte	79
Anderson, George	Pte	48
Andrews, Albert Lezanto	Corporal	42
Arnold, Basil Drake		135
Atkinson, Ernest G		114
Atkinson, George Reginald	L/Corporal	34
Atkinson, T Beecroft (Alderman)	Lord Mayor of Hull	126
Aumonier, William		125,126,195
Austin, A W		194
Backhouse, Laurence Henry	Bombadier	79,108
Backhurst, E (Mrs)		10,11
Baines, J		194
Barcroft, Jessie (Miss)		10
Barker, G E	Rifleman	206
Barton, John Woodliff	Pte	175
Barwick, Elsie (Miss)		11
Batty, Daisy (Miss)		11
Baxter, Albert	Pte	20
Beacock, George Arthur	Bombadier	175
Beckett, F		188
Beckett, George Wilson	Pte	48,175
Bell, F (Miss)		174
Bell, William Henry	Pte	62
Benstead, John	L/Corporal	206
Berridge, Arthur	Pte	208
Binks, Henry	Driver	106
Binns, William Arthur	Pte	175
Blain, James	Pte	175
Booth, William	Pte	77
Borrill, Thomas Edgar	L/Corporal	87
Bowden, John Robert	Pte	21
Bradley, C	Pte	25
Brady, John F		193

Brelsford, Lily (Miss)		11
Bricklebank, T		194
Broadley, Thomas	Pte	21
Brocher, Constant Jean Marie		194
Brocklesby, G	L/Corporal	176
Broddle, Osward	Pte	85
Broddle, Sydney	Pte	85
Bromby, Thomas Alfred	Captain	51
Brown, E		194
Bruzant, Gaston		194
Bryan, Harry	Pte	206
Butler (Miss)		10
Butters, Mary (Miss)		11
Buttery, Robert	L/Corporal	206
Caborn, Frank	Pte	73,194
Carver, Arthur	Pte	22
Cassie, J H		194
Chalmers, Ellen (Miss)		10,11
Chapman, Edward	L/Corporal	94
Chapman, Frederick J	Pte	38
Chapman, George James	Pte	77,192
Charlesworth, Mabel (Miss)		11
Charlton, George	Pte	90
Chattey, Robert S	Pte	97
Claeijs, J		194
Clare, Marion (Miss)		11
Clark, A		194
Clark, D		188
Claxton, Henry	Pte	64
Cleminson, A R		129
Coates, A V		118,126
Cobb, Harry	Pte	86
Cockerline, Ernest	Pte	100,208
Collins, John Henry	Pte	26
Connor, F J		194
Cook, (Miss)	Matron	12,13,14
Cook, Albert	Pte	61
Cooper, A (Mrs)		174
Cooper, Clifford	Pte	88
Cooper, G		197

Costello, Mark	Pte	206
Coulson, Leslie	Sergeant	49
Coupland, Frederick B	Pte	96,207
Cousins, Joseph Ernest	Pte	39
Cowell, J N	Corporal	28
Crockett, George	Driver	96
Cronk, Thomas William	Pte	60
Cropper, William Ernest	Pte	60
Cullen, Lily (Miss)		10
Curtis, G		192
Curtis, G		193
Dalton, Percival	Pte	45
Dalton, Thomas Edward	Pte	45
Darling, Charles	Sapper	37,189
Dawson, Wilfred	Gunner	93
Dean, Alfred	Stoker	40
Dean, Alfred	Stoker	189
Dent, George	Corporal	176
Dewick, George H	Pte	54
Divine, J	Doctor	12,14,16
Dobson, James	Gunner	86
Dodsworth, Alfred	Gunner	129,207
Downs, Ernest	L/Corporal	99
Downs, Harry	Pte	207
Dresser, Walter	Pte	54
Dunlin, (Miss)		129
Dunn, (Miss)		117
Earl, John	Gunner	97
Early, Harold	Pte	61
Easton	Captain	33
Eggleton, E (Mrs)		10,11
Elliot, Walter John Lester	Driver	78
Ellyard, Charles Sydney	Pte	22
Elsom, Robert	L/Corporal	97
Elsworth, A S		192
Elvin, Harold		135
Elvin, K (Miss)		17
Ely, George	Sapper	63
Emment, Thomas Clifford	Sergeant	75
Emmerson, Herbert	Pte	43,129

Evans (Miss)	Matron	13,16
Evans, Walter	Pte	176
Farrell, Emma (Miss)		10,11
Farrell, Herbert	Pte	52
Farrow, Asrthur	Pte	63
Ferens, T R (Rt. Hon)		126,129,130,196,197
Findlay, Mr.		12
Foster, Leslie C	Pte	64
Fournier, Theo		194
Fox, S T		194
Frow, Frances (Miss)		11
Fryer, Stanley Phillipps	2nd Lieutenant	98
Gall, Henry	Pte	207
Gates, John	Sergeant	49,107,194
Gill, G	Driver	63
Golden, M (Mrs)		174
Goodfellow, Frederick	Pte	62
Gorely, Reginald B	Pte	46
Grant (Colonel)	Colonel	126
Gray, Edwin	Pte	207
Green, Hilda (Miss)		11
Guest, T		11,16,17
Gurdon (Bishop)	Bishop of Hull	125
Handy, J (Rev)		174
Hardy, (Miss)		16
Hardy, C H		126,129
Hardy, E M (Miss)	Lady Supt.	10,11,12
Hardy, W C		194
Hardy, Walter Charles	Pte	69
Harris, James Alfred	Pte	208
Harrison, Arthur	L/Corporal	34,194
Harrison, Frank	Corporal	80
Harrison, Frank R		194
Harry, E J (Rev)		172
Hartley, Charles	Sergeant	99
Harvey, E J W (Rev)		174
Harvey, John James	Pte	94
Hill, Henry Ellis	Captain	50,194
Hill, Richard A	Pte	94
Hinds, John	Pte	44

Hodsworth, John ("Jack")	Sapper	29
Hogg, George Edward	Corporal	39
Holt, J L	Doctor	12,14,16
Hoodless, Goeorge	Gunner	107
Hopkinson, James	Pte	26,194
Hopper, Richard	Rifleman	93
Hotchkin, Ernest	Pte	95
Housley, John	Pte	208
Hunter, John	Pte	102
Hunter, Len	Gunner	102
Hunter, Rachel (Miss)		102
Hunter, Samuel	Pte	101
Hutchinson, Ivan	Lieutenant	95
Irwin, William Alfred	L/Corporal	79
Jacklin, John Percy	Pte	177
Jackson, Edward	Pte	129,195,209
Jagger, J W	Pte	177
Jagoe, Allen W	Lieutenant	191,194
Jarrett, Henry	Pte	58
Johnstone, Helen	Lady	17
Joy, N H		194
Jubb, William Cecil	Bugler	71
Kay, M		188
Kaye, J H	Doctor	12,14
Kellett, Albert George	Sergeant	88
Kemp, William Thomas	Sapper	177
Kirby, Ethel (Miss)		10,11,16
Lang, Daniel	Pte	30
Lawson, Howard	Sergeant	111
Layfield, A	Corporal	12
Leak, George E	Pte	85
Leake (Miss)		174
Learoyd, H A	Town Clerk	126
Leathley, N J		194
Leber, Georges		194
Lees, Harold B	Pte	68,194
Legave, Pierre	Canonier	194
Leggott, T L	Captain	197
Lesar, Thomas George	Sergeant	56,194
Lill, John	Trooper	25

Linney, B (Miss)		16
Lister, Jane		188
Lockham, John E	Pte	87
Locking, J W (Councillor)	Sheriff of Hull	126
Lockwood, Mark	Pte	2,177
Longhorn, Gladys (Miss)		11
Longley, Walter	Pte	42
Lowe, Elizabeth (Miss)		11
Lundie, Henry	Sergeant	130
Lundie, Henry	Sergeant	194
Macaulay, Thomas	Pte	177
Mace, Herbert	Pte	86
Macpherson, William A	L/Corporal	40
Magson, Walter	Pte	84
Mann, M K		174
Markham, Joseph	Rifleman	92,129
Marsden, Harry	Pte	27
Marshall, Hilda (Miss)		10,11
Martin, W H B		194
McColl, Christiana(Miss)		11
McDonald, Alice (Miss)		174
McDonald, J F (Mrs)		174
McGavin, Dora (Miss)		11,13,14,15
McKernan, Emma (Miss)		11
McLean, B		188
McLoud, John	Gunner	85
McNally, Lily (Miss)		11
Merrifield, Arthur Henry	Pte	74
Miller, Frank Lonsdale	PTE	23
Miller, Sydney	Pte	84
Millington, Raymond	Pte	68
Mills, A		194
Milner, G		194
Monks, Frank	Pte	67
Moon, W		16
Moore, William	Corporal	130,194
Morin, Andre		194
Morrill, (Councillor)		172,174
Morris, Ernest Oswald	QM Sergeant	72
Morris, Ernest Oswald	QM Sergeant	194

Munton, F A		194
Murray, Walter Stanley	Pte	20
Myers, Charles Edward	Sergeant	2,177
Myers, George William	Pte	177
Myers, S (Mrs)		174
Nasby, Laurence	Pte	47
Nasby, Valentine Percival	Pte	47
Neal, Herbert	Pte	59
Neal, M		129
Needham, Albert	Pte	178
Nicholson, Tom	Sergeant	78,194
Nix, Charles John	Sergeant	104,194
Nix, James	Corporal	106
Noble, Harold	Captain	52
Nozedar, Edward Henry	Pte	100
Ogden C		126
Parker, Gerald Pitts	Driver	91
Parker, T		188
Pattison, Elsie (Miss)		11
Payne, Bertha (Miss)		11
Peak, H T		114
Pearson, Edwin	Pte	68,129
Percy, C	Industrial Chaplain	185,187,188
Peterson, George Benjamin	Pte	92
Piercy, William A	Pte	70
Pitcairn, Henry	Pte	57
Priest Shaw, A	Doctor	12,14
Prime, Beatrice (Miss)		11
Prissick, Ada		103
Pullam, Arthur Richard	Pte	89
Pulsford, Frederick James	Pte	27,50
Raper, Fred	Pte	207
Reckitt, Albert L		126,129
Reckitt, Arnold	Captain	126,129
Reckitt, Arthur Benington		114,116,126,129,197
Reckitt, Geoffrey	Captain	197
Reckitt, Harold J		17,126,194
Reckitt, Philip B		13,15,16,126,129, 173,174,194
Reed, Albert	Able Seaman	178

Reeder, Ivy (Miss)		11
Rimmington, William		115,116
Roberts, Harold Lancaster	Pte	91
Robertson, Louisa (Miss)		11
Robinson, Percival B P	2nd Lieutenant	36
Robinson, Walter	Pte	69
Rogers, Frank Webb	Bombadier	72
Rogers, William	Driver	72
Rooms, Harold	Lieutenant	54
Rylett, William	Pte	56
Sanderson, James Thornton	L/Corporal	29,33
Sanderson, Thomas	Pte	71
Saul, George Henry	Gunner	90
Savage, Ernest	Pte	27
Scott, (Alderman)		172,174
Scott, Francis Joseph	Pte	41
Scott, Robert	Pte	56
Sedman, Herbert	Pte	70,129
Selby, Eva (Miss)		11
Sellers, Herbert	Pte	38,178
Sharman, George A	Pte	44
Sharp, Edward	Pte	89
Shepherd, A (Councillor)	Pres., Br. Legion)	126
Shepherd, Albert Edward	Pte	208
Shields, Leonard	Pte	66
Simpson, John	Pte	92
Slack, Cecil M	Captain	137,194
Slack, W H		126,129,172,173,197
Slater, William George	Pte	91
Smailes, Benjamin	Pte	209
Smith, Ada (Miss)		11
Smith, Walter Edward		132
Smith, William		194
Snow, Samuel	Pte	46
Snow, Samuel	Pte	129
Sorfleet, Dolly (Miss)		11
Spires, George	Pte	2,37,178
Spruit, J	Sapper	28
Squires, Herbert		136
Stead. A E		194

Stewart, I		188
Stokes, William James	Stoker	59
Stone, John	Pte	26
Streat, Clifford	Sergeant Major	49,130,194
Sullivan, Edward	Pte	43
Sutton, Edith (Miss)		11
Tatham, J W	Colonel	13,14
Taylor, Arthur Banfield	Rifleman	78
Taylor, Arthur Cecil	Pte	71
Taylor, Charles		194
Taylor, Robert	Pte	58
Taylor, Thomas Samuel	Pte	93
Taylor, William ("Ely")	Stoker	23
Teall, Ivy (Miss)		11
Thackery, H Ruth (Miss)		10,11,16
Thackery, Herbert Edward	Pte	61
Thomas, Elsie (Miss)		11
Thorley, Lily (Miss)		11
Thurloe, George	Pte	98
Thurnell, G W	Pte	178
Timmons, Charles	Able Seaman	77
Tiplady, Florence (Miss)		16,17,135
Todd, Elsie May (Miss)		134
Tommins, Hilda (Miss)		11
Trowell, George William	Pte	65
Trowell, John Robert	Pte	65
Tune, Charles Walter	2nd Lieutenant	98
Tunnard, (Miss)	Matron	13
Turner, Albert	Pte	62
Turner, Robert	Pte	67
Upfold, William Henry	Stoker	207
Varey, (Miss)	Sister	12,13,14,16
Varey, N		188
Veal, Arthur Jubb	Pte	208
Veal, Thomas E	Pte	208
Vickers, Roy	Pte	110
Vincent, T		194
Wade, P		188
Wadge, Ernest	Lieutenant	104
Wales, Dr.	Doctor Surgeon	10

Walsh, A		194
Walton (Miss)		16
Walton, Maurice	Pte	99
Watson, John William	Pte	65
Webster, Edward Wilson	Pte	53,54
Wells, (Mrs)		174
Wells, Albert	Pte	58
West, Robert Henry		133
Westerman, E (Miss)		10
Westerman, Mabel (Miss)		11
Wharam, William	PTe	24
Wharf, W R		194
Wheelhouse, Stanley	Pte	76
White, T R	Chaplain	113
Whitteridge, Albert E	L/Corporal	51
Wilby, W A		194
Wilkinson, Percy S (Sir)	Major General	123,125,127
Willatt, W H	Major	126,129
Williams, Thomas F		192,194
Wilson, Albert	L/Corporal	209
Wilson, Richard	Pte	88,194
Winston, Edgar	Pte	178
Witherwick, C		194
Wolfe, Harry Edmund	Pte	178
Wood, Lily (Miss)		11
Woodcraft, William Herbert	Pte	96
Woodmansey, Sydney	Pte	69
Woolias, Henry	Bombadier	81
Wright, John		174
Wright, Robert	Pte	84
Wyatt, Herbert Digby	Gunner	67
Yates, A (Miss)		11

Index of name-bearing memorials

Memorial or list	*Nature of the list*	*Page no.*
Australian House	survivors	168
Belgium House	survivors	170
Bluebell House, Fulham	survivors	165
Canister Works, Stoneferry	fallen	117
Canister Works, Stoneferry	survivors	141
Complete List of the Fallen	fallen	201
Dansom Lane Shrine	fallen and survivors	179
Dublin House	survivors	168
Garden of Remembrance: new plaque	fallen	190
General Office, Dansom Lane	fallen	118
General Office, Dansom Lane	survivors	159
Kingston Works, Dansom Lane	survivors	146
Liverpool House, Reckitt & Sons Ltd	survivors	167
London House, Bedford Square	survivors	166
London Office, Bedford Square	fallen	120
Morley Street, Reckitt's Colours Ltd	survivors	139
New York House	survivors	169
New Zealand House	survivors	168
Outside Staff, Reckitt & Sons Ltd	survivors	162
Paris House	survivors	169
Plymouth House	survivors	167
Reckitt's Boys' Club	fallen and survivors	121
Shinio Metal Polish Company	survivors	119
South African House	survivors	168